D0872288

Sep 2019

HERE ALL ALONG

HERE ALL ALONG

Finding Meaning, Spirituality, and a
Deeper Connection to Life—in Judaism
(After Finally Choosing to Look There)

SARAH HURWITZ

SPIEGEL & GRAU NEW YORK

Published in the United States by Spiegel & Grau, an imprint of Random House, a division of Penguin Random House LLC, New York.

SPIEGEL & GRAU and Design is a registered trademark of Penguin Random House LLC.

LIBRARY OF CONGRESS CATALOGING-IN-PUBLICATION DATA
Names: Hurwitz, Sarah, author.
Title: Here all along : finding meaning, spirituality,
and a deeper connection to life—in Judaism
(after finally choosing to look there) / by Sarah Hurwitz.
Description: New York : Spiegel & Grau, [2019] |
Includes bibliographical references.
Identifiers: LCCN 2019011424 | ISBN 9780525510710 |
ISBN 9780525510727 (ebook)
Subjects: LCSH: Judaism.
Classification: LCC BM45 .H87 2019 | DDC 296—dc23
LC record available at https://lccn.loc.gov/2019011424

Printed in the United States of America on acid-free paper

randomhousebooks.com
spiegelandgrau.com

1 2 3 4 5 6 7 8 9

First Edition

Book design by Susan Turner

For my parents, who have made everything possible.

CONTENTS

Why Bother with Judaism?

A decision I made in sixth grade to violate two of the Ten Commandments nearly ended my Jewish journey.

The events that led to these transgressions took place in a fluorescent-lit, industrial-carpeted Hebrew school classroom at the synagogue in the small Boston suburb where I grew up. It was a late fall afternoon, and the light was fading, as were the dozen or so eleven- and twelve-year-olds unhappily marking the beginning of their seventh year of Jewish education.

We were carrying on a timeworn American Jewish tradition whereby a couple of days a week, after regular school ended, tired, restless kids were driven to their families' synagogues, where they sat through another few hours of class during which Jewish educators attempted to teach them to read Hebrew and appreciate an incredibly complex, four-thousand-year-old religion that can be baffling for even the most intelligent adults.

Our teacher was a weary, middle-aged man whose name I've forgotten. But I do recall that he insisted we call him Mr. Shalom, the

Hebrew word for hello, goodbye, and peace, and that he wore a brightly patterned yarmulke, which struck me as incredibly dorky. So as far as I and my classmates were concerned, he was begging us to disrespect him. And we happily complied, haphazardly filling out the Hebrew worksheets he assigned, talking over his attempts to quiet us down, and misbehaving in ways we never would have dreamed of in real school, where we were generally model students.

About halfway through class on that otherwise unremarkable day, I had a sudden moment of clarity: I was done with all of this.

Maybe it was the poor grade I had gotten on last week's homework assignment and Mr. Shalom's look of disappointment as he handed it back to me. Or maybe it was the moment when several of my classmates, in a rare display of cooperative behavior, decided to gang up and make fun of me. Or maybe it was just years of accumulated boredom and the sense that while I might be stuck being Jewish, I didn't have to waste hours each week on this pointless exercise that was keeping me from worthier 1980s preteen girl pursuits, like watching mediocre TV and reading Baby-Sitters Club and Sweet Valley High books.

Whatever it was, as I walked out the classroom door that afternoon, I decided there was no way I was ever coming back.

That night, I approached my mother and launched into an impassioned speech about how Hebrew school was failing to make me into the Jew I wanted to be. The teachers didn't challenge us! The students didn't take class seriously! I wasn't learning what I needed to learn to carry on our proud tradition!

My mother was, understandably, taken aback. Neither she nor my father was particularly religious, but feeling an obligation to give me and my brother some sense of Jewish identity, they had joined the synagogue in our town and enrolled us in its Hebrew school. And twice a year, on the major Jewish holidays of Rosh Hashanah and Yom Kippur, they dragged us to services, where we squirmed through the endless droning melodies, halfheartedly recited the prayers that alternated between incomprehensible Hebrew and stilted English translations, and obeyed the seemingly random calls to stand up and sit down. The only holiday we celebrated in our home was Ḥanukkah,* but while we lit the candles and said the prayers, it was mainly about the presents.

Given our minimal Jewish practice and the fact that I had never previously displayed much interest in my Jewish education, my mother was probably suspicious of my sudden religiosity. And after some probing, she tried to stall, assuring me that she would talk to my father about it.

But I was relentless, commencing a days-long anti–Hebrew school campaign with a kind of message discipline that I find admirable today, having spent years working in political communications. At every chance I got, I let her know: This Hebrew school did not meet my needs as a Jew, and I was not going back.

Either my father bought my story or I simply wore my mother down, because within a few weeks, she found me another Hebrew school—one that mercifully met only one day a week—which agreed to take me midsemester. The following Sunday, she dropped me off for my first day of class.

Within minutes, my relief at escaping my old Hebrew school was replaced by the sinking sensation that I had done something terribly wrong, because it was clear that this new place was a bit of a loose operation. The kids were struggling to read the kind of one-syllable Hebrew words my former classmates and I had mastered years ago, and we spent much of the time singing Jewish songs with the younger children and having a meandering discussion that I think was supposed to be about Jewish ethics.

As I waited for my mother to pick me up, I thought about telling her that I'd made a mistake and the old Hebrew school was actually fine.

---

* Note that a number of Hebrew words that appear in this book, including "Ḥanukkah," begin with a Hebrew letter that has a guttural "H" sound and can be rendered as "H" or "Ch" in English. I've chosen to follow the convention of designating that guttural "H" with an "H" with a dot under it (ḥ/Ḥ) because I think "Ch" can be confusing for English speakers, who tend to mistakenly pronounce it like the "Ch" in "Chair." I have, however, kept "Ch" when quoting from others who use it and in other select circumstances.

But the memory of my former classmates' mockery and the feeling that I'd made my bed and now had to lie in it won out. And when my mother arrived, I assured her that this new Hebrew school was both top notch and the perfect fit.

Thus began the domino effect on my Judaism. My mother soon got tired of carpooling her children to two different Hebrew schools, so she pulled my brother out of the old one and sent him to the new one with me. With that connection to our synagogue severed, it was easy enough to continue down the slippery slope of disengagement and stop attending services as well.

The following year, through my new Hebrew school, I had my bat mitzvah, which, like the curriculum, was pretty light on the Judaism. Various family members read poems and quotes. I played my flute. It was a beautiful and deeply meaningful coming-of-age ceremony, one that I will always treasure, but it bore only a passing resemblance to a Jewish life cycle ritual.

And that was about it for my Jewish observance. My ancestry stretches back through a tenement on the Lower East Side, the shtetls of Eastern Europe, and presumably all the way to the ancient Near East. But without making any kind of conscious decision beyond the one I made to dishonor my mother and father by bearing false witness to them against my Hebrew school (violating Commandments Five and Nine), I was just kind of done with Judaism.

As Rabbi Joseph Telushkin and Dennis Prager point out in their writing about Jewish identity, if you grow up like I did, getting only an after-school-activity kind of Jewish education, when you get to college and have the chance to study eastern religion or western philosophy, you may think to yourself, "Now *this* is where it's at! This is so much smarter and deeper than Judaism!" That childhood Judaism just can't compete.

Maybe in a decade or so, if you get married and create a family of your own, you'll start the whole process over again. Maybe you'll send your own kids to Hebrew school because you want them to have some kind of Jewish identity. Maybe you'll drag them to services, because even if you don't really understand what's happening, the familiar melodies make you nostalgic and it feels meaningful to be connected to Jewish tradition. And maybe one day, years from now, your kids will hand down the same "pediatric Judaism," as Rabbi Lawrence Hoffman calls it, to their own kids.

But maybe you won't do any of that. Greater acceptance of Jews into mainstream American society in recent decades means Jews are now welcome in all kinds of neighborhoods, universities, and workplaces, and most Jews no longer live in tight-knit Jewish communities that enforce the norms and practices of traditional Jewish life. We also live at a time when many of us view religion* as something we can choose from a marketplace of ideas rather than an inherited obligation we must unquestioningly fulfill. Today, we're all welcome to check out the offerings at the local Unitarian church or Buddhist sangha; or we can grab some crystals or hallucinogenic drugs; or we can do nothing religious or spiritual at all.

The term "Jews by choice" is often used to refer to those who convert to Judaism. But these days, all American Jews are Jews by choice— and many of us are choosing to opt out.

A much-cited 2013 study by the Pew Research Center found that while 94 percent of American Jews feel proud to be Jewish, 22 percent of them, including 32 percent of millennial-age Jews, "describe themselves as having no religion and identify as Jewish on the basis of ancestry, ethnicity, or culture." A full two-thirds of these Jews of no religion report that they're not raising their kids with any kind of Jewish identity.

There is also a trend of moving from more observant† denomina-

---

* Though Judaism is not just a religion—we'll get to that shortly.

† In Judaism, the word "observant" is generally used to mean something like "religious," and it refers to those who observe traditional Jewish laws. Orthodox Judaism is considered the most observant denomination, followed by Conservative Judaism, and then Reform Judaism. But as we will discuss in Chapter 4, I question this definition of "observant" and will use the phrase "traditionally observant" instead (though even that phrase is problematic since, as we'll see in later chapters, Jewish tradition is constantly evolving).

tions of Judaism to less observant. Roughly one in four Jews who grew up Orthodox have switched to Conservative or Reform Judaism*; 30 percent of those raised in the Conservative movement have become Reform Jews; and 28 percent of those who grew up Reform now identify as Jews of no religion.†

That last shift—moving from Reform Judaism to considering myself a Jew of no religion—was the choice I made after my bat mitzvah. While I would always be Jewish by birth, and I couldn't quite shake the feeling that my Judaism was important in some way, I saw no reason to engage with it on a regular basis. When I got to college, my one experience attending a Shabbat‡ dinner at Hillel, the international campus organization for Jewish students, only confirmed this decision. Everyone there seemed to know each other from Jewish summer camp and be in on some inside joke to which I was not privy, and I couldn't follow any of the prayers or rituals.

A couple of years after graduating from college, I spent part of a summer traveling around Eastern Europe, and I visited several Jewish museums and Holocaust memorial sites, a searing experience that left me uneasy about my noncommittal Jewish identity. Throughout history, people had risked and sacrificed their lives to practice and preserve Judaism. Here I was with all the freedom in the world, but I just couldn't be bothered.

So in my twenties, I started once again regularly attending services on Rosh Hashanah and Yom Kippur. Like in college, I still didn't know the prayers or understand why we were saying them in the first place—and this made for some uncomfortable moments. When you have a name like Sarah Hurwitz, people assume you know what you're doing in Jewish settings, and I was too ashamed of my ignorance to admit

---

* Though the Orthodox population appears to be growing, with a birthrate more than twice as high as that of other Jews.

† The reverse seems to be rare: Only seven percent of Jews who grew up Reform have switched to Conservative or Orthodox Judaism, and only four percent of those raised Conservative have transitioned to Orthodoxy.

‡ Shabbat, the Jewish Sabbath, is celebrated each week from Friday night through Saturday night and includes a special Friday night dinner. We'll discuss further in Chapter 7.

otherwise. So I would anxiously watch the people around me and do my best to copy them, hoping I wouldn't commit some awful faux pas. I got about as much out of my time in synagogues as I had during my childhood, but I couldn't bring myself to stay home on major holidays, nor could I bring myself to go to work.

I was unable to own my Judaism, but unable to disown it either. So I mainly ignored it. And that worked out just fine for me.

After all, I was busy.

Growing up with a grandmother who was a passionate Roosevelt Democrat, a mother who is a proud feminist, and a father who, as a young man, kept a quote book filled with excerpts from speeches by the Kennedy brothers and Dr. Martin Luther King, Jr., I became interested in politics at an early age. A college internship in Vice President Al Gore's speechwriting office in the White House eventually led to speechwriting jobs on a couple of losing presidential campaigns; law school and a stint at a large Washington, D.C., law firm; and a position as then-Senator Hillary Clinton's chief speechwriter on her first presidential campaign. After Hillary conceded in June of 2008, I got a job as a speechwriter for then-Senator Barack Obama on his campaign for president, and I wound up helping his wife, Michelle Obama, with her speech at the 2008 Democratic National Convention.

That summer was a fraught time for Mrs. Obama. For months, ugly currents of racism and sexism had been swirling around her, and she had been caricatured in the media as an angry black woman—most notably in a cartoon of her on the cover of *The New Yorker* sporting combat fatigues, an afro, and a machine gun slung across her back.

As I prepared for our first meeting about the speech, I wondered whether the negative press had gotten to her. Would she be upset? Defensive? Would she want to react to it in her remarks?

None of the above, it turned out. Instead, over the course of ninety minutes in her Hyde Park living room, she simply told me about her life: her childhood on the South Side of Chicago, why she left corporate law for a career in public service, the joy she took in being a mother. Her plan for the speech seemed to be: I will simply say what is true for me and let people decide for themselves what to think. (It worked—the media narrative around her shifted dramatically after that speech.)

Months later, after her husband won the election, I got a job as speechwriter for him in the White House. But while I loved writing for President Obama, I was never fully at home in his voice. I often felt like I was straining to grasp it, mimicking what I thought it sounded like rather than hearing it in my head. And whenever I took a break from writing for him to help Mrs. Obama with a speech—which I sometimes did to assist her small communications team—I could feel the difference.

Compared with her husband's voice, Mrs. Obama's voice was more like mine—more personal and emotional—and I felt an ease in channeling it onto the page that I did not feel with his. So after the first couple of years of the Administration, in what was probably an unprecedented White House career move, I decided to transition from being a senior speechwriter for the President to being head speechwriter for the First Lady.

Over the next six years, I wrote and edited hundreds of speeches for Mrs. Obama and traveled with her across the country and around the world. Just as with that first speech, no matter what the topic, she always seemed to be asking herself, "What is the deepest, most important truth I can tell at this particular moment?" And when we met to discuss an upcoming speech, she would dictate paragraphs of vivid language that I would frantically try to capture verbatim on my laptop. Those notes would form the basis of the drafts I would send to her, which would often come back covered with edits.

At times our back-and-forth was extensive. I must have trekked from my office, through the West Wing, up to the White House Usher's office outside the First Family's residence hundreds of times to retrieve speeches marked up in her neat handwriting.

The hours were not always predictable. As one of my colleagues once said, in the White House, you never have the day you think you're going to have. And the travel could be disorienting—more than once I woke up unsure of what state or country I was in.

But I never doubted that what I was doing mattered, and I felt—and still feel—that I was part of an especially hopeful moment in the American story. At a time when history seems to be heading in the opposite direction, I try to remind myself that its arc is long. And I think often of Mrs. Obama's address at the 2016 Democratic National Convention, where she declared, "I wake up every morning in a house that was built by slaves, and I watch my daughters, two beautiful, intelligent, black young women playing with their dogs on the White House lawn."

To this day, people tell me that they try to live by the motto she shared in that speech: "When they go low, we go high." (I wish I could take credit for that line, but she came up with it—all I did was type it into the speech.)

Even as a kid who grew up dreaming of having a career in politics, I never could have imagined that I would one day work for a President and First Lady like the Obamas. No matter what else happens in the rest of my life, I'll always feel like I won some kind of lottery.

Now, in rare quiet moments, did I sometimes feel like something was missing? I did. But I don't think I could have articulated what it was. I chalked it up to the wisdom of a line Sarah Silverman delivers in the movie *Take This Waltz*: "Life has a gap in it. It just does. You don't go crazy trying to fill it like some lunatic."

So I know I disappoint people when I give them honest answers to their questions about what prompted me to start learning about Judaism as an adult. I know they're expecting some kind of major life crisis, or the culmination of a long spiritual journey. But the truth is much less exciting: At the age of thirty-six, I broke up with a guy I had been dating, found myself with a lot of time on my hands that had previously been spent with him, and happened to hear about an Introduction to Judaism class at the Washington, D.C., Jewish Community Center. I signed up less to fulfill some existential longing and more to fill a couple of hours on a Wednesday night that would otherwise have been spent feeling lonely in my apartment.

But what I discovered in that class utterly floored me.

I had always thought of myself as a good person, but the Jewish ethics we studied set a much higher bar for honesty, generosity, and basic human decency than I had ever thought to set for myself. Once I actually understood the purposes of the holidays and life cycle rituals, they struck me as beautiful and profound, honoring the lessons of the past, sanctifying moments in the present, and conveying deep moral wisdom. Seen through adult eyes, the whole sensibility of Judaism spoke to me—its intellectual rigor, its creativity and humanity, its emphasis on questioning and debate. This wasn't the stale, rote Judaism of my childhood. It was something relevant, endlessly fascinating, and alive.

That first class led me to a second, more intensive introductory class, which led me to additional classes, as well as retreats, lectures, one-on-one studies with rabbis, and countless hours spent reading about Judaism on my own. I was amazed to discover an entire universe of people doing the most innovative things with Judaism—a Jewish renaissance that had been going on for years, which, as a disengaged Jew, I knew nothing about because, well, I was disengaged.

I met rabbis who exposed me to conceptions of God that didn't strike me as childish or crazy. I encountered Jews who were leading Jewish meditation retreats, reinventing Hebrew school, creating outreach programs for interfaith families, reimagining the kosher laws* to protect farmworkers and the environment, infusing synagogue services with beautiful music and modern translations, and so much more.

I found spaces where I could wrestle with big questions: What's the deal with God? What is our purpose here on earth? What happens after we die? What does it mean to be a good person? To be true to yourself? To treat others well?

People generally do not raise such questions in the heat of a presidential campaign, or in the daily churn of life in the White House, or in polite dinner party conversation in Washington, D.C. In fact, in the final months of the Obama Administration, I was at an office happy

---

* These are the Jewish dietary laws—the ones that prohibit eating pork, among other rules. We'll discuss further in Chapter 5.

hour and approached two of my colleagues who were deep in conversation. "What are you guys talking about?" I asked. One of them replied, "Actually, we're talking about the afterlife."

I couldn't believe it—this was my kind of conversation! "That's amazing!" I exclaimed. "Can I join you guys? Can we talk about God too?" They stared back at me, baffled. And then one of them started laughing. "No, Sarah, the *afterlife* . . . like what we're going to do *after* we leave the White House."

The rabbis and Jewish educators I met, however, were thrilled to have these kinds of conversations with me. And these were smart, thoughtful people who had no interest in easy answers. They happily welcomed my questions, no matter how pointed or petulant. They patiently listened to my rants about the awfulness of Jewish liturgy and the foolishness of believing in the kind of God depicted in those prayers. And they lovingly responded—often by sharing their own struggles and doubts.

Nothing was off-limits, and there were no "because so-and-so authority figure says so" or "because God wants it that way" explanations. In fact, it was fine if I didn't believe in God at all, and nothing I said seemed to shock or upset anyone. They had heard it all before—or thought it themselves.

In Judaism, I discovered, the questions are often more important than the answers. But many of the answers are quite impressive. It turned out that Judaism had deep wisdom to offer me—teachings that have helped me be kinder and more honest, challenged my lazy and self-righteous assumptions about religion, and led me to view the values of modern secular society with a more skeptical eye.

After years working in politics, trying to keep up with the twenty-four-hour news cycle in a media environment driven by the quick "take"—the zinger on cable news or snap opinion in a tweet—I found that Judaism offered millions of pages of painstaking commentary and debate written over thousands of years. Judaism, I discovered, demands an appreciation of complexity and scrupulous consideration of opposing views.

Having endured a round-the-clock schedule on campaigns and at times in the White House, I found that Judaism says there are limits. For one day each week, on Shabbat, Judaism tells us to stop everything—stop working, stop buying, stop trying to bend the world to our desires—and simply appreciate and enjoy what we have.

In a city like Washington, D.C., where everyone is always vying for power, striving to be in the elusive inner circle, Judaism emphasizes our obligations to those on the margins. Many of the earliest Jewish laws focused on protecting the most vulnerable—widows, orphans, outsiders, and the poor.

And it turned out that some of the hottest spiritual trends in recent years—practices that have inspired numerous books and TED Talks—have actually been part of Judaism for centuries.

The gratitude movement? The first word of the first prayer Jews traditionally say when they wake up in the morning is "grateful"—they express gratitude for being alive with a prayer that begins "Grateful am I." And the Hebrew word for Jew, "Yehudi," actually comes from the same root as the word that means "to thank."

The mindfulness craze? Judaism is basically one big mindfulness practice, with countless rituals and practices (including meditation) to wake us up and help us be more present in our lives.

It's hard to overstate how surprised I was by these discoveries. None of this was evident to me during the two services I grudgingly sat through each year. And with those occasions as my main points of contact with Judaism, it had never occurred to me to look to it for answers to my big life questions or as a source of meaning and spirituality.

I had thought I didn't need religion and that serious engagement with Judaism might be valuable for others, but not for me.

It turned out that I was wrong.

If you also feel that you don't need what religion has to offer, I would ask you this: Have you ever read any kind of self-help book or books people have written about their journeys of self-discovery? Have you ever seen a therapist? Tried yoga or meditation?

Why did you do those things? Were you looking to find peace of mind or spiritual connection? Understand yourself more deeply? Become a better person? Lead a more meaningful, impactful life?

All of this happens to be precisely what religion, when done well, can provide. The problem is that it is often not done well, and it comes with a lot of baggage—both current and historic. Religion can be associated with a kind of unquestioning adherence that repels many thoughtful people, and religions generally get the most press when their followers twist them into excuses to harm others—to shun those who worship differently, or swindle people out of their hard-earned money, or even murder nonbelievers. And religious traditions have been used to justify racism, sexism, homophobia, transphobia, Islamophobia, anti-semitism, xenophobia, and other disgusting ideologies.

And it's not just these distorted forms of religion that turn people off, but the stale, uninspiring versions as well. I've met plenty of Jews and people of other backgrounds who consider themselves spiritual and yearn to belong to some kind of religious community but have trouble finding one that moves and challenges them. Or they're still scarred by memories of the dullness, materialism, rigidity, or vapidity of their childhood congregations.

So I understand why many people have an instinct to run as far as possible from organized religion, or just don't believe it's worth their time. But I think we can at least agree that lots of people actually *do* want what religion is supposed to offer—they're just looking for it elsewhere.

Many search outside of established religious traditions, drawn to individuals who offer a variety of spiritual services, including healing experiences and practices that evoke intense highs. I don't think there's anything inherently wrong with this kind of seeking. There is much wisdom and insight to be found outside of mainstream religious institutions. And one of the most renowned Jewish philosophers of all time, a twelfth-century rabbi named Moses Maimonides, once declared, "Listen to the truth from whoever said it."

But I'm thinking that religions that have been practiced by millions, even billions of people over thousands of years might also have something to offer, possibly even something more worthwhile than that one person who set up shop a few years ago.

A great many seekers have thrown themselves into exploring these established faiths, eager to take what they can from as many as possible and mix and match those traditions with other spiritual practices they've found along the way. I think the impulse here is wonderful. I have done this myself, incorporating Buddhist meditation techniques into my Jewish practice.

But I'm hesitant about an approach to spirituality where, instead of picking one religion and putting in the time and effort to engage deeply with it, we learn just a little bit about many traditions and then decide to do this thing from one tradition, and that thing from another, because each of these things speaks to us in some way—because each feels like it's "so me"—and we don't have to deal with the other parts of those belief systems that are "so not me."

When we do this, we're embracing the aspects of these traditions that reinforce our current preferences and beliefs and ignoring those that don't. In other words—and I hope this doesn't sound too harsh—we're reifying, maybe even deifying, *ourselves,* focusing on the self-discovery, self-affirmation, and self-expression parts of religion (the "comfort the afflicted" parts) and neglecting the self-discipline, self-sacrifice, and self-transcendence parts (the "afflict the comfortable" parts).

As Rabbi Danya Ruttenberg points out, in beginning and ending with ourselves this way, we're never forced to wrestle with ideas that challenge our core beliefs, hold us to more rigorous moral standards than we're accustomed to, or otherwise push us to grow as human beings. The Eastern Orthodox Christian writer Frederica Mathewes-Green describes this approach as "constructing a safe, tidy, unsurprising God who could never transform me, but would only confirm my residence in that familiar bog I called home."

This is similar to how many of us consume media today. We consult the news sources and engage with the social media that confirm our own points of view, and algorithms just keep showing us more of what we like. As a result, we're becoming narrower-minded and more convinced of our own unimpeachable rightness.

But religions do not exist solely to provide comfort and affirmation. Each, Ruttenberg notes, is a comprehensive system that is also meant to call us on our callousness and selfishness and help us become more compassionate, ethical people. So while we should certainly learn from many different traditions, there's something to be said for committing to one of them and engaging deeply with it—wrestling with it, learning from it, challenging it, and rejecting or reimagining the parts of it that have become obsolete.

So why Judaism?

For those who were not born into a Jewish family, I think the answer to this question is: Because it speaks to you in some way, and you wish to join your fate with the fate of the Jewish people—perhaps because you're marrying someone Jewish (though that certainly isn't a requirement).

While Jews do not proselytize, people who wish to convert are welcome. Conversion is a serious process that involves quite a bit of study. But once you convert, there's generally no distinction between you and any other Jew, and Jewish law forbids belittling or disrespecting someone because of their status as a Jew by choice. Following conversion, you're even considered to have Jewish ancestry—those who convert are traditionally given Hebrew names* that include "son/daughter of Abraham and Sarah." They are recognized as descendants of the very first Jews.

In every class I have taken, the people looking to convert were, by

---

* Your Hebrew name is the name you use in Jewish ritual contexts (at your bar/bat mitzvah and in your wedding documents, for example). It is composed of your first name (or a Hebraicized version of your first name) and possibly other names, followed by "son/daughter of," and then the Hebrew names of your parents. If your first name doesn't have an obvious Hebrew parallel, you may have a separate Hebrew first name. An example of a Hebrew name is as follows: "Leah Sarah, daughter of David Moshe and Tamar Devorah."

far, the most enthusiastic and knowledgeable. They brought a fresh perspective and a commitment that many of us born into Judaism lack.

I think the answer to the "Why be Jewish?" question is different—and more challenging—for those of us born Jewish.* Answers to this question from previous generations often went something like: You should be Jewish because of the Holocaust and Israel. And because if you don't practice Judaism and marry someone Jewish, Judaism will die out. And because being proudly Jewish is how we defy our enemies.

I understand where these arguments are coming from, and some of them do have resonance for me. But I worry that they boil down to little more than "You should be Jewish so that Judaism can survive," rather than a substantive case for the meaning, joy, and connection that Judaism and membership in the Jewish people can provide.

But plenty of religions and secular philosophers offer belief systems that can provide meaning, joy, and connection—belief systems that may be even more compelling to us than Judaism.

So again, why Judaism?

One of the best answers I've found to this question comes in the form of the following hypothetical scenario laid out by Rabbi Jonathan Sacks: Picture a library filled with books describing various values you could choose to embrace and lifestyles you could choose to live. You're free to pull any book off the shelf and browse its contents. If you like it, you can read other books on that topic or by that author. If not, you can just put it back and pick another.

But imagine, Sacks writes, if on those shelves, you came across a book with your family's name printed on its spine. He continues:

---

* Different Jewish denominations have different rules about whether they consider a child Jewish. The Orthodox and Conservative position is that a child is Jewish only if the child's mother is Jewish (if not, the child will have to convert). The Reform and Reconstructionist movements consider a child Jewish if either of the child's parents is Jewish and the child is raised as a Jew. And FYI, the Reform and Reconstructionist approach is not a modern innovation: Until the first century, Judaism was passed on through the father, not the mother.

Intrigued, you open it and see many pages written by different hands in many languages. You start reading it, and gradually you begin to understand what it is. It is the story each generation of your ancestors has told for the sake of the next, so that everyone born into this family can learn where they came from, what happened to them, what they lived for and why. As you turn the pages, you reach the last, which carries no entry but a heading. It bears your name.

This is what Judaism is—it's not just a religion, it is the story of a large, diverse family. Christianity is a religion (also quite diverse)—it's based on a core set of beliefs. If you're a Christian, but you one day decide that Jesus Christ was not the son of God and did not die for your sins, and that you don't believe in God at all, you may well conclude that you're no longer a Christian.

By contrast, being Jewish, as the Israeli academic Ze'ev Maghen puts it, "is a lot more like 'being one of the Goldblatt kids'." No matter how estranged you are from your family, no matter how vehemently you reject their values, no matter whether you change your name and join another family, there is nothing you can do to erase the fact of being your parents' offspring. It's the same with being Jewish: If you're Jewish, even if you disavow every single Jewish belief and convert to some other religion, Jewish law still considers you to be Jewish. You are always part of this family and its story. It is your story too.

And standing there in that library, are you really going to view the book that contains that story—your family's story—as just one of many that offer wisdom for how to live? Are you really going to put it back on the shelf and move on?

Might some of those other books have wisdom that would resonate just as much for you as Judaism, if not more so? Absolutely, and I think you should read them too. But they are not the story of your family.

Understanding our family's story helps us know who we are and where we came from (which is why, as Rabbi Sacks points out, people who are adopted are often eager to learn about their birth families). And the story of the Jewish family happens to be a pretty good one— one that has lasted thousands of years despite determined efforts to snuff it out and has shaped some of the world's most renowned people; birthed the world's two largest religions, Christianity and Islam; and set forth some of the world's most enduring ideas.

At this point, if you're not Jewish, I hope you're thinking, "Judaism sounds pretty interesting, I'd like to learn more." My life has been greatly enriched by what I've learned about other religious traditions, and "don't proselytize" doesn't mean "don't share," so I'm excited to share with you what I've learned about Judaism. While the rest of this introduction is aimed at readers who are Jewish or considering becoming Jewish, and that is the core audience for this book, I would be thrilled to have readers of all faiths and none.

If you are Jewish, I hope you're also eager to learn more about Judaism. But I know that if the me of five years ago were reading this book right now, she would not only be surprised by what I've written so far, but quite skeptical. She would likely be thinking, "It's great that Judaism is so meaningful for you, Future-Sarah, and I really am proud to be Jewish. But Judaism just isn't an important part of my life right now."

"I'm an ethnic Jew," Five-Years-Ago-Sarah might have said, or "I'm a cultural Jew," or "For me, doing social justice is how I practice Judaism."

I fully embraced each of these identities at one point or another, maybe even more than one of them at a time. But I've come to realize that much of what I used to think about being an ethnic/cultural/social justice Jew doesn't make sense.

Let's start with the notion of an "ethnic Jew." It turns out that there is no one authentic Jewish ethnicity. Jews come in every race and ethnicity. There are Ashkenazi Jews, whose family trees stretch back through much of Europe; Sephardi Jews, who can trace their lineage back to Spain and Portugal; Mizraḥi Jews, who have ancestors from the Middle East and North Africa; and others. There are African American Jews, Latino Jews, Asian American Jews, and Native American Jews—both those who were born Jewish and those who became Jewish via conversion. And there are plenty of multiracial and multiethnic Jews too.

I would also point out that ethnicity can be a dicey bet for long-term identity in a country like America with such a strong assimilationist pull. We can debate whether America is a melting pot or a salad bowl, but there is no denying that after a few generations in this country, the strength of many people's ethnic identities wanes. Generations ago, being of Irish, Italian, or German descent was an important part of how many Americans defined themselves, but that is much less true for their great-grandchildren. And a recent study of people with Hispanic ancestry showed that the longer their families had been in America, the less likely they were to identify as Latino or Hispanic.

As for being a "cultural Jew," it would have been one thing if I had meant that I loved celebrating Jewish holidays and life cycle rituals or learning about Jewish history, literature, art, or ethics, but just wasn't into the God/prayer aspects of Judaism. But by identifying as a "cultural Jew," I really meant that I felt like I had a "Jewish personality": funny in an edgy, gallows humor kind of way; anxious and convinced the worst is always going to happen; intellectual and into arguing about ideas.

But all of that is also true of many people who are *not* Jewish. And there are plenty of Jews who are humorless, laid-back, unintellectual, and nonconfrontational to a fault, and that does not make them any less Jewish than the rest of us.

By "cultural Jew," I also probably meant that I wasn't interested in practicing or learning about Judaism, but I'm fond of matzah ball soup, delight in discovering that famous people I admire are Jewish, and get a kick out of eating Chinese food on Christmas. There's nothing wrong with any of that, but I think I was selling Judaism a bit short. As Rabbi Telushkin wrote, "The purpose of Jewish existence is not to eat Jewish foods, or tell Jewish jokes, or use Yiddish* words. It is to fight evil and to reduce suffering in the world."

As for being a social justice Jew, this one is more challenging, because I agree with Rabbi Telushkin that social justice is indeed a core *purpose* of Jewish existence. But by calling myself a social justice Jew, I wasn't saying that my engagement with Judaism had inspired me to right the world's wrongs. Rather, I meant that my career in public service *was* my engagement with Judaism.

But Judaism isn't the only religion that emphasizes social justice. Consider the story of Jesus, with his passionate insistence on caring for the least among us. There is an entire religion that urges its followers to be just like him. Also, check out the Koran—one of the five pillars of Islam is "Zakat," or charity. And the Bhagavad Gita extols the value of selfless service to others. While Judaism certainly has its own unique approach to social justice, and social justice is indeed an important Jewish value, it is an important value in other traditions as well. And like those traditions, Judaism has a great deal to offer in addition to its commitment to bettering the world.

That's really the problem with being an ethnic, cultural, or social justice Jew: These are all incomplete notions of what Judaism is—notions that focus on just one aspect of it while ignoring everything else.

For me, I think these labels were a way of saying: I'm proud to be Jewish, and I sense that I'm part of something bigger that in some way explains who I am—but I can't quite articulate what that is. And while I can't figure out how to connect with Judaism in a meaningful way, I wish I could, because it feels important.

And it's not just Jews like me on the less traditionally observant end of the spectrum who struggle with their Jewish identity. Plenty of very religious Jews at times feel like they're just going through the motions, or even have full-on crises of belief and find themselves just as alienated by and disconnected from Judaism as I was.

---

* Yiddish is a language once commonly spoken by European Jews and still spoken by a small number of people today.

Yet, even some of the most disaffected Jews will admit that something inside them feels unsettled. Even if they won't go anywhere near a synagogue, it still doesn't feel quite right to attend their partners' churches on Easter or have Christmas trees in their living rooms. And even if Judaism as they know it leaves them cold, there is something about it—albeit faint and inexplicable—that still tugs at them.

There is a Yiddish phrase for this: "dos pintele yid," which literally means "that little point of a Jew" and refers to that spark of Jewishness in each of us that we can't quite manage to ignore, no matter how hard we may try.

Kindling that spark, I believe, starts with recognizing that for many of us, our understanding of Judaism is frozen in childhood, limited to what our seventh-grade minds were capable of grasping. And while Judaism offers plenty to engage children, much of its deepest, most transformative wisdom is really only accessible to adults.

I will be the first to admit that learning about Judaism as an adult is no small task. In addition to being a family, Judaism is also—as the influential twentieth-century American rabbi Mordecai Kaplan noted—a "civilization." It has its own languages, history, customs, religion, holidays, and laws (which is why it's quite unfair to expect Hebrew school teachers to give kids a decent Jewish education in just a few hours a week). Consequently, the source material about Judaism is mind-bogglingly vast—millions of pages written over thousands of years, much of it in Hebrew and other languages many of us don't understand.

There are plenty of secondary sources in English, but they're often quite sophisticated and academic, inaccessible to those without a basic Jewish education and the patience to slog through dense writing. There are a number of books geared toward beginners, many of which have been tremendously helpful to me. But because Jews don't proselytize, we don't have centuries of experience explaining Judaism to those who know nothing about it. And while some of the introductory books I read did an excellent job laying out the mechanics of Jewish practice—how to celebrate holidays, when to recite prayers, what Jewish law says about various topics—I often struggled to figure out why these details mattered and how I could map them onto the topography of my own life.

When I read books about Judaism, I'm sometimes reminded of my experience working with policy experts in the White House. If I was writing a speech about health care, a health care policy expert might have excitedly informed me, "Our health care policy is going to bend the cost curve and improve the delivery system!" That may indeed be impressive, but most people do not think about health care this way. They are not interested in the mechanics of how the policy works. They want to know whether their health insurance will be affordable and cover the care they need and the doctors they want to see. That is the beating heart of this issue for them—where they live it and feel it every day. It is a speechwriter's job to cut through the policy jargon and find that beating heart.

This is how I approach Judaism. Not as an expert—I have neither rabbinic training nor an academic degree in Jewish studies. But as a speechwriter trying to find its beating heart for myself and others—the places where we can live and feel Judaism's wisdom in our lives, the parts of Judaism that feel like its deepest, most important truths. I'm essentially trying to write the book I wish I'd had five years ago, when I first started learning about Judaism as an adult—one that teaches the basics while also uncovering some of Judaism's most profound ideas.

Back then, I realized that to engage meaningfully with Judaism, I needed to be familiar with its sacred origins and evolution over time. Only once I had some familiarity with Judaism's key holy text, the Torah, and understood how Jews have continued to interpret and reinterpret it for thousands of years, could I begin to appreciate the life-changing insights Judaism has to offer. This book is structured accordingly, with Part I focusing on the textual, historical, theological, and legal foundations of Judaism and Part II focusing on Jewish ethics, spiritual practices, holidays, and life cycle rituals. Throughout, I share not just my own struggles and thoughts but those of various rabbis, scholars, and

Jewish leaders, both modern and historic.* So this book is not just my own story, but that of Jews throughout history who have done the seeking, learning, experimenting, and grappling required to make this tradition their own.

Though I should be clear that this book is by no means a comprehensive, objective description of Judaism. I have neither the expertise nor the desire to attempt such a thing, nor do I think it's possible. Judaism is vast and deep and shaped by so many different people, and perhaps you've heard the old joke: Two Jews, three opinions.

I'm simply a Jew with some opinions—a Jew in the pew, as the saying goes, though I'm only rarely in the pew these days, so even that is probably an overstatement. While this book is informed by careful research and significant input from experts across the spectrum of Jewish practice and belief, it is simply an account of what in Judaism has most spoken to me. But I hope much of it will speak to you as well. I hope it will convince you that there is something in Judaism worth finding and inspire you to start—or continue—looking for yourself.

At a time when all Jews are Jews by choice, we have to believe that Judaism is worth choosing. I wrote this book in the hope of showing you that it is.

---

* I share their words and ideas not necessarily because of who they are, or because I agree with all of their views. Rather, I cite them because something they've written or said has helped me understand and appreciate Judaism. I thus do not include biographical information on them unless I feel that it's relevant to the content of their quotes.

PART I

CHAPTER 1

In the Beginning and In the Image: The Torah

G rowing up, I knew the Torah was the large scroll at the front of the synagogue that was sometimes unfurled and read from during services. And I had a vague sense that it was Judaism's core sacred text. But while I was familiar with some of its stories and characters, I had no idea that it is the first five books of the Hebrew Bible—known as the "Tanakh"—which Christians refer to as "the Old Testament."*

When I first read the Torah as an adult, and I learned that just about all of Judaism is rooted in its words, that did not exactly fill me with

---

* Unlike Christians, Jews do not believe the Hebrew Bible/Tanakh was superseded by the New Testament, which details the life and teachings of Jesus, so we do not use the Christian term "Old Testament." The word "Tanakh" is an acronym for the names of the Hebrew Bible's three main sections. The five books of the Torah compose the first section. The other two sections are the "Nevi'im" (which means "Prophets," and includes the books named after Hebrew prophets like Isaiah and Jeremiah) and the "Ketuvim" (which means "Writings," and includes books like Psalms, Proverbs, Job, and Ecclesiastes). T-N-K = Tanakh. While the Nevi'im and Ketuvim are important in Judaism, the Torah is our most holy text and is regarded as the source of Jewish law.

confidence. I found parts of it to be moving and relatable, but with its bizarre rituals, fallible characters, supernatural occurrences, and not so warm and fuzzy God, the Torah did not strike me as an ideal text upon which to base a major world religion.

I've since come around and now understand that the Torah is filled with revolutionary ideas, deep insights into the human condition, and profound moral wisdom. But getting there was a process—one I went through with many aspects of Judaism I encountered—from skepticism or disdain, to gradual comprehension and grudging appreciation, to outright appreciation and, often, something that feels like love.

THE TORAH'S PLOT

In my skepticism/disdain phase, I read the Torah mainly for plot, as a quasi-historical account of the exploits of my ancestors. Read this way, the Torah goes something like this:

Book One: Genesis

Creation Story #1: God brings the world and humans into being in six days via a series of verbal commands and then rests on the seventh day.

Creation Story #2: God creates Adam out of the dust of the earth, breathes life into him, settles him in the Garden of Eden, forbids him to eat from the Tree of Knowledge of Good and Evil, and creates Eve from his side.* Adam and Eve eat from the forbidden tree, and God expels them from the Garden.

Adam and Eve have two sons, Cain and Abel. God accepts a sacrifice from Abel, and not Cain. Cain becomes jealous and kills Abel.

People multiply on earth and behave badly. God sends a flood to wipe out everyone but a man named Noah, his family, and a select group of animals. God then makes a covenant with all humankind and animalkind never to do so again.

---

* Or from his "rib"—there is a debate as to how this particular Hebrew word should be translated.

God tells a man named Abram to leave his native land of Mesopotamia for a new land, the Promised Land (known as Canaan),* which his descendants will inherit[†] (and God declares that they will become "a great nation"[‡]). Abram does so, along with his wife, Sarai.

Sarai is infertile and tells Abram to take her Egyptian maid, Hagar, as a surrogate. Hagar gets pregnant. Sarai is jealous and mistreats Hagar. Hagar runs away. God comforts Hagar and tells her to return. Hagar gives birth to Ishmael. God helps Sarai conceive (at the age of ninety) and changes her name to Sarah and Abram's name to Abraham.

God threatens to kill all the inhabitants of Sodom and Gomorrah because of their cruelty and immorality.[§] Abraham pushes back on God, convincing God to relent if there are at least ten righteous men to be found. There aren't. God goes through with God's plan.

Sarah gives birth to Isaac. Years later, God tells Abraham to sacrifice Isaac as a burnt offering, but stops him just as he's about to do so.

Isaac grows up, marries Rebekah, and they have twin sons, Jacob and Esau. Jacob gets Esau (who came out of the womb first) to give up the inheritance due to him as the firstborn son and then, at Rebekah's urging, swindles him out of an important deathbed blessing from their father. Esau vows revenge, and Jacob flees to his uncle, Laban. Jacob falls in love with Laban's daughter, Rachel; is tricked by Laban into marrying his other daughter, Leah; but then marries Rachel too.[¶]

Jacob decides to reconcile with Esau. On his way to meet his brother, he encounters a mysterious being with whom he has an overnight wrestling match. Jacob prevails, and the being changes Jacob's name to "Israel" and declares, "For you have wrestled with God and man and have prevailed." Jacob and Esau have a touching reunion.

Jacob and his family settle in Canaan. Jacob's favorite son, Joseph,

---

* The Hebrew Bible also refers to Canaan as "the Land of Israel."
† This bequest becomes part of a covenant that God makes with Abram, one of Abram's sons (Isaac), and one of his grandsons (Jacob).
‡ "Nation" in this context is synonymous with "people" or "tribe."
§ Not, as some later claimed, because they are gay.
¶ Polygamy and cousin-marrying were common back then.

annoys his brothers, and they retaliate by selling him into slavery. Through a series of unfortunate, and then fortunate, events, Joseph becomes the deputy of the Egyptian Pharaoh. When a famine hits, Jacob sends his sons to Egypt to purchase food. They come before Joseph, the brothers eventually reconcile, and the whole family moves to Egypt.*

Book Two: Exodus

The Israelites are fruitful and multiply in Egypt, but then a new Pharaoh comes to power who feels threatened by their numbers and enslaves them. Pharaoh orders two midwives to kill any baby boys born to Israelites. The midwives refuse. Pharaoh then orders all Egyptians to drown any boy born to the Israelites.

An Israelite woman gives birth to a son. Unable to hide him from the Egyptians, she puts him in a basket on the Nile River while his sister, Miriam, hovers nearby. Pharaoh's daughter comes to bathe in the river, discovers the baby, realizes he's an Israelite, but rescues him anyway. Miriam helpfully offers her mother as a wet nurse for the baby. Once the baby is weaned, Pharaoh's daughter adopts him and gives him an Egyptian name: Moses.

When Moses grows up, he sees an Egyptian beating an Israelite and intervenes to defend the Israelite, killing the Egyptian. Moses flees to a land called Midian, where he defends the daughters of a Midianite priest named Jethro from shepherds blocking them from getting water for their father's sheep. Moses later marries one of the daughters, Zipporah.

God appears to Moses in a burning bush, which miraculously is not consumed by the flames, declares an intent to free the Israelites from Egypt and bring them to the Promised Land, and states that Moses will be leading this rescue mission. Moses repeatedly demurs, noting that he is "slow of speech and slow of tongue." God is irritated, but offers to appoint Moses' brother, Aaron, as Moses' spokesperson. Moses accepts the charge.

---

* These brothers are the forefathers of the twelve tribes of Israel, which are named after them (with the exception of Joseph—instead, tribes are named after his two sons).

Moses and Aaron return to Egypt and repeatedly try to convince Pharaoh to release the Israelites. Pharaoh repeatedly refuses, and God unleashes a series of plagues (Nile River turning to blood, frogs, lice, etc.) culminating in the death of all firstborn offspring (human and animal) in Egypt. Per God's instructions, the Israelites mark their doorposts with lamb's blood so God will know to pass over their homes and not kill their firstborn.

Pharaoh finally lets the Israelites go, then changes his mind and chases them down. God parts the Sea of Reeds* so the Israelites can cross, and then drowns the pursuing Egyptians. The Israelites enter the wilderness and bitterly complain about their hunger. God provides food for them in the form of a substance they call "manna."

God decides to address the entire Israelite population at Mount Sinai and outlines the terms of a covenant God would like to make with them. God starts with the Ten Commandments (which, in addition to laws against lying, stealing, and murdering, include prohibitions on idolatry and worshipping other gods, as well as instructions for observing the Sabbath). God then dictates additional laws regarding slavery, mistreatment of parents, kidnapping, assault, sorcery, gossip, bribery, and other transgressions, along with guidelines for observing festivals. God is also adamant about ensuring just treatment of the vulnerable, issuing laws to protect widows, orphans, strangers,† and the poor.

The Israelites agree to this covenant.

Moses leaves to spend forty days and nights with God on Mount Sinai, where God gives him painstakingly detailed instructions for the construction of the Tabernacle, a portable sanctuary where God will appear and receive sacrifices from the Israelites. With Moses gone for so long, the Israelites get anxious, and they create and start worshipping a golden calf, violating the no-idolatry provision of the covenant.

---

* While the Torah could have been referring to the body of water known today as the Red Sea, the biblical Hebrew actually translates as "Sea of Reeds" or "Reed Sea," not "Red Sea."

† The word "stranger" refers to a non-Israelite living among the Israelites. We'll talk more about this later in this chapter.

God is enraged and threatens to kill them all. Moses convinces God to refrain from doing so.

The Israelites build the Tabernacle, and God settles in to accompany them on their journey to the Promised Land.

Book Three: Leviticus

God issues numerous instructions for how the Israelites should worship God by making sacrifices (of animals, grains, oil)* for various purposes (to atone for sins, express gratitude). God also specifies the following: what animals the Israelites may and may not eat; how they should restore personal purity in the wake of skin diseases, childbirth, menstruation, and male ejaculation; and with whom they may have sexual relations.

In addition, God establishes various holidays; issues more laws for how the Israelites should treat each other, including a strong prohibition on child sacrifice and decrees for periodic redistribution of wealth; and details the rewards (fertile fields and people, victory over enemies) and punishments (death, disease, despair, defeat by enemies) the Israelites will receive for following/breaking these laws.

Book Four: Numbers

God organizes the twelve Israelite tribes into quasi-military formation in preparation for their impending journey through the desert and tells Moses to take a census of all men old enough to bear arms. The Israelites then set off for the Promised Land with God guiding their way.

God tells Moses to dispatch spies to scout out the Promised Land. The spies are easily spooked, and upon returning they deliver a hyperbolic report claiming that Canaan is filled with fortified cities and giant people—though two of the spies, Caleb and Joshua, disagree. The Israelites panic and demand to go back to Egypt. God is now very frustrated

---

* This practice was common among peoples in the ancient Near East.

and decrees that the Israelites will wander for forty years in the desert, and with the exception of Caleb and Joshua, only future generations will enter the Promised Land.

Moses executes an order from God not exactly as God wished, and God informs Moses that he won't get to lead the Israelites into the Promised Land.

Book Five: Deuteronomy

When the Israelites reach the border of the Promised Land, Moses addresses them in a series of speeches in which he recaps the highlights of their journey; reminds them of everything God has done for them; reviews the laws God has set out for them; warns them of the horrific things (pestilence, starvation, madness, cannibalism) that will befall them if they don't uphold their end of the covenant by following these laws; emphasizes that the choice is theirs but strongly recommends that they stick it out with God; and then dies.

Other things happen too—some very strange (there is a talking donkey), some quite fabulous (a group of women demand that Moses change property inheritance laws that favor men, and God agrees), and some deeply disturbing (God tells the Israelites to stone someone for working on Shabbat, kills thousands of them with a plague as punishment for their resistance to Moses' and Aaron's leadership, and urges them to treat their enemies in ways that we would today regard as war crimes). But I've hit the highlights.

WHAT ARE WE SUPPOSED TO MAKE OF ALL THIS?

When I read the Torah this way, focusing on plot and surface meaning, much of it seemed, to my modern sensibility, shocking, appalling, and quite bizarre.

I of course understood that the Torah is not a modern text. Scholars believe it was compiled* and edited sometime around the sixth century B.C.E.,† but the events it depicts appear to take place centuries earlier. The patriarch and matriarch narratives (the stories of Abraham, Isaac, Jacob, Sarah, Rebekah, Leah, and Rachel) seem to be set between 2000 and 1800 B.C.E., and the Exodus story around the thirteenth century B.C.E.

But while I tried to give the Torah the benefit of the doubt because of its antiquity and just focus on its beautiful and inspiring parts—stories of courage and devotion, laws that emphasize our obligations to the vulnerable—I found it hard to get beyond its disturbing aspects.

What was I supposed to do with that story about God ordering Abraham to slaughter his own son, for example? What kind of God would demand such a thing? What kind of person would be willing to obey such an order? Why is this person considered the father of the Jewish people? Why is this God the Jewish God?

This reaction is a good snapshot of how I had always approached Judaism: largely ignorant of context or history, generally assuming the worst, and quick to judge based on surface appearances.

To move from the skepticism/disdain stage of reading the Torah to the gradual comprehension/grudging appreciation stage, I first had to do some learning. I started with a classic essay entitled "Odysseus' Scar," in which literary scholar Erich Auerbach compares Homer's *Odyssey* to the Hebrew Bible. The Torah, Auerbach explains, is not written in epic poetry, as was the case with the *Odyssey* and other ancient texts, but in an unusually spare kind of prose. While in the *Odyssey,* Homer shares his characters' every thought and emotion in copious detail—with "never a lacuna, never a gap, never a glimpse of unplumbed depths"—in the Torah, by contrast, "thoughts and feeling remain unexpressed, are only suggested by the silence and the fragmentary speeches."

---

* Some amount of material in the Torah likely previously existed in the form of oral traditions, proverbs, and laws that originated centuries before they were incorporated into the text.
† C.E. stands for "common era." This acronym and "B.C.E.," "before the common era," are often used instead of B.C. and A.D., which refer to the birth of Jesus.

Auerbach actually cites as an example the story of God telling Abraham to sacrifice Isaac, so let's take a look at an excerpt from the Torah's account of their journey to the altar:

Abraham took the wood for the burnt offering and put it on his son Isaac. He himself took the firestone and the knife; and the two walked off together. Then Isaac said to his father Abraham, "Father!" And he answered, "Yes, my son." And he said, "Here are the firestone and the wood; but where is the sheep for the burnt offering?" And Abraham said, "God will see to the sheep for His burnt offering, my son." And the two of them walked on together.

When I first read this paragraph closely, I wondered: Is Isaac merely curious? Actively suspicious? Downright terrified? Totally unaware of what's happening? Does his father's response to his question reassure him or not?

What about Abraham? Does his cryptic statement about God providing the sheep indicate that he's committed to killing his son? Or is it evidence that he's confident God will not ultimately require him to do such a thing and will provide an animal for him to sacrifice instead (which God does)? Is God testing Abraham, or is Abraham testing God? Does Abraham pass the test? Does God?

Is this story a simple polemic against child sacrifice, which the Torah repeatedly condemns? Or does it have a deeper message about the complexities of faith and family (note that this scene is the last time in the Torah that Abraham and Isaac speak to each other)?

The Torah provides no clear answers to these questions. This story is not a simple morality tale, it is a provocation, an invitation to a conversation—or maybe a debate. That is true of the other stories in the Torah as well. Summarizing Auerbach's conclusions, novelist Dara Horn notes that when it comes to the Hebrew Bible, "merely to read for the plain meaning of the text is to engage in an interpretive act."

This text, I realized, is not meant to be read for plot, it's meant to be interpreted for meaning. Doing so requires serious effort on the part of the reader, because the Torah is sparing with details not just in the stories it tells but in the laws it dictates as well. For example, we're told the following about how to help the poor: "You shall surely open your hand unto him, and shall surely lend him sufficient for his need in that which he wants." What, exactly, does that mean? Merely meeting his most basic needs? Maintaining him at the average level of the rest of the tribe? Restoring him to his former level of wealth before he fell into poverty? The Torah leaves it to us to figure all of this out. It demands not just obedience, but responsibility.

And rife with ambiguity, the Torah lends itself to multiple—often contradictory—interpretations. One traditional Jewish teaching claims that there are "seventy faces to the Torah," meaning many different ways to understand it. Another declares: "Turn it [the Torah] over and turn it over, for everything is in it."

Simply by reading this text, I was implicated in it. It was like an ancient Rorschach test: What did I see? How did I fill in its gaps? What did that say about me? How have Jews understood the Torah over the years? What does that say about us as a people?

The more I read, the more implicated I felt. Rather than being a triumphalist tale about the conquests of powerful rulers, the Torah is an oddly self-critical account of ordinary people called to meet extraordinary challenges who often fall short. While Moses stalwartly leads the Israelites forward despite their endless complaints and disobedience, as historian Paul Johnson notes, Moses is also sometimes depicted as

> hesitant and uncertain almost to the point of cowardice, mistaken, wrong-headed, foolish, irritable and, what is still more remarkable, bitterly conscious of his shortcomings . . . an isolated, rather desperate and inefficient figure, struggling with the burdens of a huge role he has reluctantly accepted but grimly seeks to discharge.

And Moses is arguably the Torah's greatest hero!

Because these characters are portrayed in all their complexity,* they feel incredibly real and familiar, even today. I'm thinking of Sarah's bitter laughter and caustic retort when she's informed that she will become pregnant: "Now that I am withered, am I to have enjoyment— with my husband so old?" And the Israelites' sarcastic protest to Moses when they realize the Egyptians are pursuing them: "Was it for want of graves in Egypt that you brought us to die in the wilderness?" And the advice Moses' father-in-law, Jethro, gives him when he finds him personally adjudicating every dispute between the Israelites: "The thing you are doing is not right; you will surely wear yourself out . . . For the task is too heavy for you; you cannot do it alone."

I know these people. I *am* these people: prone to sarcasm and ingratitude; panicky about change and convinced the worst is going to happen; bad at delegating and indebted to wise mentors who have given me invaluable advice.

But as much as I was drawn in by this text, I was also distracted and put off by the parts of it that I found to be horrifying or outright absurd. What was I supposed to make of that time when God parted the sea, or Adam lived to be 930 years old, or Sarah got pregnant at the age of 90 (after, the Torah helpfully informs us, she "had stopped having the periods of women"), or God sent magical food from the sky to feed the Israelites?

Even if I set aside the miracles, there's the issue of historical accuracy. Aspects of the stories about the matriarchs and patriarchs are consistent with what we know about the lives of people in that region and era, and there is evidence that various tribes had contacts with Egypt around the time of the Exodus. But we have yet to confirm that the

---

* It's worth noting that the women in the Torah are just as complex and interesting as the men. Some are difficult, like Sarah. Some are heroic, like the midwives who disobey Pharaoh's orders to kill the Israelite babies. In fact, Moses' very existence is made possible by a series of righteous women: the midwives, Moses' mother, Pharaoh's daughter, and Miriam. Do women in the Torah get the same amount of airtime as men? No. But nor are they props. And that is impressive for a 2,500-year-old document.

particular people in the Torah existed or that the particular events took place.

Then there's the issue of the Torah's authorship. Some Jews, who I assume are mainly on the more traditionally observant end of the spectrum, believe the Torah is the word of God. Most others, myself included, believe the academic literature indicating that it was written by multiple human authors, and there is a range of views as to whether these human authors were in some way divinely inspired.

Who were these authors? Were they ancient Israel's greatest minds and most insightful spiritual leaders? Possibly, but we're not sure who exactly had the pen on this document.

So I still think it's fair to ask: Is this 2,500-year-old text, which many of us believe was written by human beings about events that may or may not have happened four thousand years ago, still a sound basis for a religion that any of us should practice today?

My answer to this question is a resounding yes. But to get there, I had to learn a little about the time and place from which the Torah emerged and then sort through its ancient language to discover its core animating ideas. Only then did I move on to the outright appreciation and love phase, realizing just how radical, wise, and important the Torah is—not just in its own time, but in ours as well.

THE TORAH'S CORE ANIMATING IDEA:
IN THE IMAGE

The Torah represented a dramatic departure from many of the prevailing theological and political norms of the ancient Near East. The many gods that people worshipped in places like ancient Egypt and Mesopotamia each had their own life history and limited powers—over a particular activity (war, healing) or aspect of nature (sun, rain)—and they were often in conflict with each other. The key was to discern which gods were dominant at the moment and what they wanted, but they could be disconcertingly capricious. In one Mesopotamian legend, for example, the gods decide to drown every human being except for one man in a flood simply because humans were too noisy and prevented the gods from sleeping.*

While rulers in ancient times were often thought to descend from or be favored by these gods, or even be gods themselves, ordinary people were generally regarded as insignificant, if not downright expendable. And rulers didn't hesitate to press their lowly subjects into forced labor on various building projects.

By contrast, the God of the Torah has no birth story or biography, but rather is simply just there from the beginning. This God creates the world alone in an orderly fashion and doesn't battle it out with any other gods.† Indeed, this God is superior to all of them, with power over not just one aspect of the world, but the whole thing.

As for human beings, the Torah pointedly declares: "God created man in His‡ image, in the image of God He created him; male and female He created them."

This belief that every single one of us is created in the image of God has been cited as the defining Jewish idea, the beating heart of the entire Jewish enterprise. And you don't have to believe in any kind of deity or higher power to appreciate its implications. Drawing on an ancient Jewish teaching, Rabbi Yitz Greenberg argues that this idea is shorthand for three fundamental truths, which he deems the "three inalienable dignities":

1. We are each of infinite worth—no one is expendable, and we cannot quantify the value of any human life.

* The biblical story of Noah and the flood is a version of this Mesopotamian story, one that seems to pointedly rewrite it to emphasize that God sent the flood because humans were violent and lawless, not merely because they were disturbing God's beauty rest.
† The Torah clearly assumes the existence of other (lesser) gods, and God constantly implores the Israelites not to worship them.
‡ Judaism does not believe that God has one particular gender. Hebrew, however, is a gendered language, like Spanish and French, so every noun has a gender associated with it. While the Torah refers to God using male pronouns, and I will do so when quoting from it (and when sharing direct quotations from other sources), as Rabbi Danya Ruttenberg notes, "The pronoun for God is God." This makes for some awkward writing, which I do not love. But I love gendered God language even less.

2. We are all fundamentally equal—no human being is any more important than any other human being.

3. We are each totally unique—there is no one else like us, and no one is interchangeable with anybody else.

When I first put all of this together, I was stunned. I had of course been exposed to these three ideas before. But I had never seen them woven together this way, rooted in one core idea tied to Divinity, and located in the most sacred Jewish text. Given my prior experience with the Torah—viewing it mainly as a prop at the front of the synagogue during services—this was the last place I expected to find such an exquisite encapsulation of such fundamental moral teachings.

I was also flooded with a feeling of recognition. This In-the-Image idea and the "inalienable dignities" that flow from it are the very values that run through just about every speech I have ever written.

We are all infinitely worthy. According to the teaching Rabbi Greenberg cites, "Anyone who destroys a life is considered by Scripture to have destroyed an entire world; and anyone who saves a life is as if he saved an entire world." Every speech I wrote about international girls' education for Mrs. Obama explicitly articulated this belief—arguing that every girl on this planet has a universe of potential within her, that she is not a statistic or a unit of GDP, but a boundlessly precious human being.

We are all equal. Each year, Mrs. Obama would deliver several commencement addresses, and she preferred to speak at schools that rarely received visits from presidents and first ladies: inner-city high schools, a high school for Native American students, colleges with many low-income and first-generation students. She would always tell these striving, dreaming graduates: You may not have had the same advantages as some other young people, but you are equally deserving and have just as much to offer.

We are each unique. Mrs. Obama delivered her final address as First Lady in the wake of the 2016 presidential election, which had been infused with all manner of racism, Islamophobia, and xenophobia. And in her remarks, she took a moment to speak directly to the young people of America, urging them to be proud of who they are, how they worship, and where they come from. "Our glorious diversity," she declared, "is not a threat to who we are, it makes us who we are." She was telling each of them: You are not a smear or a stereotype, you are gloriously unique.

This may all sound obvious, like the basic values we try to teach our kids. But none of this was obvious back in ancient times. And I don't think it's obvious today either. If we really thought the homeless man we passed by each day on our way to work was as fundamentally worthy as a CEO or celebrity, I doubt we would ignore him. While in theory we believe in equality, in practice, American children start out with wildly different opportunities depending on the families into which they happen to be born, and we do little to remedy those inequalities. And in recent years, we have become increasingly polarized, seeing "those people" who disagree with us as an undefined group, all the same, rather than unique individuals.

The Torah sounded the alarm about all of this thousands of years ago, not just with its laws, but with the very story of God choosing the Israelites for the covenant in the first place. The Israelites were, to put it bluntly, the losers of the ancient world, as were their ancestors. Abraham was not a king. Moses was not a great warrior—when God came to him in the burning bush, he was a fugitive shepherd with a fear of public speaking. And if you were a typical ancient Near Eastern god looking to create a great nation, a tribe of anxious former slaves probably would not have been your top choice.

The Israelites were an extreme test case for how serious the Torah was about this In-the-Image idea. And even *they* passed the test. These highly fallible matriarchs and patriarchs and this ragtag bunch of newly freed slaves are just as much in the Divine image as any emperor or king. And if that is true for them, then it must be true for all of us as well.

All of this had been in those scrolls at the front of the synagogue as I sat through services year after year, wishing to be elsewhere. It had been there the whole time, and I had not known.

GOD IS POWERFUL . . . BUT SO ARE HUMAN BEINGS

Once I understood "In-the-Image" as the Torah's core animating idea, I began to read its stories and laws in a new light. I had always been under the impression that the Torah was about an all-powerful, vengeful God who demands unquestioning obedience and that the Torah's main message is: Do what God says or God will smite you.

But that is actually not the case. While the God of the Torah is clearly the ultimate power, human beings are not merely subjects of God's whims. Being in God's image, they too are empowered.

In fact, the very first instruction God issues to human beings is "Be fruitful and multiply, fill the earth and master it; and rule the fish of the sea, the birds of the sky, and all the living things that creep on earth." As Rabbi Reuven Hammer puts it, "The task they are given is to rule the world."

These new humans take this power and run with it. Not even ten verses after God creates Adam and Eve, they break the one rule God has given them—to not eat from the Tree of Knowledge of Good and Evil—seeming to take God by surprise. Humans continue to confound God throughout the Torah, not just with their disobedience, but with ethical demands of their own, from Abraham pleading with God to save the people of Sodom to Moses demanding that God have mercy on the Israelites after the golden calf incident.

As Judaism scholar Christine Hayes points out, God often appears to be playing catch-up, constantly adjusting to the decisions humans make. "Humans," she notes, "are going to be a force to be reckoned with. They're unpredictable to the very god who created them."

Yet despite God's frequent frustration, God never tries to modify humans to make them more obedient. God does not want people to just be God's servants. Instead, God asks them to be God's *partners*. That's what God was doing at Mount Sinai: God was presenting the Israelites with a covenant—a mutual agreement between two parties under which each agrees to perform certain actions in exchange for something of value from the other.

The form of this arrangement is significant, because as political theorist and Bible scholar Yoram Hazony notes, in the ancient world, there was a big difference between subjects who merely obeyed a king's law and subjects who agreed to a covenant (which is a form of contract) with the king:

> The king grants a covenant to *someone whom he respects, and whose services and assistance he needs and may not be able to obtain without his agreement* . . . In other words, the covenant is a relationship that recognizes the weaker party's *voluntary contribution* to the king's order—and the king's *need* of such help.

While God is clearly the "senior partner," as Rabbi Yitz Greenberg observes, there is no question that both parties have leverage in this agreement. God is asking not merely for the Israelites' obedience, but for their help in ruling the universe, help that they freely consent to give.

And God doesn't just form this partnership with Moses, or with a small number of powerful elites. God insists on gathering the entire Israelite people at Mount Sinai so they can all hear the terms of the covenant and decide whether to accept it. Once the Israelites have agreed to the covenant, God further insists that its terms be read out loud every seven years to the entire Israelite people, "men, women, children, and the strangers in your communities." This demand for universal access to the Divine teachings seems to be a polemic against other ancient cultures in which only a small circle of priests had access to sacred knowledge. In the Torah, by contrast, God pointedly informs the Israelites that "you shall be to Me a kingdom of priests and a holy nation."

And lest the Israelites forget about their obligations under the covenant after their long journey through the desert, Moses devotes his final speeches to reminding them, declaring:

> Surely, this Instruction which I enjoin upon you this day is not too baffling for you, nor is it beyond reach. It is not in the heavens,

that you should say, "Who among us can go up to the heavens and get it for us and impart it to us, that we may observe it?" Neither is it beyond the sea, that you should say, "Who among us can cross to the other side of the sea and get it for us and impart it to us, that we may observe it?" No, the word is very close to you, in your mouth and in your heart, to observe it.

This God doesn't just order people around and reward and punish them. This God gathers them together and asks for their help. And in the Divine mind, all Israelites are equally responsible for answering that call, each expected to learn the terms of the covenant and do their part to honor it.

GOD CARES DEEPLY ABOUT THE VULNERABLE AND SO SHOULD WE

Not only, it seems, are we expected to act as if *we* are in the Image of God, we're expected to treat other people as if *they* are in the Divine image as well. In fact, the covenant is where God seems to operational-ize the In-the-Image idea, translating it into a series of laws that dictate our obligations to others, particularly those who are vulnerable.

God seems to understand that it's easy for us to treat powerful peo-ple as if they are in the Divine image. The same is true of people we know and love. But those who are powerless or helpless? Those who aren't part of our family or community? Not so much.

So God makes very clear that God is on the side of the vulnerable. God declares: "You shall not ill-treat any widow or orphan. If you do mistreat them, I will heed their outcry as soon as they cry out to Me, and My anger shall blaze forth and I will put you to the sword, and your own wives shall become widows and your children orphans." Widows and orphans were considered to be among the most vulnerable people in ancient societies, and God wants everyone to know that God person-ally hears their cries, and if you abuse them, God will take you out.

This is not the last time we see God's particular abhorrence of those who prey on the weak—indeed, this is a core theme throughout the Torah. God decries worker exploitation, insisting that an employer must pay a struggling laborer on the very day he earns his wages, "for he is needy and urgently depends on it." God puts forth measures to address income inequality, insisting that all debts be forgiven every seven years and requiring landowners to leave a portion of their crops for the needy. And God warns creditors who lend money to people and take their cloaks as collateral: "If you take your neighbor's garment in pledge, you must return it to him before the sun sets; it is his only clothing, the sole covering for his skin. In what else shall he sleep? Therefore, if he cries out to Me, I will pay heed, for I am compassionate."

This is not a removed, bureaucratic concern, but an intimate, parental kind of love. Like a good Jewish mother, God cannot bear the thought of God's children being inadequately clothed for those chilly desert nights.

This concern for the vulnerable, while inspiring, wasn't unprecedented. Other ancient Near Eastern societies also had laws protecting their widows, orphans, and economically disadvantaged members. What was unusual about the Torah was its concern not just for vulnerable *Israelites,* but for vulnerable *non*-Israelites as well. They too, the Torah insists, are in God's image.

Time and again, God demands equal and loving treatment for the "ger," a Hebrew word that is usually translated as "stranger."* This term refers to a non-Israelite living among the Israelites, someone who, as Rabbi Shai Held puts it, "is not part of the kin group, and therefore not part of the in group." Some scholars have suggested that these strangers were immigrants and that some may have been refugees fleeing difficult circumstances in their native lands.

---

* Later commentators came to understand the word "ger" in some contexts to mean someone who converted to Judaism. But that is not its meaning in the Torah (the Torah is not saying: "Love the stranger, for you were converts to Egyptian religion in the land of Egypt").

Such people are among the most vulnerable in any society—including our own today—and the God of the Torah is obsessed with protecting them. God tells us just once to love our neighbor, but insists no fewer than thirty-six times that we care for the stranger. And as Held points out, God's demands regarding strangers only intensify over the course of the Torah.

At Mount Sinai, Held notes, God merely instructs the Israelites: "You shall not oppress a stranger, for you know the feelings of the stranger, having yourselves been strangers in the land of Egypt." In the next book of the Torah, we're told not just to refrain from oppressing the stranger, but that "the stranger who resides with you shall be to you as one of your native born; you shall love him as yourself, for you were strangers in the land of Egypt." This verse comes just sixteen verses after the one that tells us to "love your neighbor as yourself." Whatever "love" entails in that earlier verse, Held concludes, seems to be owed to the stranger as well.

Even more is asked of us in the final book of the Torah, where Moses declares that God "befriends the stranger, providing him with food and clothing. You too must befriend the stranger, for you were strangers in the land of Egypt."* Loving the stranger, observes Held, has now been elevated to what's known as "imitatio Dei," imitating God, and he concludes that the Torah is telling us, "You can't love a God who loves the vulnerable and not love the vulnerable yourself."

As Held points out, the Torah could easily have said: You were strangers and were terribly mistreated, and no one helped you, so you have no obligation to help anyone else—in fact, your prior mistreatment actually gives you license to mistreat others. But God's message to the Israelites is exactly the opposite: You were strangers, so you know—intimately, viscerally—what it means to be mistreated. And

---

* This isn't just talk. Think back to God's interactions with Hagar, Sarah's maidservant, who, interestingly, is Egyptian and a stranger among the Israelites. When Hagar flees from Sarah, God appears to her and lovingly reassures her. In her grateful reply, Hagar addresses God as "El-roi," meaning "God of seeing," or as Rabbi Held translates it, "God who sees me."

that experience should strengthen your commitment to treating others well, particularly those who are vulnerable.

I find all of this to be very moving, but also confusing. God seems to be getting way ahead of Godself here, addressing a problem the Israelites do not currently face. The Israelites are not in a position of power from which they can abuse strangers—far from it: They *are* the strangers, constantly under threat from hostile peoples and rulers. But the Torah seems to be anticipating a time when the Israelites will be something other than strangers, or at least powerful enough to determine how the strangers among them are treated.

You wouldn't think it would be necessary to exhort strangers to care for other strangers. But the Torah seems to understand how quickly former victims can become indifferent to current ones, or even become oppressors themselves. And again and again, it tells us: No matter how powerful or secure you may one day become, your fundamental moral orientation must always be in the direction of the outsider. Their struggles must always be your concern. For in some essential and eternal way, the plight of the stranger was, and always will be, your own.

LET'S ALL CALM DOWN ABOUT "CHOSENNESS"

It should now be clear that while the God depicted in the Torah may have chosen the Israelites for a particular covenant and mission, that does not mean God cares any less for those outside of the covenant. This came as a relief to me, because the "chosen people" idea has always made me uneasy, with its whiff of Jewish superiority.

As Rabbi Avi Weiss points out, "It was not Abraham, the first Jew, who was created in the image of God, but Adam, the first human being, from whom all peoples are descended." In fact, the opening chapters of the Torah are about *all* human beings. And God's covenant with *all* humankind after the flood (in which God promises never to wipe everyone out again) came first, before God's specific covenants with Abraham and the Israelites.

In addition, some of the Torah's greatest heroes are *non*-Israelites.

The midwives who refuse to kill the Israelites' firstborn sons may well have been Egyptian,* and the Torah states, "God dealt well with the midwives." And none other than the daughter of Pharaoh himself rescues and raises Moses. Let's also remember that after Moses flees Egypt, the first thing he does is defend a group of *non*-Israelite women and then marry one of them. Six verses later, God comes to him in the burning bush and chooses him to be the Israelites' leader with nary a word about his interfaith marriage. And as Moses struggles to manage his unruly people during their desert wanderings, his father-in-law, also not an Israelite, shows up and advises him to start delegating some of his leadership responsibilities, likely saving him from burnout.

The Torah also explicitly warns the Israelites against becoming arrogant because of their unique relationship with God. In one of his speeches near the end of the Torah, Moses informs them:

> It is not because you are the most numerous of peoples that the Lord set His heart on you and chose you—indeed, you are the smallest of peoples; but it was because the Lord favored you and kept the oath He made to your fathers that the Lord freed you with a mighty hand and rescued you from the house of bondage.

This pretty much boils down to "God loves you because God loves you, and also God keeps promises."

While Jews have traditionally believed that they have a special relationship with the Divine, so do people of other religions. That's the point: Each religion has its own unique approach to, and relationship with, Divinity.

Have Jews often embraced this "chosen people" idea? Absolutely. It is woven throughout traditional Jewish liturgy and thought. Have some

---

* Traditional interpretations often assume that the midwives were Israelites. But the Hebrew is actually unclear. It could be translated either as "Hebrew midwives" or "midwives to/of the Hebrews"—and a number of commentators, both historic and modern, have argued that the midwives were actually Egyptian.

Jews done so in ways that were chauvinistic, influenced by passages of the Torah and other ancient Jewish texts that condemn pagans and idolators or express hostility toward non-Jews? Unfortunately, yes. And while, historically, that may have reflected an understandable attempt to find solace during times of persecution, and I don't judge my ancestors for this, I think it reflects a misinterpretation of the idea of chosenness.

Chosenness should never be understood as a declaration of Jewish superiority or a statement that Jews have a monopoly on religious truth. Quite the contrary. Judaism asserts that there is one God who loves and cares for all of humanity, and while Jews have a particular relationship with that God, we recognize that others also have their own relationships with the Divine. Jews do not feel the need to convert people to Judaism because we do not think that others need to act and believe like we do to be saved or morally acceptable.

A better name for us would be "the choosing people"—the people who chose to accept a particular covenant with the Divine, and who must continue choosing, in each new generation, to honor it.

THE JEWISH MISSION IN THE WORLD—THEN AND NOW

If I were going to tell the story of the Torah in a nutshell, it would be as follows: God chose a powerless people for a particular relationship, rescued them from slavery, and gave them a mission: To create a society that is the very opposite of Egypt, one based on the belief that we are all created in the Divine image—all infinitely worthy, fundamentally equal, and totally unique.

This is still very much the Jewish mission today, and we regularly acknowledge that it is nowhere near complete. That's what we're doing each week when we read and study one section of the Torah and chant it out loud during services in our synagogues. Over the course of a year or three years (different congregations have different practices), we read the entire Torah, and then we start over again at the beginning. So no matter where in the world you go, if you find your way to a synagogue for a prayer service on a Saturday morning, you can hear a portion of the Torah—a moment from our founding story—a retelling that has been ongoing for thousands of years.

This isn't just ceremonial—some nostalgic ritual for old times' sake. It's a weekly reminder of what we agreed to at Mount Sinai. You read that correctly–*"we"* not *"they."* "We" as in Jews right now, today. Jewish tradition holds that the souls of all Jews, including those who converted to Judaism, were present at Sinai.

Despite their flaws and fears, the Israelites accepted the sacred charge they were given to honor the Divine image in each other and to never forget their origins—and obligations—as strangers and slaves. And according to Jewish tradition, so did we.

This is why I'm not persuaded by those who argue that Judaism shouldn't be "political"—that rabbis shouldn't refer to public policy issues in their sermons or apply what they believe are the moral lessons of the Torah to current events.

The Torah strikes me as an unavoidably political document—a passionate protest against the old hierarchies and abuses of power. Time and again, the younger son usurps the firstborn to carry on the family line, and God consistently favors the powerless over the powerful—slaves over pharaohs, widows and orphans over those who would oppress them. And the sacred teachings are shared with all Israelites—all standing on equal footing at Mount Sinai, all giving their consent to be governed by God—rather than just an elite few.

You can cite the Torah and other Jewish texts to support many different opinions on issues like immigration and health care. But it does not strike me as a particularly Jewish approach to ignore these issues because they are too "political." That would, I think, be missing the point.

BUT WHAT ABOUT THE AWFUL PARTS OF THE TORAH?

This is all well and good, but what about the questions I raised at the beginning of this chapter?

What about the horrifying parts of the Torah? And if we don't think the Torah is the word of God or believe in God at all, aren't sure it's historically accurate, and know it's not scientifically accurate, how can we take it seriously? Why should we look to it for guidance on how to live our lives?

As for the Torah not necessarily being the word of God, neither are the Declaration of Independence and the U.S. Constitution. And I don't value those founding documents because of who wrote them, but because of certain ideals enshrined within them. I think something similar can be said of the Torah, which can be understood as Judaism's founding document.

As for the Torah's dubious historical accuracy, most of us have at some point read a book of fiction that taught us important truths about the human condition and conveyed profound moral wisdom. That the actual events in the book never happened is irrelevant. I'm not saying the Torah is fiction, but even if it is, I don't think that should be disqualifying. In fact, I would be moved to learn that instead of making up a story about descending from kings and warriors, my ancestors claimed that they were once strangers and slaves and insisted that this heritage imbued them with special obligations to other vulnerable people.

As for whether the Torah is scientifically accurate, I think that's asking the wrong question. The Torah is best read not as a book of scientific truths, but as a book of moral truths. You can embrace the moral truth in the Torah's claim that human beings all descend from the same ancestor (Adam)—that we're all part of the same human family—while still firmly believing in the scientific theory of evolution. You can appreciate the moral truth implied in the story of God creating the world in six days and resting on the seventh—that there's value in ceasing our constant production and consumption and taking time to appreciate the world around us—and still believe in the big bang theory. Plenty of very religious Jews are doctors, scientists, and engineers who are able to distinguish between scientific truths and moral truths and appreciate the value and necessity of both.

As for what to do about the horrifying parts of the Torah, I have devoted the entire next chapter of this book to that very question. But the short answer is: We've interpreted them, as the text demands of us. This means confronting the Torah's difficult parts—rather than ignoring them—and understanding them in new ways. This is why, for example, while many Jews still embrace the practice of taking a day of rest each week, we no longer think it's acceptable to stone people for working on Shabbat.

From the very beginning, we've been interpreting Judaism: challenging it, wrestling with it, and reimagining and retranslating it for the times in which we live. This ongoing process has been the key to Jewish survival and success for thousands of years, and it is the subject to which we will now turn.

CHAPTER 2

The Process of Judaism: Questioning, Debating, and Interpreting

One of the speeches I most loved writing with Mrs. Obama was a commencement address she delivered at a high school for Native American students in Santa Fe, New Mexico, in the spring of 2016.

This school had a painful history. It was one of the boarding schools established by the federal government in the nineteenth century to strip Native American children of their cultures and languages and "Americanize" them. Eventually the school was turned over to tribal leaders, and it is now a first-rate educational institution that teaches students to embrace and celebrate their heritage.

Here is how Mrs. Obama started her remarks:

I am the great-great-granddaughter of Jim Robinson, who was born in South Carolina, lived as a slave, and is likely buried in an unmarked grave on the plantation where he worked. I am the great-granddaughter of Fraser Robinson, an illiterate houseboy who taught himself to read and became an entrepreneur, selling newspapers and shoes. I am the granddaughter of Fraser Robinson Jr., who left the only life he'd ever known to move his family north, seeking a place where his children's dreams wouldn't be so limited by the color of their skin.

And I am the daughter of Fraser Robinson III and Marian Robinson, who raised me and my brother in a tiny apartment on the South Side of Chicago . . . And while my parents were products of segregated schools, and neither of them had an education past high school, they knew with every bone in their bodies that they wanted their kids to go to college . . . And let me tell you, I will never forget the look of pride on [my dad's] face and on my mom's face as I walked across the stage at Princeton University, and three years later at Harvard Law School to accept my diplomas—degrees that have given me opportunities that my parents never could have dreamed of for themselves.

So, graduates, this is my story. And I'm sharing this with you because . . . I heard that when you were first brainstorming about who to invite to your commencement and someone suggested me or my husband, some of you thought that that was an impossible dream, that it just wasn't realistic to think that people like us would ever visit a school like yours. Well, today, I want you to know that there is nowhere I would rather be than right here with all of you.

The Robinson family's journey over the generations in some ways reflects a broader American story—one that has wound through plantations, battlefields, lunch counters, classrooms, courtrooms, and the halls of Congress as we've struggled to understand our founding documents and apply their centuries-old words to modern dilemmas. For more than two centuries, we have been reinterpreting these texts in light of the moral progress we've made as a nation, struggling to keep faith with their animating ideals in our own time—and we obviously still have a great deal of work left to do.

I think something similar can be said of the Jewish people and our founding document, the Torah. We did not stick the Torah behind glass in a museum simply to be admired from afar. Instead, from the moment the Torah was canonized, we were already arguing about what it meant. And since then, we have interpreted and reinterpreted it, continually breathing new life into it—and allowing it to breathe new life into us—in each new era.

Jews today no more live by a literal surface reading of the Torah than Americans live by the original version of the Constitution. Thanks to our Jewish interpretive tradition, we no longer make animal sacrifices or stone people for working on Shabbat; women and LGBTQ people now serve as rabbis; and I attend Jewish meditation retreats, feminist Torah study classes, and Shabbat services where we sing ancient prayers to the tunes of Stevie Wonder and John Legend songs.

Our interpretive tradition is the reason why Judaism still exists— the reason why I am here today typing these words—and it is the tradition that I honor as I type them.

TAKING A STEP BACK . . . WAY BACK: A BRIEF ACCOUNT OF ANCIENT JEWISH HISTORY

But we're getting ahead of ourselves. How exactly did we go from the Torah's account of Moses lecturing the Israelites at the border of Canaan, which seems to be set around the late thirteenth century B.C.E., to me praying to pop song tunes and meditating in the twenty-first century C.E.? And how is that history relevant to the project and process of Judaism?

It's a long story, and the historical evidence is spotty at times, but at some point, possibly in the twelfth century B.C.E., the Israelites wound up in Canaan.* By the late eleventh century B.C.E., they seem to have formed a monarchy there. According to the biblical narrative, they

---

* The books of the Hebrew Bible following the Torah detail a series of conquests, but archaeologists and scholars have disputed the biblical account.

had a series of kings, including Saul, David, and Solomon, and Solomon built a massive Temple in Jerusalem that served as a central site where the Israelites worshipped God via animal sacrifices, yearly pilgrimages, and other devotional activities.

Around 928 B.C.E., the Israelite kingdom split into two kingdoms, one in the north and one in the south. The Assyrians conquered the northern kingdom in 722 B.C.E.* In 586 B.C.E., the Babylonians conquered the southern kingdom, known as Judah, and they leveled Jerusalem, destroyed the Temple, and deported many of Judah's citizens to Babylonia.†

The Babylonian conquest and exile appear to have been devastating for the Israelites. Judaism without the Temple must have seemed inconceivable, because, as historian Shaye Cohen notes, by then the Temple had become "the sole institution in which the Israelites could worship God." It was the place where they celebrated their holidays, atoned for their sins, expressed their gratitude, and asked God for help.

The usual reaction to this kind of conquest in the ancient Near East would probably have been something like "Clearly, our god has abandoned us" or "Our god must not have been so powerful after all." The conquered people would then start worshipping the conqueror's gods.

But the exiles did something unexpected. They stuck with their own God, bringing that God with them into exile. And about fifty years later, when Babylonia was conquered by the Persians, a number of the exiles returned to Judah, where they rebuilt the Temple in Jerusalem and began referring to themselves as "Yehudim" or "Jews" (and I will similarly make this switch, using "Jews" from now on, instead of "Israelites").

This Second Temple period, as it is called, saw the rise of Jewish sects and scholars who developed non-Temple forms of worship, creating synagogues where they would gather to pray and study the Torah.

---

* Ten of the twelve Israelite Tribes lived in the northern kingdom. After the Assyrian conquest, the northerners were exiled, and they assimilated into the surrounding populations, hence becoming known as the "lost tribes" of Israel.
† Babylonia was in what is modern-day Iraq.

It was also a time of considerable political upheaval. Judah was a valuable little strip of territory, located squarely on the path to many of the lands that rulers back then sought to invade, and it was frequently conquered. Other than a period of Jewish self-rule in the second and first centuries B.C.E., Jews found themselves living under a variety of outside powers, including the Greeks and later, the Romans, who conquered Judah in 63 B.C.E. A century later, Jews tried revolting, but by 70 C.E., after several years of struggle (including with each other, as many Jews opposed the revolt), the Romans prevailed and destroyed the Second Temple.* The Jewish death toll was staggering.

Reeling from this tragedy, Jews faced an existential dilemma. While they had their synagogues, their religious practices seem to have been tied to the Temple. Prayer services were timed around the daily animal sacrifices (and were in no way considered a substitute for them)—and the congregations faced toward the Temple as they prayed—and Jewish holidays still revolved around rituals performed at the Temple.

Now that the Temple was gone, how exactly would Jews continue to practice Judaism?

THE RABBIS TO THE RESCUE

But all was not lost. Jewish tradition has it that, realizing the Jews' revolt against Rome was doomed to fail, a scholar named Rabbi Yoḥanan ben Zakkai faked his own death and convinced his students to smuggle him out of Jerusalem in a coffin, ostensibly for burial outside the city walls. Once he escaped, he sought out the Roman general Vespasian and requested permission to establish an academy in Yavneh, a town to the west of Jerusalem, a request that Vespasian granted.

It was in Yavneh, and later at similar academies nearby and in Babylonia, that a small group of Jewish scholars, who came to be known as "the

---

* The Western Wall in Jerusalem was one of the outer retaining walls of the Temple, which is why it is considered one of Judaism's holiest sites.

Rabbis" or "the Sages,"* would devote themselves, over the next several centuries, to reinterpreting the Torah for this new post-Temple era.

How would Jews follow the Torah's instructions to worship God by making animal sacrifices without a Temple at which to make those sacrifices? How would they continue to celebrate holidays without a Temple where they could perform their holiday rituals and that would serve as the destination for their holiday pilgrimages?

To answer these questions and countless others about what Judaism should look like in this post-Temple era, the Rabbis employed a distinctively Jewish approach, one that had been developed by sages before them: They argued about it.

They started with the assumption that the Torah came from God and every word of it was there for a reason, but its true meaning was often hidden and needed to be unearthed. To that end, they undertook a microscopically close kind of reading, and no detail of the law was too tiny to debate. How exactly should one say a key prayer known as the "Shema"? How loudly must one recite it? How carefully must one articulate its words? When, exactly, should it be said? In what position should one's body be when reciting it? Is it permissible to interrupt the prayer to greet someone? They also considered what one should do if, when it comes time to pray, one happens to be riding a donkey. Later Rabbis asked, can laborers say the Shema in a tree? On a stone wall that they're building? Must they cease their labors when they pray, or can they pray while working?

The more disagreements aired, perspectives heard,† and audacious

---

* They were not rabbis as we think of them today, working in congregations, organizations, schools, and hospitals. They were more like scholars, interpreters, and teachers of Judaism. And note that references to these ancient Rabbis are capitalized, unlike references to modern rabbis.

† At one point, the Rabbis recounted the debates of their predecessors, the sages Hillel and Shammai, whose students strongly disagreed on many matters of Jewish law. The Rabbis claimed that a heavenly voice had announced that the arguments from both houses of study are "the words of the living God," but that the House of Hillel's arguments have prevailed. Why? Because Hillel's students were "agreeable and forbearing" and studied opinions from the House of Shammai before forming their own.

questions asked, the better. Even the most revered Rabbis could be challenged and were expected to defend their opinions.

The Rabbis had these debates both in group settings and in pairs (a pairing for the purpose of study is known as a "ḥavruta," an Aramaic word meaning "friendship" or "fellowship"), with each partner thoughtfully considering the other's points and pushing him* to sharpen his arguments and clarify his views. This was not argument for the sake of argument, or to "win," but rather what is known as "argument for the sake of heaven," where the goal is to arrive at a richer, deeper understanding of the text. (Jewish study is still commonly done this way today.)

The Rabbis referred to these debates as the "Oral Torah," and they insisted that this Oral Torah had *also* been dictated by God at Mount Sinai. Instead of being written down like the other Torah, however, this Oral Torah had been passed down through the generations by word of mouth—from God, to Moses, to Joshua, all the way to the prophets,† and eventually to the Rabbis themselves.

So it wasn't just those Israelites at the foot of Mount Sinai or a select group of prophets who could hear the word of God. In this new Rabbinic era, it could also be discerned by those with the commitment, character, and skill to study and interpret the Torah.

Around 200 C.E., a Rabbinic leader known as Judah ha-Nasi sought to compile and edit a comprehensive account of the debates he and his colleagues had been having. The resulting work was called the "Mishnah." Over the next few centuries, Rabbis proceeded to study the Mishnah and create a voluminous commentary on it called the "Gemara."

---

* Yes, the Rabbis were all men—we'll discuss later in this chapter.

† Prophets were people with whom God had communicated directly. Some of them are featured in books of the Hebrew Bible that bear their names (Isaiah, Ezekiel, Jonah)—these are the prophets the Rabbis are referring to (though people like Abraham, Sarah, Moses, and Miriam are also considered prophets). According to the Hebrew Bible, prophets often served as powerful voices of conscience in Israelite society, insisting that God is on the side of the poor and oppressed and demanding justice on their behalf.

The Mishnah and Gemara were then published together in what is known as the "Talmud."*

While the Talmud contains extensive debates about how to follow the laws in the Torah, it is not a legal textbook or code of law that lays out clear, bright-line rules. Rather, the Rabbis recorded both majority and minority arguments and opinions from which later rabbis could draw to decide on matters of Jewish law. The Talmud also includes a number of stories referred to as "midrashim" (plural of "midrash") to fill in gaps or elucidate points made in the Torah—to imagine, as Rabbi Lawrence Kushner puts it, "what might have happened before and after, above and below the biblical story." Many midrashim were also collected in separate volumes.

Midrashim can be quite fanciful. Two of my favorites have to do with the Israelites' escape from Egypt. The first imagines that they reached the Sea of Reeds and were seized with fear, refusing to move forward. Moses unhelpfully stands at the shore, praying to God for help. Finally, a man named Naḥshon ben Amminadab decides to take the plunge, followed by other members of his tribe, and only when he's nearly in over his head does God intervene, bellowing at Moses, "My beloved ones are drowning in the sea and you prolong your prayer to me?" God then parts the sea to let the Israelites cross.

Just standing around praying isn't enough, and sometimes you have to get far beyond your comfort zone before things work out.

The other midrash is about how, after the Israelites cross the Sea of Reeds and it crashes down on the Egyptians, a group of angels want to break into celebratory song. But God rebukes them, declaring: "My creations are drowning in the sea, and you are singing?"

Again, chosenness does not mean God loves Jews more than other people.

---

* There are actually two Talmuds: the Jerusalem Talmud, compiled in the late fourth century C.E. in the Land of Israel, and the Babylonian Talmud, compiled by Rabbis in Babylonia in the sixth century C.E. The Babylonian Talmud is generally the version people are referring to when they talk about "the Talmud."

Over the years, all these stories and arguments started to add up. The Talmud is divided into six sections, each of which is broken down into subsections known as "tractates," and it weighs in at roughly 1.8 million words—or 2,700 double-sided pages (about 16,000 pages in the English translation).* Compare this with the 80,000 words of the written Torah on which it was commenting, and you can appreciate Rabbi Abraham Joshua Heschel's observation that "Judaism is based upon a minimum of revelation and a maximum of interpretation."

The Rabbis, however, didn't seem to recognize Heschel's distinction. Rather, they seem to have acted as if their interpretations *were* a form of revelation, one that had come from God and been handed down generation after generation to finally be discerned through their careful study and spirited debates.

To understand what the Rabbis were doing, I want to flesh out the analogy with which I started this chapter: The Torah is the founding document of the Jewish people just as the Constitution and Declaration of Independence are the founding documents of the American people. Just as Americans have interpreted the Constitution through our courts and amendment process, the Jewish people have interpreted the Torah through our debates in the Talmud and many other texts since then. So the Constitution is to Supreme Court cases and Constitutional Amendments as the Torah is to the Talmud and the many Jewish interpretive efforts that followed.

Let's start with an example from the Constitution. While our founders had declared that "all men are created equal," the original version of the Constitution allowed white men (and women) to buy, sell, and brutally enslave black men (and women and children). It took us an obscenely long time and an unspeakable amount of bloodshed, but we eventually amended the Constitution to abolish slavery. Through Su-

---

* There is a regimen for studying the Talmud known as "daf yomi," which means "page of the day," that many Jews undertake today. It involves studying a page of Talmud (technically two pages, since it's the front and back of the page) each day until you get through the whole thing. It takes about seven and a half years.

preme Court cases, including those outlawing segregation, efforts have been made to dismantle slavery's ugly legacy, a process that is ongoing and obviously far from finished.

Another example: The Constitution grants us freedom of speech. But new developments over the years have led to new questions about what exactly counts as "speech." Is pornography speech? Flag burning? Donations to political campaigns? The Supreme Court has issued opinions to answer those questions.

Now let's turn to the Torah. The Torah itself prohibits amendments to its language, so the Rabbis couldn't cut from or add to it. But there was nothing to stop them from interpreting it in a way that essentially accomplished the same end, and they certainly did plenty of that.

For instance, the Torah offers the following guidance about how to handle a "wayward and rebellious son, who does not heed his father or mother and does not obey them even after they discipline him": His parents should take him out to the town square and have him stoned to death. Seriously.

Yet, through pages of sometimes torturous reasoning, the Rabbis construed this verse so narrowly—insisting that it applied only during a three-month period at a certain stage of the boy's development; and only to a boy who ate a certain kind of meat and drank a certain kind of wine; and, according to one view, only to a boy whose parents were identical to each other "in voice, appearance, and height"; among other requirements—that it was virtually impossible to enforce. They basically interpreted a biblical law out of existence.*

The Torah also states that "if anyone maims his fellow, as he has done so shall it be done to him: fracture for fracture, eye for eye, tooth for tooth. The injury he inflicted on another shall be inflicted on him."

---

* Two of the Rabbis even declared that "there has never been a stubborn and rebellious son and there will never be one in the future." They then wondered: Why was this provision included in the Torah in the first place? The answer: It was put there for the purpose of study! Or as the poet and literary critic Adam Kirsch puts it, "God makes unenforceable laws simply so that scholars can analyze why they are unenforceable!"

But the Rabbis insisted that a literal interpretation of this verse "should not enter your mind." Rather, through a series of interpretive maneuvers, they concluded that it really meant that if you physically injure someone, you have to compensate that person monetarily for the harm you caused.

As for that language about stoning people for working on the Sabbath, the Rabbis made the evidentiary standards for imposing capital punishment so high—demanding testimony from at least two witnesses who had actually *seen* the defendant commit the crime, as the Torah instructs, as well as proof that someone had previously counseled the defendant against doing so, among other requirements—that this punishment became nearly impossible to carry out.

The Rabbis also reinterpreted the Torah's sections on worship, decreeing that prayer could be a substitute for sacrifices made at the Temple.* And they reimagined the Torah's instructions for how to observe the holidays. No longer able to perform their rituals of atonement at the Temple on Yom Kippur (which involved symbolically assigning all the sins of the Jews to a goat and sending it out into the wilderness—hence the origin of the word "scapegoat"), the Rabbis came up with a process of repenting that individuals could perform without a Temple. Passover had previously required pilgrimages to the Temple, complete with festive meals and special sacrifices of lambs (which reminds us of how the Israelites smeared lamb's blood on their doors back in Egypt to protect their firstborn from the final plague). The Rabbis moved these rituals to the home by creating the Passover Seder, a way for Jews to retell the Exodus story over dinner with their families. The focal point for worship thus shifted from one central location in Jerusalem to any synagogue or home where Jews could gather.

So as Jonathan Rosen notes in his book *The Talmud and the Internet,* "Jews, contrary to general understanding, have a New Testament— it is called the Talmud, and it is, in fact, numerous new testaments all

---

* Though the Rabbis didn't give up hope that the Temple and its sacrifices would one day be restored, and they included pleas to that effect in the liturgy.

unfolding one into the other and circling back to that first biblical testament."

It is in no way an overstatement to say that with the interpretive process they developed, the Rabbis rescued Judaism in one of its darkest moments and ensured its continuation for the next two millennia. Thanks to the Rabbis, Rosen notes, "Jews became the people of the book and not the people of the Temple or the land," all now bound together by the same foundational interpretive text and process.

Judaism thus became entirely portable—through space and time. Now that it was no longer so closely tied to a particular structure, Judaism could be fully practiced anywhere in the world. And as times changed, Judaism could adapt.

In the ensuing centuries, pursuing economic opportunities and fleeing various forms of persecution, Jews came to live all across the globe. And nearly everywhere they went, they set up academies, or "yeshivot" (plural of "yeshiva"), where, like the Rabbis, they continued studying sacred texts and translating traditional Jewish values and practices for new circumstances.

The standard publication of the Talmud captures a number of interpretations from scholars at these later yeshivot, and it does so in a visual format that beautifully illustrates the interpretive nature of Judaism. The original Talmudic texts—the Mishnah and Gemara—are in the center of the page. On one side of them is a column of commentary from an eleventh-century French Rabbi named Shlomo ben Isaac, who is known by the acronym "Rashi." On the other side is commentary from twelfth- and thirteenth-century scholars (which prominently features contributions from Rashi's sons-in-law and grandsons). Then there is a ring of commentary around that commentary, which includes references to codes of Jewish law compiled by Maimonides in Egypt in the twelfth century and Rabbi Josef Karo in what is now Israel in the sixteenth century that sought to distill Rabbinic debates into clear laws for Jews to follow. This layer also includes notes from seventeenth-, eighteenth-, and nineteenth-century European rabbis.

You have commentary, surrounded by commentary, surrounded by commentary in a spirited debate across time. A single page of Talmud could include a fifth-century Rabbi disagreeing with a statement made by a fourth-century Rabbi and using an argument from a first-century Rabbi to prove his point . . . and then an eleventh-century rabbi might jump in to explain what that fifth-century Rabbi meant . . . and then an eighteenth-century rabbi could take issue with the eleventh-century rabbi, and so on.

This is one of the strangest and most wonderful features of the Talmud: It's as if, within its pages, the barriers of time and space do not exist. No matter when or where we live, we can listen in on this epic, centuries-long argument for the sake of heaven. We can witness our ancestors' continuous striving to tune their minds and hearts to the Divine frequency and perhaps even hear its faint echo for ourselves.

HOW JEWS HAVE, AGAINST ALL ODDS, CONTINUED THE CONVERSATION

That this conversation has continued unbroken for so long is utterly remarkable, particularly given the various efforts throughout history to snuff it out.

As Rabbi Bradley Shavit Artson points out, "There are no weekly meetings of Edomites in Brooklyn, or of Hittites in Los Angeles"; yet after thousands of years, Jews still exist as a distinct people, still studying the same ancient texts and practicing some form of the same ancient rituals. Generation after generation, in the wake of tragedy and persecution, and in moments when Judaism became unresponsive to the times, a critical mass of Jews chose not to abandon Judaism, but to iterate on it.

It's true that there were times and places where Jews lived relatively untroubled lives. And over the centuries, Jews have built thriving communities around the world, establishing strong religious, charitable, and educational institutions and producing some of the world's most renowned individuals.* But there is no denying that they have done so in the face of all manner of persecution.

Jews have been blamed for the death of Jesus and accused of murdering Christian children and using their blood in religious rituals, a lie known as "the blood libel." They were required to live in ghettos and forbidden from owning land and working in certain trades and professions. They were frequently expelled from the countries where they lived, and many were killed in the Crusades, the Spanish Inquisition, and pogroms in Eastern Europe.

The Jewish Emancipation that took place in Europe in the eighteenth and nineteenth centuries provided a brief moment of hope. During this period, a number of countries rescinded discriminatory laws and granted Jews citizenship, freeing them from the ghettos and allowing them to attend universities and pursue occupations from which they had previously been barred.

But as Jews became more integrated into European society, other antisemitic tropes took hold, which, as many students of history have noted, were oddly contradictory. Jews were genetically inferior—a threat to the Aryan race—but also on the cusp of taking over the entire world.† They were both depraved atheists and religious fundamentalists; both dangerous radicals and backward traditionalists opposed to the progress of modernity.

In the twentieth century, drawing on various strands of antisemitism throughout history, Adolf Hitler and his collaborators orchestrated a genocide in which millions of Germans and other Europeans participated. They murdered six million Jews, wiping out two-thirds of European Jewry.

Jews have fared far better in America, which has undoubtedly been

---

* One example that makes me proud: While Jews are 0.2 percent of the world's population, 22 percent of Nobel Prize winners are Jews. (There are about 14 million Jews on earth, compared with 2.3 billion Christians, 1.8 billlion Muslims, 1.1 billion Hindus, and 500 million Buddhists.)

† In the late 1800s, the secret police in Russia published "The Protocols of the Elders of Zion," which they claimed were the minutes from a meeting of leading Jews plotting to take over the media and the global economy. It was a complete forgery, but it was—and sadly, still is—widely circulated and believed to be real.

a land of opportunity, with the first Jewish settlers arriving in 1654.* But the United States has its own history of antisemitism. Up until my parents' generation, companies still frequently discriminated against Jews in hiring, and universities had quotas limiting the number of Jewish students they would admit.

And just when many of us, myself included, had assumed antisemitism was largely a thing of the past, in 2017, antisemitic incidents rose 57 percent. Between late January 2017 and late January 2018, approximately 4.2 million antisemitic tweets were sent or retweeted from roughly three million accounts.†

And in October 2018, a man with a history of virulently antisemitic writings online stormed into the Tree of Life synagogue in Pittsburgh on a Shabbat morning wielding three handguns and a machine gun and screaming, "All Jews must die," and murdered eleven people. Six months later, another man—also with a machine gun, also having posted antisemitic writings—stormed into the Chabad of Poway synagogue near San Diego and opened fire, killing one person and wounding three others.

I initially hesitated about including a section on antisemitism. I think we sometimes focus a bit too much on the negative, the "lachrymose theory" of Jewish history, as historian Salo Baron put it. But I included this section to make a different point—about Jewish creativity and resilience. Despite centuries of persecution, Jews have somehow managed to continue the conversation that allows that ancient revelation to keep unfolding. And we have often done so at great risk: from fifteenth-century Spanish Jews who performed Jewish rituals in secret, knowing they could be tortured or killed in the Spanish Inquisition if

---

* A handful of Jews came before then—as early as 1585—but none of them stayed.
† It is likely not a coincidence that this uptick in antisemitism occurred in tandem with the rise of a national political leader and others who have employed rhetoric that appeals to various hate groups, members of which do not appear to be all that discerning in their hatred. You generally do not hear them saying, "I adore Mexican immigrants, but I can't stand Muslims," or "African Americans are wonderful, but boy do I hate Jews." And when influential public figures embolden them by stoking animus against any minority group, it affects other minority groups as well, including Jews.

caught, to Jews who smuggled sections of the Torah into a Nazi labor camp, hiding them in hollow bedposts and under floorboards in their barracks, and studying them together late at night.

While a number of Jews over the years sought to escape their fate by converting—with mixed results—many others seem to have sensed that they were part of something bigger and more enduring than the reign of any one king, czar, or führer, something they could not bring themselves to abandon.

I'm thinking in particular of a story that took place in 1946 at a displaced persons camp in Germany where survivors of the Holocaust were waiting to be resettled. Among these Jews was a group of rabbis who approached the American general in charge and asked if the U.S. Army might help publish a set of Talmuds for them and others to study. The Army agreed.

Unable to find a single complete Talmud in all of western Europe (the Nazis had made a point of burning Talmuds and Torahs), they had to import one from New York. The Army then commandeered a printing press in Heidelberg that had previously been used to churn out Nazi propaganda and printed one hundred copies of this massive, ancient Jewish text.

These survivors had lost their homes, families, communities, and nearly their lives. And conditions in the displaced persons camps were by no means luxurious. I imagine there were quite a few things they could have asked for to improve their living circumstances and help secure their future prospects. But these rabbis seemed to believe that the key to their survival lay in continuing this sacred conversation with generations past and generations to come—a conversation that has sustained and renewed Judaism in each new era.

From Jews who kept Judaism alive in exile in Babylonia; to the Rabbis who reimagined Judaism after the destruction of the Second Temple; to Jews expelled from Spain in the fifteenth century who embraced a mystical form of Judaism called "Kabbalah"; to eighteenth-century Jews who, frustrated by the intellectual elitism and spiritual deficiencies of traditional Judaism, developed a populist approach to Judaism known as "Hasidism," which emphasized passionate spirituality rather than legalistic scholarship;* to Jews who became Zionists and fought to establish the State of Israel, we have always come up with new arguments for Judaism and new ways to be Jewish.

Jews in nineteenth-century Germany questioned the value of ancient ritual practices like keeping kosher. Seeking to modernize Judaism, they focused more on its ethical aspects, developing the first iteration of Reform Judaism, which would later catch on in America. In response, a traditionalist movement that became known as Orthodoxy arose, emphasizing adherence to Jewish law and opposing the reformers' innovations. By the mid-nineteenth century, in response to both the Reform and Orthodox movements, a new denomination known as Conservative Judaism took shape, which sought to preserve traditional Jewish laws and rituals but interpret them in a more contemporary way.

In the early twentieth century, an American rabbi named Mordecai Kaplan founded Reconstructionist Judaism, which emphasizes Jewish customs, culture, literature, history, and language in addition to ritual and ethics. And in the 1960s, another American rabbi, Zalman Schachter-Shalomi, created the Renewal movement—a transdenominational movement that draws heavily from Kabbalah and Hasidism and seeks to revitalize Jewish spirituality.

I used to think there was just one "traditional" form of Judaism and that only in recent decades had we started reimagining it. But that is clearly not true. Throughout history, in communities across the globe, we have continued to reinterpret what Judaism is and reimagine what it could be.

---

* This upstart resistance movement later developed into a kind of ultra-Orthodoxy that is still practiced in some Jewish communities today.

WHY WE MUST JOIN AND CONTINUE
THE CONVERSATION TODAY

While Judaism has evolved significantly over the centuries, there is no denying that the Talmud, the text that has shaped Jewish tradition for the past two thousand years, was created by men.* Though often ahead of its time,† some of the Talmud's content very much reflects the era in which its debates took place. And Talmudic law has been interpreted to bar women from religious leadership roles, prohibit them from serving as witnesses in Jewish legal proceedings, and require them to stay in marriages against their will when their husbands refused to grant them divorces. LGBTQ individuals have also faced discrimination and degradation.

I find it heartbreaking and infuriating that these practices continue in some traditional communities. As is the case with the Constitution, the legacy of the painful parts of our historic texts is still with us today.

Fortunately, like the ancient Rabbis, numerous modern rabbis and scholars have studied and interpreted Jewish texts in the context of the time and place in which they live, taking into account current understandings of gender and sexuality. This is why today, in every denomination except Orthodoxy, women can officially participate equally in all aspects of Jewish life, serving as rabbis‡ and heads of rabbinical schools, most of which currently have more women than men as students. And in recent years, a segment of the Orthodox community in

---

* Though the Rabbis' views were surely shaped by the opinions and experiences of the women in their families. There are even accounts of at least one Rabbi's wife—a woman named Berurya—participating in their debates.

† The Rabbis were sometimes surprisingly enlightened, assuming, for example, that women desire and enjoy sex, are entitled to sexual pleasure, and should never be forced into sexual activity. In fact, the Rabbis explicitly forbade men from coercing their wives into having sex, thus banning marital rape many centuries before we did so in the United States (marital rape did not become illegal in all fifty states until 1993). They also insisted on marriage contracts known as "ketubot" (plural of "ketubah"), which outlined men's financial and conjugal obligations to their wives.

‡ The first female American rabbi was ordained in 1972, though in Germany, a woman became a rabbi back in 1935. She did not get to serve for very long, as she was murdered in the Holocaust in 1944.

America has become more open to women in leadership roles. There is now even a school that ordains women as Orthodox clergy (though while its graduates adhere to Orthodoxy's rules about gender roles and refrain from duties traditionally only performed by men, it is still quite controversial in much of the Orthodox world). And every denomination except for Orthodoxy* officially ordains openly gay rabbis, performs gay marriages, and has taken significant steps to welcome trans and nongender-conforming people.

Some of my more traditionally observant friends have objected to these developments, viewing them as attempts by some Jews to change Judaism simply to suit their own tastes. But I don't think that's fair. The individuals who undertook these interpretive efforts were not trying to make Jewish law conform to their own personal values, but rather to their understanding of *Judaism's* values. While, like the Rabbis, these modern rabbis and scholars are products of their times, they did not make changes lightly, or as a knee-jerk reaction to evolving mores. Like the Rabbis, they painstakingly analyzed sacred texts, carefully considered Judaism's core ideals, and argued vigorously with each other for years.

I would also respectfully point out that in ancient times, only after the Second Temple was destroyed did the Rabbis decide that God would accept prayers in lieu of animal sacrifices. Why had they and their predecessors never previously discerned this from the text of the Torah? Was the timing a mere coincidence? I don't think so. I think the Rabbis understood that if Judaism was going to continue without a Temple, they would need to adapt its practices to their new reality.

This is something I love about Judaism: When Temples fall, we don't just stand around trying to make sacrifices at the ruins. We re-translate our tradition to create something more enduring. We understand, as Rabbi Donniel Hartman puts it, that "the anthropocentric nature of revelation—its intended audience is human beings—requires that it be bounded in a particular place and time and speak the language of the human beings of that culture and era, with all their moral and

---

* Though there is a range of opinions on LGBTQ issues among Orthodox Jews themselves.

psychological imperfections." Revelation thus cannot be viewed as "a pure expression of God's will," but rather "as an expression of God's will filtered through the mindset and mores of its intended audience."

In other words, at Mount Sinai, God spoke to people in a way that they could understand *at the time.* "Scripture is thus inherently constituted as a compromise between divine will and human limitation," Hartman concludes. Or as Rabbi Alan Lew put it: "The Torah has a very strong sense of what is, and an equally strong sense of what ought to be, and it recognizes very clearly that if the second ever gets too far away from the first, the Torah will become a repository of irrelevant and impossible ideals." So the Torah pushes people with its demands, but not so far that they give up and don't bother trying to meet them.

The "eye for an eye" law is a good example. This law may have been quite progressive for biblical times, a departure from other ancient law codes that specified different punishments depending on the victim's social class.* But it also wasn't wildly out of sync with prevailing norms that permitted bodily injury to perpetrators as punishment.

Centuries later, however, the Rabbis generally weren't even willing to entertain the thought that this law might be construed literally—that couldn't possibly be the will of God. And using the process they had established, they interpreted it as being about monetary compensation. They went through a similar process with the wayward and rebellious son and stoning people for working on Shabbat.

With their debates in the Talmud, the Rabbis ensured that the core truths of revelation would not be forever trapped in the specifics of ancient laws developed for an ancient people. And this process was not meant to end in the sixth century. The Rabbis seemed to think that Judaism would continue to evolve over time. At least that appears to be the implication of one of their most famous midrashim, which imag-

---

* The Code of Hammurabi, for example, states that if a wealthy man puts out another wealthy man's eye, he should lose his own eye—but if a wealthy man gouges a poor man, monetary compensation will suffice.

ines the moment when Moses went up to Mount Sinai to receive the Torah from God.

According to this midrash, Moses finds God adding little ornamental flourishes to the tops of the letters in a Torah scroll. God explains that many generations from now, a Rabbi named Akiva ben Joseph (who was one of the most renowned Rabbis) will derive all sorts of legal interpretations solely from these decorative markings.

Moses asks to see this Akiva figure, and he's suddenly transported centuries into the future to Akiva's classroom, where he finds himself seated near the back with the least advanced students. As Moses listens to Akiva's lesson on the Torah, he doesn't understand any of it and becomes distraught. But then one of the students asks Akiva about the origins of the material he is teaching—and Akiva replies that it comes from a law given to Moses at Sinai.

It seems as if the Rabbis were admitting that they were reinterpreting the Torah so radically that even Moses wouldn't recognize it! And this process is still ongoing today, unfolding in countless books, articles, sermons, podcasts, and social media posts. Like previous generations of Jews, we continue to make choices about which parts of our ancient texts to embrace, and which to deemphasize or reject. As Rabbi Hartman writes:

> Which narrative will ultimately prevail? Which passages will nurture and comprise the beating heart of faith, and which will be relegated to the ideological dumping ground of verses that, according to the Talmudic adage, "never were nor were ever meant to be implemented, but were written only as objects of theoretical study."

And it's not just scholars and rabbis who are participating in these interpretive efforts, but laypeople as well. In that spirit, the former CEO of Timberland, Jeff Swartz, who came to serious Jewish study later in life and now teaches Talmud to others, will ask his students: What is the most important section on any page of Talmud?

It is not, he tells them, the Mishnah, or the Gemara, or the later commentaries, but rather the slim columns of empty space between them. His point is that these pages are not full. This process is not finished. There is room for our voices too.

I hope it's now clear that if you're simply looking for rules to memorize or dogma to unthinkingly accept, you should look elsewhere. If you're a dictator looking for a religion to be, as Karl Marx once put it, the "opium of the people," I would not recommend Judaism. As Jonathan Rosen noted of the Rabbis, "Theirs was a system that made a virtue of ambivalence and built uncertainty into bedrock assertions of faith. No wonder fundamentalists and fascists have hated it so."

While I cherish Judaism's embrace of nuance and complexity, I sometimes find it frustrating. Often, the answer to a question like "What does Judaism think about X?" isn't some bright-line rule, but rather, the contours of a debate: "Well, most people think Judaism says this about X, but some think Judaism says something totally different." And there always seems to be an exception, and an exception to that exception, and, often, two totally opposite things are true at the same time.

But I also appreciate that this endlessly argumentative, iterative process is the reason why Judaism is still around today. Questioning, debating, and interpreting aren't merely tolerated in Judaism—this *is* Judaism, and this process is the key not just to our survival, but to our success as well. The same, I think, can be said of America. Generation after generation, Jews and Americans have shaped our founding texts and stories—and they have shaped us—and ultimately their purpose is not to provide eternal and unchanging answers, but rather to spur us to ask the right questions.

I cannot imagine what America's founding fathers would have thought had they been in the audience for Mrs. Obama's commencement speech at that school in New Mexico. I'm guessing they would have been both shocked and baffled as they sat there, listening to an address given by a First Lady of the United States—the great-great-granddaughter of a man who was regarded as someone else's property—to a graduating class of Native American students headed for some of the top universities in this country.

I also cannot imagine what my great-grandparents would think about how I practice Judaism today, let alone what Jews sacrificing animals at the Temple in Jerusalem two thousand years ago might think. I'm guessing that if Moses or Rabbi Akiva sat in the back of the classes, retreats, and services I attend, they would be quite confused and likely scandalized. But I believe that these forms of Judaism also come from the Torah given to Moses at Sinai (metaphorically speaking). And I imagine—and hope—that I would be just as confused and scandalized if transported centuries into the future to see what Judaism looks like then.

CHAPTER 3

Freeing God from "His" Human-Shaped Cage in the Sky

Before we explore some of the topics the Rabbis were debating about—like ethics, prayer, holidays, and life cycle rituals—we first need to talk about God, because for me, this was a real sticking point.

And it appears that I'm not alone.

One recent study found that 72 percent of American Jews believe in "God or a universal spirit,"* compared with 97 percent of Christians, and 68 percent of religiously unaffiliated people. But only 34 percent of American Jews are "absolutely certain" of that belief, compared with 78 percent of Christians, and 30 percent of the religiously unaffiliated.

Take that in for a moment: Jews' certainty about the existence of God is roughly as strong as that of the "Nones."†

---

* I have no idea what the survey meant by "a universal spirit," but that is apparently what they asked people about.

† "Nones" is a term that refers to those who are not religiously affiliated.

I can't speak to why other Jews struggle with the idea of God, but for me, with two yearly synagogue services and a Passover Seder as my main interactions with Judaism, my conception of the Jewish God came largely from the Jewish prayer book. And without the background necessary to understand Jewish liturgy, I got the impression that God is a Father/King in the sky who performs miracles, rewards us if we're good, punishes us if we're bad, and really enjoys our repetitive prayers to "Him." I would often look around during services and wonder whether others believed in this kind of God or were just dutifully pretending like I was.

I did not (and do not) believe that God is a supernatural being up there who controls things down here—either by intervening or choosing not to intervene—and rewards and punishes us according to our merit. I generally find attempts—no matter how thoughtful and well intentioned—to square such a view with reality and explain why God permits things like genocide, child abuse, and pandemics to be both unpersuasive and disturbing. And if there is such a God—if all the suffering in the world is Divinely willed or permitted—then I certainly did not (and do not) wish to worship that God.

I appreciate the "free will" defense of this kind of God—that bad things happen because *people,* not God, choose to make them happen, and God can't intervene without undermining our free will and turning us into puppets or pawns. But if that's the case, then what, exactly, is this all-powerful God doing all day?

Believing that this particular deity was my only Jewish God option, I found myself toggling between exasperated atheism, hazy agnosticism, and "spiritual but not religious-ism"—thinking there must be something out there, but not something I was comfortable calling "God." To be honest, I felt like I was too smart to believe in God—like God is fine for other people, who need that sort of thing to comfort themselves in times of distress, or to incentivize them to behave morally. But not me. I was above that.

I've heard people talk about having a "God-shaped hole" in their lives. What I had was more like a God-shaped wall—one with the contours of a controlling old man with a beard that I simply could not get beyond.

But then I went on a weeklong silent Jewish meditation retreat that I found one night on the Internet and read a stack of books about Jewish theology, and just about everything I thought and felt about God changed.

This retreat had all the makings of a bad idea.

No one I knew had ever heard of it. It was located in a remote part of Pennsylvania where I'm confident few, if any, Jews actually live. And it had a name—"Awakening the Divine"—that struck me as ridiculous and made me think this probably wasn't the kind of holiday vacation I would be able to discuss with my White House co-workers around the office watercooler.

In my defense, I was still struggling to get over the breakup that had led me to my first Judaism class, still feeling lonely and anxious. I had previously taken meditation classes and found them useful for dealing with anxiety, and I figured that if thirty minutes of meditation once a week could help, thirty hours all packed into one week would be even better. This kind of reasoning often leads to poor life choices, but the thought of rattling around the halls of an empty White House over the holidays was depressing, and the woman who took my registration information for the retreat over the phone was friendly and assured me that it wasn't a cult.

So unable to think of anything better to do, in late December of 2014, I found myself sitting on a cushion on the floor of a retreat center in the woods, surrounded by about sixty other Jews, none of whom I was allowed to talk to. Free from the distractions of work, friends, books, and screens, I had an unobstructed view of what was happening in my brain, and it wasn't pretty.

Hour after hour, I watched my mind jump from one anxious thought to another, questioning whether I had made the right decision about ending that relationship and whether I could trust myself to make good life decisions in general; wondering whether the guy next to me was going to continue breathing like Darth Vader for the entire retreat, and whether that would be distracting and ruin the whole experience, and whether I should try to switch seats, and whether if I did I would hurt the guy's feelings.

Despite the instructions from the teachers to view our thoughts with compassion and nonjudgmental awareness, I couldn't help but judge myself to be completely pathetic. I had all the trappings of a wonderful life: good health, amazing family and friends, and a job that involved walking through the gates of the White House every morning. But every so often, generally in the face of big life decisions about relationships or my career, I would be subsumed by anxiety, unable to enjoy any of my abundant blessings. This was definitely one of those times.

By the third night of the retreat, I was exhausted, frustrated, and thoroughly sick of myself. And when one of the teachers announced that we would be doing a practice called "hitbodedut" (pronounced "heet-bo-deh-doot")—which was developed about two hundred years ago by Rebbe* Naḥman, a Ḥasidic rabbi, and involves going out into nature alone and talking to God—my first thought was something like "Are you @*#$% kidding me?"

The rules of hitbodedut, she informed us, are as follows:

1. Go somewhere secluded outdoors where no one else can hear you.
2. Speak out loud to God—not in your head, but in an audible voice—for an allotted period of time. We would be given forty-five minutes. If you don't believe in God, that's fine, just do it anyway, along the lines of "Hi, God, I don't believe in you, so I'm basically talking to empty air . . ."

---

* "Rebbe" is a Yiddish word used by Ḥasidic Jews to refer to their most revered rabbis. The term can also be used colloquially to refer to someone you view as particularly wise and spiritually insightful (e.g., "She is totally my rebbe").

3. Speak without pauses. If you run out of things to say, you can say "I've run out of things to say" over and over again. But whatever you do, keep talking.

Despite its Jewish roots, this hitbodedut practice sounded like new age nonsense to me. But I am an inveterate rule follower, and when the bell rang to signal that the exercise had begun, I trekked up to a spot in the woods overlooking the retreat center, cleared my throat, and started talking.

"Um, hi, God. So . . . yeah . . . I don't really believe in you. I guess you do good work—the nature out here is nice. Except, again, I don't think there's a 'you' there. So it's not really clear who I'm talking to right now."

I began to wonder, could there be security cameras out here? I nervously scanned the trees. "I look like I'm insane. This is stupid. Why am I doing this?"

Pacing back and forth, I found myself growing increasingly agitated. Why was I even at this retreat? Why was I still losing hours of my life to the same senseless anxiety that had driven me to pace the floor of my college dorm room just like this two decades ago? What was the point of having a fancy title and ID badge if I was going to wind up alone in the woods ranting like a lunatic?

"This is so stupid. What is the point of this? I don't want to be out here. I don't know what I'm doing. I just . . . I don't know." And suddenly, I was crying. "I don't know, okay? I just don't know." And that was all I could say, over and over again, "I don't know."

What didn't I know? To this day, I'm not sure. But I just kept saying it, until I finally blurted out: "I don't know, but I cannot do this alone. I just can't. I can't do this alone."

And with that—"I don't know, but I cannot do this alone"—like something from a depressed greeting card writer or a middle school health class video, I heard the bell calling us back to the retreat.

. . .

The next day, I decided to request a meeting with the head teacher on the retreat, a rabbi named James Jacobson-Maisels, who, as my Internet-search luck would have it, turned out to be one of the world's leading Jewish meditation teachers and scholars.

Holding his hand over his heart, James nodded sympathetically as I did my best to describe what had happened out in the woods.

"I mean, this just isn't me," I stammered. "I don't talk like this. I don't believe in a God who I can call 'you.' So why did I get so worked up like that? This just feels crazy."

"Let me ask you something," James said, once I'd tapered off into embarrassed silence. "Have you ever been to a black church?"

I don't think James knew that I had worked in Democratic politics for years, including as a speechwriter for the first African American President and First Lady. But if he was surprised when I replied that I'd been to plenty of black churches, he didn't let on.

Instead he asked, "What do you think they're doing there?"

I began to see where he was going with this. "I don't know . . . I mean, I guess they're talking to God?"

"And do you think they're crazy?"

I was taken aback. "Of course not!" I had always loved visiting black churches. I loved the music and the energy. People seemed to be experiencing something I had never felt in a synagogue, and it didn't seem crazy to me at all.

"So," he replied, an amused smile spreading across this face, "what's the problem here?"

Wasn't it obvious? The people in those churches actually seemed to *believe* in God, so what they were doing made total sense. I did *not* believe in God, so what I was doing out in the woods did not make any sense at all.

But by this point, I was too tired to argue. "I guess there isn't a problem?"

"Nope, no problem here," James cheerfully replied as he ushered me out the door and back into the meditation hall for more time alone on the cushion with my increasingly agitated brain.

. . .

But despite my resistance, something had shifted. And as I continued to sit, hour after hour, observing my anxious ruminations and feeling no small amount of contempt for the brain that had generated them, out of nowhere the following thought popped into my mind: "You created me like this."

This was, of course, absurd. My parents created me. I did not believe in any kind of "You." This thought made no sense, and I had no idea where it came from.

Yet at the same time, in some fundamental way that I can neither explain nor defend, it felt true and also somehow connected with being boundlessly loved.* It was like stumbling upon an ancient holy site in an unkempt backyard. I had no idea what to make of it, but I couldn't escape the feeling that, amidst the rotting tires and overgrown weeds, I had uncovered something sacred, something that had been here all along.

I sat with that feeling for several hours, at which point I began to feel something else: a rising sense of annoyance. It's true that my brain had served me well in many ways, but who would deliberately build in this kind of anxiety design flaw? Why would I be created like this? If there was some kind of "You"—and as far as I was concerned, there was not—couldn't that "You" do any better?

And then, once again out of nowhere, a thought arrived—one that felt much like the first: "Thank you."

* The closest I have come to approximating this feeling was during an exercise I once did where the instructions were to close your eyes and spend ten minutes thinking about all the people in your life who have loved you. And you should define "love" broadly as "displayed some kind of care and concern for you"—so not just your family and friends, but your teachers, babysitters, childhood neighbors, coaches, professors, doctors, and colleagues, as well as the school bus driver who greeted you warmly each morning, the barista who always remembers your coffee order, and the person who ran after you for two blocks to return your wallet when you dropped it. Start from the moment you were born and continue to today, briefly picturing each person and remembering how they made you feel.

This also made no sense. I have never been in any way grateful for feeling anxious—just the opposite. But again, this thought felt undeniably true and deeply moving, like realizing that something that had been done for me a very long time ago—something I had never understood and often resented—had actually been an act of love.

I continued doing hitbodedut on my own each night, and on the final night of the retreat, I returned from the woods long after everyone else had gone to sleep and went to sit by myself in the meditation hall. After all those hours of meditation, my anxiety had finally lost its grip, and I was calmer than I'd been in years. I couldn't shake the feeling that this whole retreat was nuts and definitely not something I would ever tell my colleagues about. But whatever this was, I did not want to lose it. I did not want to go back to being tense and closed off to the world. So I found myself moving on from "I don't know" and "Thank you" to another equally unsophisticated but honest prayer: "Stay with me."

That's what I was saying over and over in my head—"stay with me"—when I had another thought: "I'm with you even when you can't feel me." As if it were being said to me.

I want to be clear that I did not hear this as a booming voice, or as any voice at all. It was more like a realization or an insight that came unbidden. I do not believe some being in the sky was speaking to me. Rather, I think these words were simply how my brain translated a feeling of deep connection using the closest available language, that of human relation.

I'm fully aware of how crazy this may sound. If someone had described an experience like this to me at the time, I would have said something like "Oh, that's your beautiful truth, how wonderful," while feeling incredibly uncomfortable and totally judging them. Like my earlier thoughts, though, this one also felt profoundly true. And to this day, I cannot think of a more loving or reassuring sentiment that could have entered my mind at that moment.

What exactly was happening here? Was this just my own subconscious mind? The power of suggestion from the talks about love and compassion the rabbis had given? The influence of the prayers we had sung with verses like "My God, the soul that you have given me is pure" and "With a great love you have loved us"?

I have no idea. It was probably all of those things. But for reasons I still cannot articulate, it felt right to me then—and still feels right to me now—to go ahead and call it God.

I wish I could translate my experience on that retreat more clearly—none of what I've written really captures it. In fact, sharing it somehow cheapens it, reducing it to the kind of thing that makes me and others in the circles I travel in uneasy. All I know is that I touched into something that felt indescribably big and also intimate—something that had always been there, and is still in some way with me, but is beyond the reach of my skill as a writer.

That retreat was when I first realized that I had been approaching the question of God backward. I had been starting with theology rather than experience. And even worse, I had been focusing on one particularly difficult theology—a theology that serves as a wall to the Divine for many modern Jews.

Rabbi Edward Feinstein shares a story to this effect about a rabbi who polled a class of Jewish teenagers about whether they believed in God. None of them did, and despite his best arguments, they remained unpersuaded.

At the next class, the rabbi asked them, "When in your life did you ever feel that God was close to you?" They had all kinds of answer to that—at Grandpa's funeral, when Mom lights the Shabbat candles. They didn't buy the *theology*—they didn't believe in the *concept* of God—yet they could admit that they sometimes *sensed* God in their lives.

We've all experienced moments that feel transcendent, whether or not we associate them with the Divine—moments when, as Rabbi Art Green writes:

In the midst of life, our ordinariness is interrupted. This may take place as we touch one of the edges of life, in a great confrontation with the new life of a child, or of an approaching death. We may see it in wonders of nature, sunrises and sunsets, mountains and oceans. It may happen to us in the course of loving and deeply entering into union with another, or in profound aloneness. Sometimes, however, such a moment of holy and awesome presence comes upon us without any apparent provocation at all. It may come as a deep inner stillness, quieting all the background noise that usually fills our inner chambers, or it may be quite the opposite, a loud rush and excitement that fills us to overflowing. It may seem to come from within or without, or perhaps both at once. The realization of such moments fills us with a sense of magnificence, of smallness, and of belonging, all at once.

Astronauts have experienced moments like these when they gaze down at planet earth, a phenomenon the author Frank White deemed the "overview effect." Some scientists also speak of their work in such terms. As the renowned astrophysicist Carl Sagan once wrote, "I would suggest that science is, at least in part, informed worship."

These experiences are impossible to fully capture in words, and they seem to have little to do with a being in the sky controlling everything. So why, I wondered, did Judaism appear to be so stuck on that particular theology?

To answer this question, I started reading. I read basic books providing overviews of Jewish God concepts. I read sophisticated books by Jewish thinkers and theologians. I read books that translated those sophisticated books into clear, accessible language, for which I am eternally grateful. And it wasn't long before I realized that, to paraphrase an old saying, the simplistic old-man-in-the-sky-who-controls-everything-God that I don't believe in is the God that Judaism doesn't believe in either.

If anything, when it comes to God, Judaism embraces complexity—

almost to a fault. While there are few things Jews agree on, there seems to be consensus that we cannot fully understand or adequately describe God.

Jews don't even pronounce God's name. The word that is considered to be God's proper name is spelled with Hebrew letters that come out in English as "YHWH." But we pronounce it "Adonai," and translate it as "the Lord," both because we no longer know the correct pronunciation for these letters and because many Jews believe God's real name is too sacred to say aloud. Even back in Temple times, when we apparently did know the correct pronunciation, this word was uttered only once a year, on Yom Kippur, by the most senior priest in Jerusalem in the most sacred part of the Temple, known as the "Holy of Holies."

Today, many traditionally observant Jews won't even write out the English word "God," and instead use abbreviations like "G-d," "Gd," or "G!d." Some won't even use the euphemistic word "Adonai" unless they're praying, preferring "Hashem," meaning "the name."

It may seem like we're getting hung up on semantics, but when it comes to God, language really matters. Frankly, I don't like the word "God" in the first place. To me it feels so inextricably linked to the image of a judgy, bearded puppet master in the sky that to utter it is almost to commit a kind of slander.

I thought about trying to use one of the alternatives I've come to prefer—phrases like "the Source of Life" or "That Which Is." But all names for God reflect the namer's theology, and I don't want to impose my God concepts on anyone else. For convenience, I'm going to use the words "God" and "the Divine" in this book, but please know that I'm talking about something I believe is indescribable in human language. In fact, just about all I can say with any clarity about the Divine is that beyond our unwavering insistence on monotheism, Judaism has no one official doctrine about God.*

---

* While some have argued that Maimonides' "Thirteen Principles of Faith"—a list of thirteen statements about the nature of the Divine—is Judaism's doctrine of God, this doctrine is nowhere near universally accepted in Judaism.

Let me repeat that, because it's really important: *Other than mono-theism, there is no universally accepted Jewish creed or article of faith defining the Divine.*

An often-cited medieval midrash asserts that each of the Israelites at Mount Sinai heard God's revelation differently according to their own capacity to understand it. They each had their own individual experience of the Divine.

Rabbi Elliot Dorff fleshes out this idea with an analogy to his own relationships with the people around him. He notes that different people have different conceptions of him—as a father, friend, teacher, colleague, board member—based on their own particular interactions with him. If these people were asked to describe him, each would give a different answer based on their personal experience. Rabbi Dorff concludes, "If various people can and do have multiple and widely varying conceptions of a person, all the more should that be true of God, who presumably is open to interaction with everyone."

For centuries, Jews have struggled to articulate conceptions of God that reflect their personal experiences and their understanding of Jewish tradition. And when you combine the Jewish emphasis on thinking for ourselves with the fact that people experience the Divine in very different ways, it's not surprising that Jewish thinkers have come up with a mind-bogglingly diverse set of ideas about God. The choices are not just "Man-in-the-Sky-Who-Controls-Everything" or atheism.

For me, learning about some of the many Jewish theologies was no less of a game changer than what happened on that retreat. Initially, experience was a gateway to theology, inspiring me to investigate various Jewish conceptions of God and allowing me to recognize my own felt sense of the Divine within them. And as I studied, I found that theology could be a gateway to even greater experience, expanding my sense of where and how the Divine could be.

Here are very brief summaries of some of the Jewish God conceptions that have most resonated for me as I've explored—perhaps some of them will resonate for you as well.

GOD AS ALL-POWERFUL, ALL-KNOWING, AND ALL-GOOD (MORE OR LESS)

The "traditional" Jewish God is sometimes understood as all-knowing (aware of everything that happens, including our thoughts and feelings), all-powerful (in control of everything, either through direct action or choosing not to act, knowing exactly what the consequences of such action or inaction will be), and all-good (if God does something, it must be for a morally warranted reason). This God rewards and punishes us according to how faithfully we uphold our end of the covenant by following the laws of the Torah.

But the God depicted in the Torah doesn't seem to fit this description. This God often appears surprised by the choices humans make and not fully in control of what's happening in the world, despite having created it.

While Rabbinic ideas about God may be closer to this all-powerful/knowing/good conception, one would be hard-pressed to find any kind of systematic theology in the Talmud. In fact, the Rabbis used numerous names for God that reflect a diversity of thought: "Hamakom," literally "the Place," but often translated as "the Omnipresent," a God who is present in every place at all times. "Ribbono Shel Olam," "Master of the world," a God who is the ultimate authority. "HaKadosh Barukh Hu," meaning "the Holy Blessed One," which connotes a God who is separate from and beyond us and the world. "Raḥmana," "the Merciful One," a God of compassion. And they used the word "Shekhinah," from the root word that means "to dwell," to describe God's presence with us in the world. (This term later came to be associated with feminine aspects of the Divine.)

The Rabbis thus seemed to understand God as both transcendent (separate from the world, unbound by time or space, beyond human comprehension) and immanent (acting within us and the world and available for personal relationship).

As for the reward-and-punishment idea, the Rabbis generally believed that God holds people accountable for their behavior—another name they used for God is "Elohim," which implies a God of justice. But they realized that sometimes innocent people seem to be unfairly punished (i.e., bad things happen to good people), and vice versa. The question of why God permits such injustices is known as "theodicy," and Jews have wrestled mightily with it throughout the ages, including in the Hebrew Bible itself, which contains an entire book—the Book of Job—devoted to this very topic.

Rabbinic attempts to resolve this theodicy problem include the following: Righteous people who suffer here on earth will be greatly rewarded in the afterlife.* It's a mystery, sometimes we just can't understand God's workings. There are certain natural laws of the universe that operate regardless of morality—if I steal seeds and plant them, for example, crops will still grow despite the immoral act that led to their existence.

So the "traditional" view is complicated. But there is one aspect of it that I want to emphasize: the idea of God as loving and compassionate. The old claim that Christianity is a religion of love while Judaism is a religion of law is simply not true. As we discussed in Chapter 2, the God of the Torah chose the Israelites not because they were particularly law-abiding, but out of love. And the Rabbis emphasized this aspect of the Divine, regarding the giving of the Torah to the Jews as an act of great love and invoking the metaphor of God as a loving father. The following midrash describing how God led the Israelites through the desert is a good example:

> It is like a man who was walking on the way and letting his son go before him; came robbers in front to take the boy captive, the father put him behind him; came a wolf from behind, he put him in front; came robbers in front and wolves behind, he took him up

---

* There is an idea of an afterlife in Judaism, many ideas actually. We'll talk more about this in Chapter 9.

in his arms; did he begin to be troubled by the heat of the sun, his father stretched his own garment over him; was he hungry, he gave him food; thirsty, he gave him to drink.

GOD AS RADICALLY TRANSCENDENT

Maimonides, the renowned twelfth-century Jewish philosopher, embraced a radically transcendent idea of God as a perfect, eternal deity who is the source of everything that exists but totally separate from the world and completely unlike human beings.

God is so unlike us that the kinds of words we use to describe people—that they are "intelligent" or "unintelligent," for example—simply do not apply to God. As Maimonides expert Kenneth Seeskin writes, "The difference between God's intelligence and ours is not one of degree but of kind. God's intelligence is so unlike ours that it cannot be measured according to the same criteria." Or as Maimonides himself put it, "We do not say this heat is similar to that colour, or this voice is similar to that sweetness." Maimonides thus concluded that we cannot make any statements about who or what God *is* at all—that God is powerful, loving, just, or wise—we can only make negative statements about what God *is not,* such as "God is not a corporeal being."

Since we and God have nothing whatsoever in common, it is not possible for us to have a direct relationship with God. We can, however, know, love, and emulate God by knowing, loving, and emulating the effects God has in the world. "It is as if God is a black box," Seeskin explains. "We have some acquaintance with the things that come out of the box, but not with the mechanism by which they are generated." Seeskin invites us to imagine an anonymous donor who generously contributes to a number of charities, and soon afterward we see homeless people in shelters and hungry people receiving meals. Since we know nothing about the donor and have no idea why they decided to give, we cannot necessarily claim that they are "just" and "merciful" (perhaps they donated to impress a potential love interest or because they lost a bet). But we *can* say that their contributions have led to "just" and "merciful" outcomes in our community. We can be grateful for, and moved by, those outcomes. And we can seek to imitate the donor's actions by choosing to support charities ourselves.

Therefore, notes Seeskin, "The point is not to comprehend the internal nature of God but to understand and eventually to imitate the qualities which flow from it." To that end, Maimonides urged the pursuit of secular learning in science, philosophy, and other disciplines. Such knowledge, he believed, helps us better comprehend and appreciate God's workings in the world, which leads us to more deeply love God.

GOD AS EVERYTHING

Theologians who are sometimes referred to as "nondualists" don't view God solely as a supernatural being "up there" who is separate from, and rules over, human beings "down here"—an idea that creates a duality between the Divine and the human. Instead, everything is God—you, me, skyscrapers, grass—it's all God. There is no separation between us and God, or us and each other, or us and anything else. We're all one.

This theology has its roots in the mysticism of Kabbalah and later found expression in the eighteenth-century Ḥasidic movement. Nondualists often cite a line from the Torah: "There is none beside Him [God]." This statement has traditionally been understood to mean that there are no gods other than the supreme God, but nondualists believe it means that there is nothing in the world other than God—God is everything. They also cite a verse that reads, "The whole world is filled with God's glory." The founder of Ḥasidism, a rabbi known as the Baal Shem Tov, interpreted this verse to mean "There is therefore absolutely nothing that is devoid of His [God's] essence."

Nondualists also emphasize that God's proper name, YHWH, is actually an amalgam of various tenses of the Hebrew word "to be"—

perhaps best understood as "was–is–will be." And they note that during the burning bush incident, when Moses asks God what God's name is, God responds, "Ehyeh-Asher-Ehyeh," meaning "I will be what I will be," or as Rabbi Jonathan Kligler translates it, "I am becoming that which I am becoming," which he renders "Life Unfolding." God is not *a* being, but rather the *process of being.* Connecting with this kind of God is less about addressing an entity and more about simply being present with what is. As Rabbi Alexander Schindler described it, "The closer I feel to life at each lived moment, the closer I feel to God."

This notion of the Divine is hard to wrap one's mind around, and nondualists often resort to phrases like "the great force of life, the cosmic breath that dwells at the center of all being . . ." or "the inner force of existence itself . . . the single unifying substratum of all that is."

A more accessible explanation comes from the spiritual teacher Ram Dass, in the form of a story about two ocean waves—a tall one and a short one—heading toward the shore. The tall wave sees what's up ahead—waves crashing and dissolving back into the ocean—and starts panicking. "We're going to die!" it cries. The short wave is untroubled. The tall wave repeatedly tries to convey the gravity of the situation. "Seriously! This is the end!" But the short wave remains unconcerned, responding: "What would you say if I told you that there are six words, that if you really understood and believed them, you would see that there's no reason to fear?" "Fine, fine, tell me the six words!" pleads the tall wave. The short wave replies: "You're not a wave, you're water."

For most of us, such moments, when our sense of separateness dissolves and we feel deeply connected to everything and everyone—part of the entire ocean rather than a separate wave—are rare and fleeting, if we have them at all. But in these moments, nondualists believe, we are in touch with the actual nature of reality. Some report that this feels like being held in a boundless kind of love—that, as Rabbi Art Green puts it, "in some mysterious way Being *loves me,* that it rejoices for a fleeting instant in dwelling within me, delighting in this unique form that constitutes my existence, as it delights in each of its endlessly diverse manifestations."

As wonderful as this sounds, however, the point is not to feel this way all the time, but rather to bring what we learn from these moments to the rest of our lives—as Rabbi Jay Michaelson explains, "to return to the experience of duality while maintaining the consciousness of unity." Doing so has implications for how we relate to others, spurring us to treat them well, not because we fear punishment from, or seek the approval of, a supernatural deity, but because we recognize our fundamental interconnectedness with them. As Michaelson writes, "How might we approach strangers on the street, if we were convinced that we and they were God?" Bringing the experience of unity to our daily duality also has implications for how we go about our lives. "If every moment, every object, and every being is the Divine before us," notes Rabbi James Jacobson-Maisels, "we bring a freshness and openness to our experience, ready to find God in every moment."

GOD AS AN ACTUALIZING FORCE

The idea of God as an actualizing force comes from Mordecai Kaplan, the twentieth-century American rabbi who founded Reconstructionism. Kaplan recognized that many Jews simply could not get behind the idea of a supernatural God, or as he described it, "a sort of invisible superman, displaying the same psychological traits as man, but on a greater scale."

But he also understood that some concept of God was still important for modern Jews. Observing that "man normally veers in the direction of that which makes for the fulfillment of his destiny as a human being," Kaplan concluded, "That fact indicates the functioning of a cosmic Power which influences his behavior." That power, "the power that makes for salvation," as Kaplan famously deemed it, is God. God is not a supernatural being, but rather a kind of force.

Kaplan wasn't using the word "salvation" in the Christian sense of redemption from sin. Rather, he was talking about the process through which all living beings take on their highest form. A psychologist might call this "self-actualization," what happens when we cultivate our talents, strengths, and passions to become the truest, best version of ourselves. Or as Rabbi Elliot Dorff describes it, "God is the force that transforms the acorn into the oak tree, a bad baseball player into a good one, and an immoral person into a moral one."

GOD AS FOUND IN RELATIONSHIP

Twentieth-century Jewish philosopher Martin Buber argued that God is found in relationship. We connect with God by connecting deeply to others—and not just humans, but animals and things in nature as well.

Buber distinguished between two kinds of relationships: "I-It" relationships and "I-Thou" relationships. When we have I-It relationships with people, we don't see them in their full humanity. Rather, we experience them as objects to be evaluated and used by us: the colleague whom we judge as competent or incompetent, the waiter whom we regard as a means to obtaining a meal. Even our closest relationships take on this quality, such as when we hurriedly ask our partner to pass the salt or take the dog for a walk.

In I-Thou relationships, by contrast, we see the other person not in terms of what they can do for us, and not, as Buber writes, as a "He or She, limited by other Hes and Shes, a dot in the world grid of space and time, nor a condition that can be experienced and described, a loose bundle of named qualities." Rather, we see the person as a "You" who "fills the firmament. Not as if there were nothing but he; but everything else lives in *his* light."

In this kind of profound interaction between two people, when they open themselves up to each other and receive each other in the fullest possible way—when "deep calls unto deep"—each of them encounters God. What is happening between them is a manifestation of the Divine—or as Buber declared: "Every particular Thou is a glimpse through to the eternal Thou." And both people walk away changed:

"The man who steps out of the essential act of pure relation has something More in his being," Buber wrote, "something new has grown there of which he did not know before."

GOD IN SEARCH OF MAN

Twentieth-century American rabbi Abraham Joshua Heschel was horrified by the distant, impersonal idea of God articulated by Maimonides, a God he felt was "unknown and indifferent to man . . . conscious of Himself, but oblivious of the world."

Heschel's God embodies the opposite of indifference. This is a God who knows each of us intimately, loves and cares about us deeply—particularly those of us who are downtrodden or oppressed—and feels our sorrows and joys intensely. This is a God to whom we can reach out. And this God reaches back, yearning for our partnership in the work of improving the world, constantly, as the title of one of Heschel's books states, "in search of man."

As a result of this move to form relationship with us, to *need* us, explains Heschel expert Rabbi Shai Held,* God is quite vulnerable to us. So while God's core emotion is love, when we spurn God by acting selfishly and callously toward others—failing to emulate God's care and compassion for us and our fellow human beings—God suffers, and even becomes angry. Heschel assures us, however, that God's anger is not irrational and uncontrolled like human anger can be; rather, it is a kind of "righteous indignation . . . it is impatience with evil." It is the anger that parents feel when someone harms their child—or one of their children harms another. God's anger, in other words, does not reflect a lapse of God's love for us—it is actually a manifestation of that love. God gets angry because God cares.

Understanding God in this way requires us to fundamentally reori-

---

* I am deeply indebted to Rabbi Held, whose remarkable book on Heschel, *Abraham Joshua Heschel: The Call of Transcendence,* led me to each of the Heschel quotations in this section.

ent our perspective such that we see ourselves not as subjects, but as objects—as recipients, understanding that we did not do anything to deserve our life. Rather, it is a "transcendent loan" we have been given. When we internalize that truth, we regard our life and the world around us with a sense of wonder, even "radical amazement." And we have a feeling of "indebtedness . . . an awareness that something is asked of us." Holocaust survivor Viktor Frankl put this insight in secular terms when sharing a key lesson from his time in concentration camps: *"It did not really matter what we expected from life, but rather what life expected from us."*

When we make this shift, Held explains, "the human project now becomes not to ask but to answer; not to assert but to respond; not to think, but to be thought of; not, finally, to know God, but to be known by him." We let up with our "relentless self-assertion" as Held puts it, and "move from ego-centeredness to other-centeredness." We stop viewing the world as something to be exploited and manipulated, but rather as something to be regarded with awe and appreciation. And instead of focusing only on our own needs, we open ourselves up to the needs of others, responding to them with the same kind of loving concern with which God responds to us.

GOD AS ALL-GOOD, BUT NOT ALL-POWERFUL

Rabbi Harold Kushner takes on theodicy directly in his bestselling book *When Bad Things Happen to Good People,* arguing that God is all-good, but not all-powerful. The bad things that happen to us are not punishments from God; God does not cause disease, violence, earthquakes, car accidents, and the deaths of innocent children. Rather, Kushner writes, some of these tragedies "are caused by bad luck, some are caused by bad people, and some are simply an inevitable consequence of our being human and being mortal, living in a world of inflexible natural laws."

But while God "neither causes nor prevents tragedies," Kushner asserts, God *does* inspire human beings to respond—to rush into harm's way to rescue others, to become medical professionals and heal people. God also gives us the courage and support we need to endure and recover from hardships:

> I believe that God gives us strength and patience and hope, renewing our spiritual resources when they run dry. How else do sick people manage to find more strength and more good humor over the course of prolonged illness than any one person could possibly have, unless God was constantly replenishing their souls?

Kushner acknowledges that his detractors believe his theology depicts God as "a weakling." He responds: "I don't think that's true. But even if it were, there are worse things than being a weakling, and one of them is being a child murderer."

GOD AS FOUND IN THE PREDICATES OF GOD

Rabbi Harold Schulweis outlines what he calls a "Predicate Theology." Instead of seeing God as a noun/subject whom we must affirm—a "God-as-person" conception—we focus on affirming the *attributes,* or predicates, of God as Jewish tradition understands them. So instead of saying that "God is just, merciful and good," we declare that "justice, mercy and goodness are godly."

When we express these attributes by being kind to others and working to create a more just and compassionate world, we "express Godliness." And when we experience these traits from others, we experience God. As Schulweis puts it, "Does God console me and comfort me? The answer is yes. Through you."

GOD AS IN PROCESS

Process theologians like Rabbi Bradley Shavit Artson argue that everything in the universe is constantly changing, including us and God.

"We aren't human *beings,* so much as human *becomings,*" Artson writes, and we are in a continuous dynamic relationship with God.

Rather than shaping our behavior through coercion with rewards and punishments, argues Artson, "God works through persuasion and invitation." At every moment, God offers each of us the best possible choice for action—the "divine lure"—that will best help us "attain the divine goals of maximal relationship, engagement, love, compassion, and justice." We have the freedom to accept that choice, or make a different choice, and God doesn't know in advance what we're going to do. Once we choose, God incorporates that decision and then offers us the best possible choice in the next moment, taking into account the previous choices we have made—so God changes and evolves as we do. In this way, Artson explains, "God is persistently, tirelessly luring creation toward its optimal expression—greater love, greater justice, greater engagement."

Once I began learning about the many Divine options other than the being in the sky, I was able to start mapping them onto various moments in my life.

After studying Buber, I had a much deeper appreciation of those rare moments of profound vulnerability (mine or others') when one person shows up for the other in a no-questions-asked, no-judgment-rendered, "I'm here with you no matter how ugly this gets" kind of way. I like the phrase chaplains use for this—"the ministry of presence." It reminds me of the moment in the Torah at the burning bush when Moses asks God, "Who am I that I should go to Pharaoh and free the Israelites from Egypt?" and God reassures him, "I will be with you."

The idea of God as found in the predicates of God comes to mind when I meet or hear about people who commit transcendent acts of love: the couple that quietly takes in foster child after foster child, caring for them as if they are their own; the lawyer who works for years to free an innocent client, doggedly gathering evidence and filing motions long after everyone else has given up; ordinary people who run up the stairs of burning buildings to rescue complete strangers. As Rabbi Schulweis might put it, I feel "Godliness" in the courage and devotion these people embody.

The nondualist notion of God as everything resonates for me in those fleeting moments of flushness with life when I'm fully present—actually noticing and appreciating everything and everyone around me rather than caught up in my own thoughts and worries.

And in moments of deep flow, when I sense that I'm doing what I'm meant to be doing on this earth, I think of Kaplan's notion of God as an actualizing force. I share the intuition that he and many other Jewish thinkers have that there is a connection between God and my truest, deepest self—that that self actually *is* the spark of the Divine within me. And I love the old Ḥasidic story about a rabbi named Zusya who was on his deathbed, weeping as his students tried to comfort him. Finally, one of them said to him, "Rabbi, why are you so upset? You've been nearly as kind as Abraham and as wise as Moses—surely, you'll be rewarded in heaven!" Zusya replied, "Yes, but when I get to heaven, God isn't going to ask me why I wasn't more like Moses or Abraham . . . He'll ask me, 'Zusya, why weren't you more like Zusya?' And then what will I say?"

Articulating all of this—and implying that I believe God is a force, or loving, or found in relationship—makes me deeply uneasy. I think Maimonides was wise in urging us to refrain from such characterizations of God. Too often, when people insist that they know what God is or what God wants, they're really talking about what *they* want and just cloaking it in Divine terms.

The Torah tells us that we are created in the Divine image, *not* the other way around. That means we should never be creating God in *our* image,* reducing the Divine to human proportions and attributing to God all our prejudices and failings. A good rule of thumb, courtesy of

* This is outlawed in the Ten Commandments—the Second Commandment prohibits making any graven images of God. No statues. No paintings. No visual depictions whatsoever. That "old man with a beard" image that so many of us have may have originated centuries ago in Christian art. It is not a Jewish conception.

the Christian writer Anne Lamott (who attributes it to her "priest friend Tom"), is as follows: "You can safely assume you've created God in your own image when it turns out that God hates all the same people you do."

But while I gravitate toward Kaplan and the nondualists, I find it difficult to relate to the Divine as simply what *is,* or as a force, even if that's all my rational mind will tolerate. My heart cannot feel God merely as an abstract, intellectually respectable concept. Instead, I've found, as Rabbi Jay Michaelson puts it, that "what appears to the mind as Being, appears to the heart as God." And as much as I recoil from anthropomorphic God imagery, I have to admit that I do sometimes think of and feel the Divine in distinctly human terms—as a "You."

This doesn't give me as much peace of mind as you might think. While I'm not sure I buy the specifics of Rabbi Harold Kushner's theology—how is God powerful enough to help millions of people re-cover from horrific traumas but not powerful enough to jam the trigger on a single mass shooter's rifle?—his notion of the Divine as all-good but not all-powerful resonates with me. I don't believe in a God who can intervene to change events in my life per my request, which is too bad because turbulence would probably scare me less if I thought God could save me from a plummeting airplane. And while I envy people who think everything happens for a reason and is all part of a larger plan—I can see the power of such a belief—I do not think there is such a plan, and I generally assume things are *not* going to work out and worry accordingly.

In being so instinctively resistant to the idea of an interventionist God, I sometimes wonder whether I'm falling into the same ungrateful trap as the ancient Israelites, still doubting and distrusting even after this God has done so many amazing things on my behalf. An acquain-tance of mine once told me that he thinks the survival of the Jewish people is so improbable that there has to be a God up there looking out for us. I'm more inclined to believe that our faith in, and ways of wor-shipping, this kind of God gave us the courage and skills we needed to survive. That might be saying the same thing, but I find it easier to swallow when stated that way. Though I can imagine an exasperated old-school God looking down from the heavens, thinking, "Seriously, people, what will it take???"

I'm aware of the incoherence of my thinking about the Divine.* I appear to believe in a largely powerless God who somehow animates all things. And while I *think* God is a cross between a force and simply what is, I sometimes *feel* and address God personally as a "You."

That's the problem with theology: Unless you're an atheist or a fundamentalist, when you actually try to articulate what you think about God, you can find yourself tangled in a web of contradictions.

I can relate to a woman I once met who, when describing her prayer practice, said something like "When I'm connecting to . . . well . . . that which I connect to" and just left it at that, without trying to define what she meant. I also like Rabbi Jay Michaelson's description of God as "the mystery that is rendered banal by explaining, the poetry lost in translation." And I love this declaration from Buber: "If to believe in God means to be able to talk about him in the third person, then I do not believe in God. If to believe in him means to be able to talk to him, then I believe in God."

Finally, I appreciate this statement from Rabbi Jeremy Gordon characterizing his own theology:

> I am sometimes asked, usually by those who disavow a faith in God, if I ever have crises of faith . . . I don't have crises of faith because my theology is built off existential crisis. It is a theology immune to being shattered by the slings and arrows of outrageous fortune precisely because it comes pre-shattered.

---

* I'm also aware of its incompleteness: You'll notice I haven't even touched on questions of cosmology. I have no idea how we got here or what, if anything, that has to do with God.

That is how my theology feels as well—like a number of separate pieces, each of which is meaningful to me even if they do not form a complete system.

While this lack of clarity about God can be confusing, even exhausting, it is also inescapably Jewish. As Rabbi Elliot Dorff observed of the Rabbis' approach to understanding God, "Their way of thinking typically prefers truth to consistency, describing experience in all its fullness even if the facts do not fit neatly together."

I suppose this is how they got away with insisting that God is beyond time, space, and human comprehension, but also right here in the world with us, loving each of us individually. This makes me feel better about my own beliefs, which are also contradictory, but which feel like they gesture at some kind of truth.

Even with all the theological options out there and no requirement to develop something unified out of them, for some people, the God idea just doesn't resonate. Maybe they can briefly access it in moments of crisis—times when, as Rabbi Michaelson writes, "theology and atheism go out the window, and the heart cries in a language the mind may neither approve nor understand." But otherwise, God talk doesn't feel like a native language to them, or may even sound like gibberish, and they consider themselves atheists, firmly believing there is no God—as opposed to agnostics, who aren't sure whether or not there is a God (and I would include in the agnosticism category those whose view on God is "doesn't resonate with me, but who knows?").

Is atheism compatible with committed Judaism? Many traditionalists would say that it is not, but I believe it is. Judaism is not just a religion, and there are many ways to engage with it that do not require a belief in God. I imagine many of the rabbis I know would say that the only theological requirement for Judaism is, as Michaelson puts it (citing a teacher of his), "one God or fewer."

I also do not think belief in God is necessary to incentivize moral behavior. Some of the most ethical people I know are atheists. They fully embrace and embody the moral values handed down from religious traditions without believing in the God to whom adherents ascribe those values.

That said, I find the righteous certitude some atheists have about their beliefs to be unnervingly similar to that of many religious fundamentalists. I'm also not all that impressed by atheists who automatically deem anyone with spiritual inclinations a moron. These folks often assume the most simplistic, least plausible notion of God—as a heavenly Santa Claus/ATM who rewards the nice, punishes the naughty, and allows us to make withdrawals whenever we please. They then triumphantly cite the endless evidence that such a God could not possibly exist.

I do not believe in this kind of God, nor, I imagine, do many other "believers." Yet I often find, as Rabbi Rachel Timoner observes, that just saying the word "God" sometimes makes people think I am "a different kind of person than they are." People assume, she writes, "that I'm a Believer, capital *B,* someone who has stopped thinking because she knows she has all of the answers."

I do not have all the answers, and I do plenty of thinking and struggling—probably too much. But that in itself is quite Jewish. Just consider our name—the people *Israel.* As you may recall from Chapter 1, that name comes from the story in the Torah about the all-night wrestling match Jacob has with a mysterious being. When Jacob prevails, the being gives him a new name—Israel—declaring, "for you have wrestled with God and men." Note that the being did not say "for you have blindly believed in God no matter what." Or "for you find the whole God thing to be ridiculous and look down on those idiots who believe." Or "for you don't think much about God because you're busy with work and the kids and everything." But "for you have *wrestled* with God."

And Jacob isn't alone in his struggle. Abraham doesn't hesitate to argue with God on behalf of the people of Sodom, declaring: "Far be it from You . . . to bring death upon the innocent as well as the guilty . . . Shall not the Judge of all the earth deal justly?" Similarly, after the Israelites worship the golden calf, Moses vehemently objects to God's plan to kill them, demanding that God "turn from Your blazing anger, and renounce the plan to punish Your people."

And consider one of my favorite stories from the Talmud, which is about a Rabbi named Eliezer who was debating with some other Rabbis about a point of Jewish law involving an oven (I'll spare you the details). They weren't buying his arguments, so Rabbi Eliezer declared that if he was right, a nearby carob tree would prove it. And indeed, the carob tree uprooted itself and moved to a different location. The Rabbis were unimpressed, retorting that a moving carob tree offered no proof for his point.

Rabbi Eliezer tried again, stating that if he was right, a nearby stream of water would prove it. As if on command, the stream started flowing in the opposite direction. Again, his fellow Rabbis were unmoved.

Rabbi Eliezer then insisted that the walls of the room in which they were studying would affirm his position. The walls responded by caving inward, at which point one of the other Rabbis stood up and yelled at the walls, telling them they had no right to interfere in this argument.

In a final attempt to convince his colleagues, Rabbi Eliezer asserted that support for his arguments would come from heaven. Right on cue, God chimed in, affirming that Rabbi Eliezer was indeed correct.

Unpersuaded by this voice from above, the Rabbi who had yelled at the walls snapped, "It is not in heaven!" by which he meant that it is not up to God to decide this debate, but to the Rabbis themselves.

God's reaction? God laughed and exclaimed, "My children have defeated me, my children have defeated me!"

But I realize that struggling with God is different from denying the existence of God. Our biblical ancestors were not atheists, and I think

Rabbi Joseph Telushkin and Dennis Prager raise a fair point when they state that "atheists replace God with gods of their own choosing: humanity, art, reason, the state, secular ideologies, science, progress, revolution, culture, education, happiness, the self . . . The issue is not belief or nonbelief, but belief in God or belief in other gods."

They seem to be talking about idolatry—the belief in false gods, including the belief that you yourself are essentially God, in control of everything. Religious gods have a mixed track record, but these other "gods" aren't much better. While leading to extraordinary human progress, science has also been manipulated to carry out horrors like the Holocaust. Pre-Holocaust Germany was renowned for its intellectual culture—its universities were widely regarded as the best in the world. And I would like to see someone argue that a godless movement like Stalinism that was responsible for millions of deaths was somehow better than the Crusades or the terror perpetrated by groups like ISIS.

Also, things generally don't go well when someone decides that *they're* God. So I appreciate Jewish educator Avraham Infeld's point that if you believe in God, when someone starts acting like they're God, you can respond, "No you're not, that job is taken."

I think about people of faith who risked their lives to assist Jews during the Holocaust, who looked at the Nazis and understood that they were not God.

I think of the role churches played in the Civil Rights movement, and how civil rights leaders like Congressman John Lewis and *The Reverend* Dr. Martin Luther King, Jr., seemed to believe in a power far greater than those hateful mobs and rows of officers wielding clubs.

I think about the rabbis I know who have been arrested as they've protested attacks on immigrants and refugees, believing that the political leaders who make those attacks are not God, and that the people whose plight they're protesting are very much in the Divine Image.

And I think about Nobel Peace Prize winner Malala Yousafzai, a committed Muslim who continues to advocate for girls' education after nearly being killed by terrorists who sought to silence her. "They think that God is a tiny, little conservative being who would send girls to the hell just because of going to school," she said in a speech at the United Nations. "The terrorists are misusing the name of Islam . . . for their own personal benefits."

You don't get to define God. You're not God. That job is taken.

But despite my best arguments and my own lived experience, I can't quite escape the sense of unease I feel about being a "believer." It feels irrational, and a little silly. And more than one thoughtful atheist has pointed out to me that many of the moments and experiences I label "Divine" could also be labeled "aesthetics" or "neurons firing in my brain."

But I also want to be careful about categorizing a belief in God as "not rational," as if that makes it baseless or meaningless. There's nothing particularly rational about being in love with someone. You don't get there by doing a numerical assessment of their strengths and weaknesses. There is something mysterious and ineffable about love, but I still believe it exists.

I guess we could reduce love to a bunch of chemical reactions in our brains. But looking at it like that diminishes it. It's like looking at a beautiful home and saying, "Well, that's just a bunch of lumber, nails, and glass," or looking at the Sistine Chapel and saying, "Well, that's just some paint on a ceiling." It's technically accurate, but it's a pretty depressing way to live. I prefer to appreciate the transcendent—both the once-in-a-while kind and the everyday kind—and elevate it by calling it God rather than degrade it by defining it solely by its component parts or scientific basis.

I once confided to a teacher of mine, Rabbi Jordan Bendat-Appell, that while my belief in the Divine felt true, it also felt ridiculous, and I couldn't figure out how to reconcile that tension. He responded: "Maybe you're asking the wrong question. Maybe the question isn't whether believing in God is ridiculous or not. Maybe you should ask yourself: When I run this belief in God on my operating system, what happens?

Am I more loving? More honest and courageous? More true to myself and present in my life?"

For me, the answer to each of these questions is yes. When I remind myself of the Divine in others, I'm kinder and more patient with them. When I remind myself of the Divine within me, I'm more willing to listen to that inner voice that tends to whisper inconvenient truths about who I am and what I should be doing with my life ("Pssst, you should take a break from being a speechwriter, a job for which you are actually qualified, and write a book about Judaism that no one but your parents might ever read"). And when I believe that the Divine is present in everything at every moment, I'm more able to approach my daily life from a posture of gratitude and wonder.

No theology totally hangs together. They all have inconsistencies and gaps in their logic. But logic and spirituality have different languages and different purposes. And I think Rabbi Bendat-Appell is right that when it comes to judging theology, the question is not "Which one of these theologies is most logically sound?" but rather "What happens when we run these theologies on our operating systems?"

As is now obvious, I have no grand unified theory about God, and I will not be resolving my questions about the Divine in the pages of this book—or, I'm confident, ever. And I think that's a good thing.

While I admire the unselfconscious way some people of faith speak about God, their certitude about what they're saying makes me nervous, and I appreciate the skepticism with which many Jews approach the Divine. As Rabbi Emanuel Rackman stated (and note that he was an Orthodox rabbi), "A Jew dare not live with absolute certainty, not only because certainty is the hallmark of the fanatic and Judaism abhors fanaticism, but also because doubt is good for the human soul."

When we stray from our tradition of questioning and wrestling, we can easily slide into extremism, believing that we alone possess the truth and distorting the Divine image to fit our own small purposes. This is a most unfortunate form of idolatry.

Even more important, obsessing over belief in God is missing the point because, as far as I can tell, Judaism's primary concern is not how strongly we *believe,* but how we *behave*—not just what we *think* and *feel,* but what we actually *do.* So next up: the Jewish focus on how we act.

CHAPTER 4

Mitzvot and the Spirituality of Doing

love studying theology and yearn for a deeper, more frequent sense of that force/what is/You that I call God. I'm also endlessly curious about other people's conceptions of the Divine, and I wish it were socially acceptable to ask people I've just met, "So, where do you come out on the whole God situation?"

But I've also come to understand that in Judaism, if you believe you're a deeply spiritual person but do nothing to reflect that in how you actually act, no one will be all that impressed—including God. In fact, at one point, the Rabbis imagine God declaring: "Better that they [the Jews] abandon Me, but follow My laws." (Observing the laws, the Rabbis then assure us, will naturally lead people back to God.) And while the old saying that Judaism is a religion of "deed, not creed" is an oversimplification, I can report that from my first day of Hebrew school to every retreat, class, service, and one-on-one meeting I've had with a rabbi, I have never been asked whether, or to what extent, I believe in God.

In fact, I once went on a date with a guy who had been raised Muslim, but now considered himself a "None." When I told him I was learning about Judaism, he was intrigued and asked, "So, are you a believer?" I was baffled by the question. I think I may have actually responded, "In what?"

In Judaism, that's just not the question. When other Jews are trying to suss out how religious I am, they want to know whether I keep kosher, observe Shabbat, and am a member of a synagogue. These are questions about what I *do,* not what I *believe.*

This approach goes all the way back to the Torah. When God presented the covenant to the Israelites on Mount Sinai, God wasn't just asking them to believe that God *existed.* God was asking them to *act* in a certain way—to enter into a covenantal partnership and follow a set of laws. As Rabbi Abraham Joshua Heschel put it, "A Jew is asked to take a *leap of action* rather than *a leap of faith* . . . We do not have faith in deeds; we attain faith through deeds."

This emphasis on action-based faith is also reflected in another Jewish concept, "tikkun olam," which means "repair of the world." While this expression has had various meanings over the centuries, the most well-known stems from a version of the creation story developed by a group of Kabbalists, the Jewish mystics, back in the sixteenth century.

In the beginning, the Kabbalists claimed, God was the "Ain Sof," which means "Endlessness" and is exactly what it sounds like: boundless, infinite, taking up all the space there is. When God created the universe, God had to contract to make room for it, a process known as "tzimtzum." God then attempted to inject God's presence into the universe by sending down vessels filled with Divine light. But this Divine content was too powerful for the vessels to contain, and they shattered, scattering sparks of Divine light throughout the universe. It is our task as human beings to gather up these Divine sparks and return them to their source. We do this by following the laws God laid out in the Torah (not just those that have to do with social justice, though that has become the focus today). This is how we repair our broken world.

If we do this repair job well enough, we can—brace yourself— hasten the coming of the Messiah. This is yet another Jewish idea that speaks to the importance of human action, one that caught me off guard since I thought Christianity had a monopoly on this area of religious thought. But according to Jewish tradition, there will be a Messiah: a human being who will be a descendant of King David, and will be sent by God to usher in a new golden age—possibly a restoration of the united Israelite monarchy of three thousand years ago or a kind of utopia where everyone lives in peace and prosperity. Historically, many Jews believed that we can hasten the Messiah's arrival by following the laws of the Torah. In the early years of the first millennium C.E., a sect of Jews who later became known as Christians declared that a Jew named Jesus* was the Messiah. This opinion was not shared by other Jews then—and it is not shared by Jews today.†

Today, outside of traditionally observant circles, you'll be hard-pressed to find many Jews who believe literally in the concept of the Messiah. I definitely do not. Instead, many Jews now understand messianism *metaphorically* to mean that if we succeed in righting the world's wrongs—ending things like poverty, violence, and discrimination—then we can usher in a messianic *era,* a new, better time for humanity.

All three of these concepts—covenantal partnership with God, tikkun olam, and messianism—emphasize that Jewish worship isn't just about contemplation or petition, it's about action. We shouldn't just sit around believing in God or asking God for things and waiting for a response—we're empowered and expected to act. Recall the midrash about Naḥshon and Moses, with Moses standing at the edge of the Sea of Reeds praying and God exhorting him to not just pray, but actually do something. It wasn't until Naḥshon took action, plunged into the sea, and was nearly in over his head that God parted the waters. A human being had to lead the way.

Similarly, there is a wonderful midrash about a farmer who is ill

---

* Jesus was a first-century Jewish rabbi/preacher. While Christians believe he was the son of God, Jews do not.

† Jews for Jesus is a missionary Christian organization that seeks to convert Jews to Christianity. No Jewish denomination or mainstream Jewish institution recognizes it as a Jewish organization.

and approaches two Rabbis to ask them for help. The Rabbis tell him to take some medicine. He objects, asking them, "But who brought this disease upon me?"

The Rabbis concede that it was God. The farmer replies, "And you have stuck your head into a matter not your own. God struck and you dare to heal? Are you not violating God's will?"

The Rabbis then ask the farmer, "Who created the fields and the vineyard?" When he responds that God did, they throw his argument back at him: "And you stick your head into something which does not concern you? God has created the field and you pick its fruits?"

The farmer tries to defend himself, saying, "If I did not plow and clear and fertilize the field, it would not bring forth anything."

Exactly, the Rabbis respond. "Just as the tree will die if you don't weed and fertilize the field, so also the human body. Medicines can be compared to weeding and fertilizing and the physician to the farmer."

Again, we're partners, not pawns. We're expected to act.

So what, exactly, are we supposed to do?

The traditional Jewish answer to that question is that we should perform what are known as the "mitzvot," which means "command-ments" and is the plural form of the word "mitzvah" (which is some-times also used to mean "good deed"). Remember the laws from the Torah that the Rabbis were debating and interpreting in the Talmud? Those laws are the mitzvot. The Rabbis went through the Torah and found a whopping 613 of them, though around 250—such as those about making sacrifices at the Temple—can no longer be observed.

The mitzvot include well-known laws, such as the Ten Command-ments, as well as more obscure ones, such as the prohibition on con-tacting the spirits of the dead. Some of the mitzvot are positive—the "do's" (do celebrate various holidays); some are negative—the "don'ts" (don't commit incest). Some are more about ethics (love strangers, help the poor), while others are more ritualistic (don't eat certain animals, don't work on Shabbat). Some are between people (don't gossip, do return lost property to its owner), some are between people and God (don't worship other gods, do pray). Some have obvious reasons for them (don't commit murder), while others don't (don't wear clothes made of linen and wool mixed together).

In addition to these Torah mitzvot, the Rabbis added some of their own, which we refer to as "Rabbinic mitzvot," including lighting a menorah on Ḥanukkah.

Taken together, the mitzvot form what is known as the "halakhah," meaning "the way" or "the path"—the overall body of Jewish law—or as Rabbi Bradley Shavit Artson describes it, "the systematic effort of the rabbis to translate the Torah into action."

By performing the mitzvot, Jewish tradition tells us, we uphold our end of the Divine-human partnership and return the Divine sparks to their source—and we usher in a better era for humankind. In other words, performing a mitzvah is actually considered a *spiritual* act—this is how we connect to the Divine. In fact, while the Hebrew word "mitzvah" is translated as "commandment," it is related to a word in Aramaic* that means "connection."

I initially found this to be a counterintuitive approach. I had always associated spirituality with prayer and contemplation and with places that are separate from ordinary life, like temples, mosques, ashrams, churches, and sacred spaces in nature. While Judaism certainly includes this kind of spirituality, in Judaism, spirituality generally isn't something we seek out separately from the activities of everyday life. Rather, it is *within* these activities that spirituality is found.

Every moment of our lives can be sacred, if we choose to make it so. When I do a mitzvah like digging into my wallet to help someone in need or refraining from passing on a juicy piece of gossip about a colleague, Judaism sees that as a spiritual moment, one in which I'm bringing myself closer to the Divine and bringing the Divine down to

---

* Aramaic is a language that was spoken by Jews in ancient times.

earth. By saying certain prayers, doing certain rituals, and observing certain rules, we can perform the mitzvah of transforming a seemingly ordinary day into a sacred holiday like Yom Kippur or Shabbat.

This may all seem primitive and weird, but is it any different from singing a certain song, eating a cake topped with candles, and receiving gifts to mark a particular day each year that happens to be the anniversary of the day we were born? Is it any different from conducting a ceremony in which we exchange rings with another person and say special vows to indicate that our relationship with each other is different from our relationships with all other people?

The particular day on which our birthday falls is no different from any other day. And we can have a lifelong monogamous relationship without conducting any kind of ceremony. But we perform these rituals to distinguish that day and that relationship—to indicate that they are different from all other days and relationships. Are we primitive weirdos? Maybe, but I think we do things like this because they signify to ourselves and others what is important to us—what we hold sacred—and they fill our lives with meaning and connection. Same with the mitzvot.

For me, learning about the purpose of the mitzvot was similar to learning about the various Jewish conceptions of the Divine: The concept was a gateway to experience and vice versa. It had not occurred to me that helping those in need or speaking kindly could be spiritual acts. Now that I see them that way, they feel more meaningful to me—like more than just nice gestures or the right thing to do, but like acts of love and devotion to something greater. And I think it's possible to experience the mitzvot this way regardless of what—if any—conception of the Divine you might hold.

If you're comfortable with the traditional notion of God as a supernatural being who gave us the Torah, expects us to perform the mitzvot, and will reward or punish us accordingly—then go with that.

If you believe in God as the force that draws us to fulfill our highest potential, per Rabbi Mordecai Kaplan, then you can view the mitzvot as a way to facilitate that process and help you become your best, truest self.

If you're more of a nondualist, believing that God is everything, the source of all life, then you can, in the words of Rabbi James Jacobson-Maisels, see the mitzvot as "a series of practices to bring us to the awareness of the divinity of all experience."

If you don't buy any God concept, then you can regard the mitzvot as a way to connect with something higher in a more secular sense, understanding them as Judaism's guidance for how to be a decent person, lead a meaningful life, and honor Jewish tradition.

Regardless of where you stand on the Divine, this is what spirituality in Judaism looks like: It's less a pursuit of once-in-a-lifetime highs, and more a series of routine practices, the effects of which build slowly over time.

It is not flashy. It generally doesn't make for amazing social media posts. And it is unlikely to provide a life-altering rush during which all the secrets of the universe are suddenly revealed. But while experiences like that can be powerful, I'm skeptical of spirituality that is based solely on seeking out rare highs ungrounded by any kind of continuous effort to build character, treat others well, and serve something greater than ourselves.

Of course, 613 mitzvot, of which several hundred are still operative, is a lot—and the mitzvot are actually understood to be a floor, not a ceiling. The Rabbis urged us to "make a fence for the Torah," meaning do a little extra to be sure we're not violating the laws. And they were clear that sometimes, we should go beyond the letter of the law.

For example, the Talmud includes a story about a man named Rabba bar bar Hanan, who employed porters to carry barrels of wine. When they accidentally dropped a barrel, he confiscated their cloaks as compensation for the spilled wine.

A Rabbi rebuked him, commanding him to return the cloaks. Rabba bar bar Hanan objected, asking, "Is this the law?" The Rabbi retorted that it is indeed the law, as scripture tells us to "walk in the way of good men."

The Rabbi then demanded that Rabba bar bar Hanan immediately pay the workers their wages. Again, he protested, asking, "Is this the law?" The Rabbi again responded in the affirmative and quoted from the Hebrew Bible: "Keep the paths of the righteousness."

Even if employment law were on Rabba bar bar Hanan's side, this Rabbi seemed to be saying, treating workers this way is unacceptable as a matter of human decency. As one medieval commentator noted, it is possible to be a "scoundrel within the limits of the law," and Judaism is definitely not in favor of that.

So you might be wondering: Do Jews really have to observe all the mitzvot?

The answer to this question, more than just about any other, is what distinguishes the various Jewish denominations from each other.

Orthodox Jews—who are 10 percent of the American Jewish population—believe we do have to observe all of the mitzvot (though there are a range of views within Orthodoxy as to what that entails).

The Conservative movement—to which 18 percent of American Jews belong—agrees that the mitzvot are binding. But they have interpreted them in a way that allows the full participation and equal treatment of women and LGBTQ people and that accounts for some of the practical realities of modern life, permitting people to drive to a synagogue on Shabbat rather than walk, for example (which is a violation of traditional Jewish law but takes into account the rise of car-dependent American suburbs in the twentieth century). In practice, however, Conservative congregations take a variety of approaches to these issues.

Reform Judaism, the largest movement—made up of 35 percent of American Jews—does not view the mitzvot as binding, but urges Jews to study them and leaves it up to each individual to choose which ones to follow (though the fundamental ethical mitzvot—being kind to others, not lying/stealing/murdering—are not considered optional in any denomination of Judaism; those are all mandatory).

Like Reform Jews, Reconstructionists—who are about 1 percent of American Jews—see the mitzvot as nonbinding (their founder, Rabbi Mordecai Kaplan, famously stated that "The ancient authorities are entitled to a vote—but not to a veto"). But the Reconstructionist movement urges its members to consider them communally, rather than individually, and Reconstructionist congregations sometimes make recommendations as to how they believe mitzvot should be observed.

That said, an increasing number of American Jews today—30 percent, myself among them—don't consider themselves part of any denomination, and even those who do have a wide range of practice. A friend who used to identify as Orthodox was strict in his observance in many ways, but when he hosted Shabbat dinners at his house, he skipped one of the rituals because it confused his non-Orthodox guests. A Conservative friend of mine does her best to maintain a rigorous Shabbat practice, but she makes exceptions for urgent work matters. One rabbi I know told me he observes Jewish laws that he considers moral or amoral, but not ones he thinks are immoral.

I currently observe a grand total of two of the rules of keeping kosher—I don't eat pork or shellfish. I don't observe the laws around Shabbat (which prohibit working on Shabbat, among many other things), though I do have regular Shabbat dinners with friends. I don't spend much time in synagogues, but I do attend services for the major holidays, and I celebrate others. I also try to observe the ethical mitzvot and feel guilty about my frequent lapses in doing so. And I care enough about Judaism to devote thousands of hours to studying it (which is a mitzvah) and writing about it.

I know this confuses people. One of my friends recently observed, "You're so interested in Judaism, you're even writing a whole book on it, but . . . well . . . you don't seem to want to *practice* it."

Like my friend, many Jews evaluate someone's commitment to Judaism by their level of compliance with ritual mitzvot—whether they keep kosher and observe Shabbat, how often they attend services at a synagogue—rather than by their observance of ethical mitzvot like giving money to those in need and being honest in their business dealings.

It's true that ritual observance is often a decent proxy for how serious someone is about Judaism. And I get that it's harder to assess—and more awkward to ask about—someone's commitment to Jewish ethics. But I also think focusing solely on ritual is an odd way to measure Jewish observance. Using this method, a Jew who would never dream of eating nonkosher food or working on Shabbat and who dutifully prays three times a day—but frequently gossips, lies, and cuts corners in business dealings—is considered "observant." Whereas a Jew who has no ritual practice—but scrupulously follows the ethical mitzvot, taking great care to speak kindly and truthfully and behaving with impeccable personal integrity—is considered "nonobservant."

Neither of them is observing all the mitzvot—they're just observing the ones they think are most important. Yet the first person is "observant" and the second person is not? I find this especially confusing given that many Jewish thinkers believe that instilling an ethical sensibility is the goal of *all* the mitzvot, ethical and ritual.

In practice, the mitzvot don't break down so cleanly between ethical and ritual. Even seemingly ritual mitzvot—such as those that call us to be thoughtful about the food we eat and take time off each week on Shabbat to reflect and be with loved ones—have an ethical component. And both ethics and ritual are critical for the practice of Judaism. I also don't think it's constructive to compare people's Jewish practices for the purpose of deciding who's "observant" and who's not. I bring up these issues merely to make the point that there are many ways of being a committed Jew, and perhaps it's time we rethought our idea of what it means to be "observant."

Regardless of how we choose to observe, Judaism, when taken seriously, demands a lot. But I appreciate that it challenges us this way, insisting that what we do matters, that the world *can* and *must* be improved by human action. As the one of the Rabbis put it: "It is not your responsibility to finish the work, but neither are you free to desist from it."

In the remaining chapters of this book, we will explore what, exactly, this work entails.

PART II

CHAPTER 5

Becoming a Great Person: Self-Restraint and Self-Transcendence

I used to think that I didn't need Judaism—or any religion—to tell me how to be a good person. I know not to lie, cheat, and steal. I have spent most of my career in public service. And I've always had an overactive guilt reflex such that I am totally the person who walks ten blocks back to the store when I discover they've given me an extra thirty-seven cents in change.

Having now learned a little bit about Jewish ethics, I stand by my original belief that I don't need Judaism to teach me how to be a good person, or at least a good enough person. But I've come to realize that I *do* need it if I ever want to become a *great* person.

It turns out that Judaism sets a much higher ethical bar than I ever would have thought to set for myself. And as I study Jewish law, I am forced to confront the numerous daily ways in which "good enough" isn't all that great.

I feel this particularly when I come across Jewish texts about speech.

From the beginning, words have held great power in Judaism. The Torah depicts God creating the entire world using words alone: Starting with "Let there be light," God just speaks the whole thing into being. And a verse from the biblical book of Proverbs warns, "Death and life are in the power of the tongue." From the blood libel to the Holocaust, this verse has proven to be prophetic. As Rabbi Abraham Joshua Heschel noted (as recounted by his daughter), "The Holocaust did not begin with the building of crematoria, and Hitler did not come to power with tanks and guns; it all began with uttering evil words, with defamation, with language and propaganda."

Words can also cause considerable harm in our everyday lives. As Rabbi Joseph Telushkin* writes in his wonderful book, *Words That Hurt, Words That Heal: How the Words You Choose Shape Your Destiny:*

> Unless you, or someone dear to you, have been the victim of terrible physical violence, chances are that the worst pains you have suffered in life have come from words used cruelly—from ego-destroying criticism, excessive anger, sarcasm, public and private humiliation, hurtful nicknames, betrayal of secrets, rumors, and malicious gossip.

Jewish law takes a dim view of such speech. In fact, noting that someone who is humiliated turns pale as the blood drains from their face, the Rabbis state: "Anyone who humiliates another in public, it is as though he were spilling blood." While it may be a bit much to compare shaming to murder, take a moment to recall a time from your childhood when you were humiliated in front of others. Even if it happened decades ago, you can still feel it, can't you—that bottoming-out feeling in your stomach accompanied by a desperate wish to disappear.

---

* I am deeply indebted to Rabbi Telushkin, whose books on speech and Jewish ethics guided me to many of the texts quoted in this chapter.

Shame cuts deep, leaving a visceral trace on our hearts that is very hard to expunge, and Jewish law tells us to do everything possible to avoid inflicting this kind of wound on others. The Rabbis approvingly cite the example of a Rabbi named Ḥiyya in the following story: Rabbi Judah ha-Nasi (the Rabbi who compiled the Mishnah) was giving a lecture when the smell of garlic assaulted his nose. Finding this odor intolerable, he demanded that the person with the garlic breath leave immediately. Rabbi Ḥiyya left the room—and all the other Rabbis followed out of respect for him. But Ḥiyya later admitted that he actually hadn't eaten the garlic. He was just trying to spare the person who had from being humiliated.

Jewish law also strongly condemns gossip. The Torah states: "Do not go about as a talebearer among your countrymen." When I first read this verse, I assumed it referred to slander—false and malicious speech about others. As for gossip—sharing unkind or embarrassing things about others that happen to be true (details of their messy divorce or problems at work, an account of something they did that annoyed me)—I saw that as unseemly, but a relatively minor transgression.

The Rabbis and later commentators strongly disagreed, referring to gossip as "lashon hara," meaning "evil tongue," and they considered it a grave offense.* A classic Jewish story illustrates why:

In a small town, a man who disliked the rabbi went about spreading malicious reports about him . . . At a certain point the man realized that what he had said was unfair and had immensely damaged the rabbi's reputation. Full of remorse, he confessed to the rabbi what he had done, and begged for forgiveness. The rabbi, shocked at what the man had said, told him, "Go home and take a feather pillow, then go outside, cut it open, and scatter its feathers to the winds.

* Though note that there are many exceptions. For example, it is permissible to share negative, true information about someone if you are asked for an employment reference for that person, or to report wrongdoing so as to protect yourself and others from harm (and in both cases, Jewish law offers additional guidance about how and with whom such information should be shared).

After you have done that, come back to me." The man thought the request bizarre, but, relieved that this act would gain the rabbi's forgiveness, followed the instructions precisely. When he returned, he asked the rabbi, "Am I now forgiven?" "One more thing," the rabbi replied. "Now go and gather up all the feathers."

This was, of course, impossible, which illustrates why gossip is such a serious sin: Unlike with many other transgressions, there's often no way to undo the damage you've done to someone's reputation. Even if you go back to those with whom you've shared the gossip, they may have already shared it with others, who have shared it with others—and in the age of social media, this ripple effect can quickly build into a tidal wave.

Even worse, the people you gossiped about weren't there to defend themselves from your words. This is unfortunate because, as a medieval rabbinic commentary points out, "If a man takes a sword in hand to slay his fellow, who then pleads with him and begs for mercy, the would-be slayer can change his mind and return the sword to its sheath. But once the would-be slayer has shot an arrow, it cannot be brought back even if he wants to."

This quote highlights another problem with gossip: We often say things from afar that we would never dream of saying to people's faces. And we're not particularly even-handed about it. As one fifteenth-century text on Jewish ethics vividly notes: "A gossip always seeks out the faults of people; he is like the flies who always rest on the dirty spot. If a man has boils, the flies will let the rest of the body go and sit on the boil. And thus it is with a gossip."

This may all sound a bit hyperbolic, but consider the following scenario: I'm at a party, and I start venting to some of the other guests about how my colleague, Jon Doe, screwed up his part of a project the two of us were working on. I'm still furious at Jon, and I rant about how he missed his deadlines, was incoherent in the meeting where we presented our work to our boss, and still hasn't responded to my emails or calls. My fellow partygoers are sympathetic, and I feel better after air-ing my frustrations. By the time I leave the party later that night, I've forgotten about this conversation.

A few weeks later, one of the people to whom I complained about Jon at that party happens to receive Jon's résumé because he's applying for a job at her company. The name rings a bell. She remembers my story about Jon's incompetence, and she quickly shuffles his résumé to the back of the pile.

A couple of months after that, another one of the people I vented to gets an email from his friend saying, "Hey, I know this great guy—his name is Jon Doe. He's cute and really smart, and I think you guys would hit it off. Can I set you up?" He too remembers that night at the party, and while he can't recall the exact details, he writes back to his friend: "I've actually heard some bad stuff about that guy—he sounds like kind of a mess, so I'll pass on this one."

You might be thinking: Well, that's unfortunate for Jon, but these folks clearly dodged a bullet since Jon doesn't sound like a great colleague or romantic partner.

But what if I told you that before Jon's shoddy performance on that project, he had gotten several promotions and was widely regarded as a rising star in our company, but I was so angry at him that I hadn't bothered to mention that at the party—I just focused on his "boils." And what if I also told you that the day after the party, I found out that Jon's sister had recently been diagnosed with terminal cancer, which probably explained his subpar work and nonresponsiveness.

That's the danger of lashon hara—in five minutes at a party, you can do some real damage to someone's life and livelihood. If I had just given Jon a chance to explain himself face-to-face, I would have been able to return my sword to its sheath. But instead I went ahead and shot a bunch of arrows, and there was no way to get them back.

While this is a made-up scenario, I find studying texts about lashon hara to be excruciating, because I worry that—especially in a gossipy, one-company town like Washington, D.C.—I could very well have harmed someone like this without even knowing it.

. . .

But perhaps you are a better person than I am, and you're thinking to yourself, "Well, it's obviously bad to shame people and gossip—I don't need Judaism to tell me that." Fair enough. But I invite you to consider the Jewish thinking about something called "g'neivat da'at," which means "stealing the mind."

Imagine the following scenario: You're putting together the guest list for your housewarming party, and you decide not to invite your annoying co-worker. The next day, you find out that she'll be out of town the day of the party. You therefore decide to send her an invitation figuring that she'll think you wanted her there and will feel good about being invited . . . but you won't actually have to deal with her presence at your party. Everybody wins!

Another example, courtesy of Rabbi Nachum Amsel: You're a store owner during a recession, and you cut prices to compete with other businesses in the area or to get rid of overstocked inventory . . . but you tell your customers that you're giving these discounts to help them during this difficult economic time.

In both scenarios, according to Jewish law, you're deceiving people by making them think you've given them something of value to you when you really haven't. You're thus getting credit for being generous that you don't deserve.

When I first learned about g'neivat da'at, I had a sinking feeling of being busted. I have absolutely done this. And while I've had a vague sense that it wasn't quite on the up-and-up, I don't know if I could have clearly articulated why.

But there it was, all spelled out for me: I was stealing people's minds, misleading them into feeling indebted to me when they really weren't, and that was wrong.

My speech-related transgressions were just the beginning.

I briefly experimented with a Jewish ethical training system known as "Mussar," meaning "instruction" or "correction." Mussar is about improving your character by working to develop various "middot" or character traits. Each person has what Mussar expert Alan Morinis calls their own "spiritual curriculum," the character traits they most need to work on. And let me tell you, it was sobering to look at the list of middot a decent person should have—like patience, equanimity, loving-kindness, and trust—and realize just how many of them I needed to work on. In fact, of the eighteen middot listed in Morinis's book *Everyday Holiness,* there was only one in which I did not feel deficient: enthusiasm. I am very enthusiastic.

All of this was far more sophisticated than the basic be-nice-to-others, don't lie/cheat/steal rules I was taught growing up. That might suffice for children, but adulthood presents more complicated ethical challenges—situations where two or more values collide, and we struggle to balance honesty with kindness, or justice with mercy—and many of us never get any advanced instruction. So we improvise, trying to infer the right thing to do from the basics we know, and we often just go with our gut.

We might look to American law for guidance, but our legal system is primarily designed to protect our rights and freedoms and keep our economy running rather than to ensure that we're honest, generous, and kind. For example, under American law, which values freedom of speech, we can generally say whatever we want about someone, even in national media outlets or on social media (though there are exceptions—statements about others that are untrue could be considered libel or slander). Such freedom is, obviously, crucial for maintaining a functioning democracy.

Jewish law, however, requires us to carefully consider the impact our speech will have on others, even if what we say is true. Will it humiliate them? Unfairly harm their reputation? Cause them to feel indebted to us when they're really not?

While American law forbids us from being murderers, rapists, and thieves, it does little to stop us from being cruel, selfish, and gossipy. We can do a whole lot of tale bearing and mind stealing within the letter of state and federal laws.

We could also look to American cultural norms for ethical instruction, but I think we'll find a similarly low standard. These days, our culture is focused mainly on what columnist David Brooks refers to as "résumé virtues"—like wealth, fame, and professional accomplishment, rather than "eulogy values," which "are the ones that are talked about at your funeral—whether you were kind, brave, honest or faithful. Were you capable of deep love?"

When you focus only on résumé virtues, Brooks writes:

> Years pass and the deepest parts of you go unexplored and unstructured. You lack a moral vocabulary. It is easy to slip into a self-satisfied moral mediocrity. You grade yourself on a forgiving curve. You figure as long as you are not obviously hurting anybody and people seem to like you, you must be O.K.

The most celebrated people in American public life today—athletes, business leaders, Hollywood stars, politicians—are generally known for their résumé virtues, not their eulogy virtues. They're admired for their physical attractiveness, charisma, and professional success—not for their kindness, decency, and generosity. In fact, when we learn that a celebrity has those latter traits, we're often amazed. It's like a special bonus when it turns out that someone famous is also a good person; their goodness is generally not the reason for their fame.

Jewish law, on the other hand, is all over eulogy virtues. Judaism tends to focus less on rights and freedoms and more on obligations, and it outlines a great many affirmative duties beyond tending to our own life, liberty, and happiness. 613 of them, to be precise, each of which has inspired centuries' worth of commentary on how, exactly, it should be carried out.

I'm not going to go through all of the mitzvot in this chapter, but I do want to highlight two ethical themes that seem to weave their way through Jewish law:

Self-restraint: "Do whatever feels good" is not a Jewish approach. Rather, Jewish law puts a great many limits on how we satisfy our appetites for things like power, money, sex, and food.

Self-transcendence: Judaism is passionately concerned with how we treat others. Do we take their needs and feelings into account? Do we notice their suffering? Do we respond?

Until I started learning about Judaism as an adult, other than having a vague sense that Judaism is pro–social justice and anti-lying/cheating/stealing, I don't think I could have articulated what, exactly, Judaism says about how to be a great person. But now, I think much of it comes down to these two ethical demands: self-restraint and self-transcendence.

SELF-RESTRAINT

There is no such thing as original sin in Judaism. We are not born sinners. The Hebrew word for sin is "ḥet," which refers to something that misses the mark or goes astray—it is something we *do,* not something we *are.* According to Jewish tradition, we each have two competing inclinations: the good inclination (the "yetzer hatov") and the bad inclination (the "yetzer hara"). While some strands of classical Jewish thought regard the bad inclination as stronger and more innate than the good one, at each moment of our lives, we have the freedom to choose which of these two impulses we will honor. As the God of the Torah puts it when Cain's jealousy of his brother, Abel, threatens to turn fratricidal: "Sin crouches at the door, its urge is toward you, yet you can be its master." Cain can exercise self-restraint and contain his envy and rage . . . or not. (He chooses the latter and kills his brother, much to God's anguish.)

By self-restraint, I don't mean asceticism. The Rabbis and other Jewish thinkers throughout history certainly believed in self-discipline, and some did engage in acts of self-denial. But Judaism is not based on the idea that the body is dirty and bad, the soul is pure and good, and the key to cultivating the soul is to renounce the pleasures of the body by taking vows of poverty, abstaining from sex, and sequestering ourselves away for a lifetime up on a mountaintop.

Quite the contrary: Jewish tradition is generally not hostile to people making money; Jewish rituals and prayer mainly happen in family and community contexts; and sex is not viewed as inherently dirty or bad. The Rabbis held that it's perfectly fine—a good thing, even—for married couples to have sex for enjoyment and intimacy, and not just for the purpose of procreation* (though traditional Judaism is very big on that as well). And they even state that in the World to Come, people will have to answer for all the times when they could have enjoyed life's pleasures (within the bounds of Jewish law, of course), but decided not to. As Rabbi Elliot Dorff puts it, we will have to answer "for the ingratitude and haughtiness involved in denying ourselves the pleasures that God has provided."

One of the best-known Talmudic stories to this point is about Rabbi Shimon bar Yoḥai and his son, Rabbi Elazar, who hide out in a cave for twelve years, studying, praying, and living off a carob tree and spring of water that miraculously appear. When they finally emerge and see farmers sowing and plowing their fields, they are appalled that people would spend their days on such mundane activities rather than the holy work of studying Torah. Everything these two Rabbis look at is immediately consumed by flames. But instead of being impressed by their piety and asceticism, God is furious at them for burning up everything around them, bellowing, "Did you emerge from the cave in order to destroy My world? Return to your cave."

But while asceticism is not our thing, neither is hedonism. We can-

---

* Remember, the Rabbis had wives, so they understood the role sex plays in a marriage. They also understood just how complicated marriage can be, which may be why, in Judaism, divorce has never been considered a sin—very sad, yes, but not sinful.

not just do whatever we want—say whatever we want, treat people however we want, make money however we want. There are limits, and a core purpose of Jewish law is to articulate those limits, helping us discipline ourselves without becoming ascetics and enjoy ourselves without becoming hedonists.

Judaism sees the yetzer hara, the bad inclination, as the source of our most base, animalistic impulses—to be selfish, gluttonous, lustful, greedy, and aggressive. And the Rabbis believed that this inclination, when properly managed and channeled, can actually be quite constructive. Greed and aggression can fuel great professional achievements; lust can lead to the creation of beautiful families. Indeed, they observed that were it not for the evil inclination, no one would get married and have children or build homes and businesses. There's even a charming story in the Talmud about people who caught and imprisoned the yetzer hara for three days—and as a result, all the chickens stopped laying eggs.

So as Rabbi Harold Kushner notes, rather than suppressing our desires (like the folks who imprisoned the yetzer hara), or mindlessly indulging them, we can *sanctify* our desires with the mitzvot—elevating them and ensuring they're in the service of something beyond mere bodily satisfaction. Kushner offers the following examples: You want to make lots of money? Go for it! But please sanctify that materialistic impulse by observing the mitzvot that require you to give generously to those in need and refrain from working one day a week on Shabbat. You want to enjoy a good meal? Wonderful! Just be sure to sanctify that desire by following the mitzvot that limit what animals you can eat and how you prepare them. You want to have lots of sex? Excellent! But do sanctify that desire by observing the mitzvot that put some limits on whom you can have sex with (e.g., no adultery).

Rather than acting on every urge and indulging every appetite, we refuse to be at the mercy of our most base instincts, and we take the needs of others into account. This approach definitely bucks modern trends in spirituality that emphasize freeing ourselves from limitations and obligations and are more about self-discovery and self-expression than self-restraint. But it is very much in line with the approach that many of us take to other areas of our lives.

When we want to become more physically fit or lose weight, we'll observe all sorts of restrictions on what we eat, doing a Talmudically close reading of every food label, and we'll spend hours at the gym. When we want to succeed in our careers, we'll jump through all kinds of hoops, slogging through advanced degrees and running ourselves ragged to please our bosses. And we'll happily heed advice from a personal trainer, nutritionist, or career coach.

But for some reason, the idea of submitting to any kind of regimen to improve our character seems like a serious infringement on our personal freedom, and we balk at following guidelines on how to be a great person that have been shaped by countless thoughtful people over thousands of years. Many of us automatically associate such systems with judgment and shame, particularly in a religious context. And there is no doubt they can serve such ends (as can certain diet, workout, and career plans). But when done reasonably, I see the value of being pushed to make deliberate decisions not just about what kind of body or professional achievements I wish to attain, but about what kind of person I want to be.

Much like diets can make us painfully aware of our impulses and habits around food, my time studying Jewish ethics and doing Mussar opened my eyes to my impulses and habits of character. With each trait I focused on as part of my Mussar "spiritual curriculum," I was instructed to pay attention to how it arose in my life each day—to stop and notice when I was about to speak unkindly or act ungenerously. The results were sobering but worthwhile. During these brief pauses, I would sometimes (though not nearly often enough) reconsider what I was about to do or say. And I would sometimes (again, not nearly often enough) make a different decision.

I could use more of this kind of character cross-training in my life.

SELF-TRANSCENDENCE

When asked to capture the essence of Judaism, Hillel, who was one of the greatest Jewish sages, replied, simply, "That which is hateful to you, do not do to another: this is the whole Torah. The rest is commentary—now go study." Another sage, the renowned Rabbi Akiva, declared that the key principle of the Torah is "Love your neighbor as yourself."

Transcend the narrow straits of the self, Hillel and Akiva seem to be imploring us. Turn your gaze outward and notice the plight of others. Resist the convenience of that "not my problem" callousness you may have developed in the face of the suffering around you.

Rabbi Donniel Hartman refers to this core Jewish ethic of self-transcendence as the "ethic of non-indifference," which he defines as the obligation "to see the needs of others and to implicate oneself as part of the solution."

As Hartman notes, this ethic is the central characteristic of the Torah's greatest heroes, starting with Abraham. When God announces a plan to wipe out the people of Sodom and Gomorrah, Abraham doesn't just shrug his shoulders and say, "Too bad for those folks." He pleads with God to save them. Moses had been raised as Egyptian royalty, but when he witnesses an Egyptian beating an Israelite slave, he intervenes. At this point, Moses may not even know he is an Israelite, but as Hartman writes, "from his perch of royal power, he chooses to see, and like Abraham he can neither ignore nor rationalize away what is in front of him."

This same ethic of non-indifference, argues Hartman, also animates many of the laws God dictates in the Torah, and he cites the following examples: If we see someone we know sinning, we should rebuke them. If we find someone's lost property, we can't just ignore it but must make an effort to find its owner and return it. And we must not "stand idly by the blood of your neighbor," which the Rabbis understood to mean that if we come upon someone in danger—"drowning in a river, or being dragged away by a wild animal, or being attacked by bandits"—we should step in* and try to help.†

In addition, the prophets were non-indifference evangelists, vividly condemning those who "turn justice into wormwood and hurl righteousness to the ground!" or "defraud men of their homes, and people of their land," or "trample the heads of the poor into the dust of the ground."

It's as if, notes Rabbi Telushkin, the Hebrew Bible is one long answer to the question Cain asked in its earliest pages: "Am I my brother's keeper?"‡ (Spoiler alert: The answer is yes.)

This is what the ethic of non-indifference is about—the belief that we are each other's keepers, implicated in some way in each other's suffering, obligated to not just stand idly by, but do our part to help. And I want to focus on two Jewish ways of embodying this ethic in our daily lives: "tzedakah" and "ḥesed."

Tzedakah

The word "tzedakah" is sometimes translated as "charity," but it comes from the Hebrew word that means "justice," and knowing the distinction between the two is the key to understanding how tzedakah works.

"Charity" is something we give out of the kindness of our hearts when the spirit moves us. Tzedakah is mandatory—we give money to those in need regardless of how we feel about doing so (though it's

---

* This is very different from American law, which is loath to assign an affirmative duty to rescue. So generally, if you happen to look out your window and see someone being brutally assaulted, it's perfectly legal for you to do absolutely nothing. You're not even required to call 911 if you don't feel like it.

† Though note that Jewish law does not require you to intervene in a way that risks your own life, and if you do intervene, you're exempted from responsibility for any harm you inadvertently cause.

‡ There are many libraries' worth of Jewish texts seeking to define what, exactly, this responsibility entails: Who counts as our brothers and sisters—people in our neighborhood? Our city? Our country? Only other Jews? And what exactly does it mean to be someone's keeper? To ensure that their rights and freedoms are protected? To provide financial support? I'm not going to get into these details in this book, but know that a great deal of thought has gone into trying to answer these questions.

considered best to give willingly and out of genuine concern for the recipient). In Judaism, supporting the poor is not viewed as an above-and-beyond act of generosity. It's more like ensuring fair procedures in a courtroom, which we should do not only when we're feeling generous, but all the time, because it's necessary to ensure justice.

This is a different approach to economic justice than many of us are used to, one that reflects a different understanding of our relationship to our wealth: the belief that what we have isn't really ours to begin with. The God of the Torah makes very clear to the Israelites that the land they are being given "is Mine." In other words, we don't truly own any of our possessions—our house, our car, the money in our savings account—God does and is merely allowing us to hold them in trust during our time on earth.

As the true owner of our property, God has every right to tell us what to do with it, including telling us to give it to those in need. And God does so, insisting in the Torah that the Israelites should not pick every last sheaf of wheat from their fields or every last grape from their vineyards, but rather let those in need come gather the gleanings and fallen fruit. God also informs them that every seven years, they should let their fields and vineyards lie fallow so that the poor can come and harvest whatever happens to grow. Further, every seven years, all debts must be forgiven (which protects people from being doomed to decades of poverty because of crushing debt), and every fifty years, the land must be returned to its original owners* (which helps alleviate generational poverty and limits hereditary wealth since, in agricultural societies, wealth was often tied up with land).

This conception of ownership struck me as a little out there when I first learned about it. *God* owns everything?

But then again, can I really claim that what I own is *mine* in some profound moral sense? Was I one hundred percent responsible for

---

* In the Torah, God distributed the land among the Israelite tribes, and it would go back to that original allocation.

everything that went into acquiring my possessions? Didn't my good health, which is at least partially determined by the luck of my genetics, play a role? How about being born into a loving, financially secure family in a relatively peaceful and prosperous country? Even "self-made" successful people can usually point to someone who helped them—a teacher who believed in them or a boss who gave them their start.

I'm certainly not suggesting that we all become communists—and neither is Judaism. There are long sections of the Talmud devoted to protecting property rights, and Hillel actually developed a loophole to get around the debt forgiveness sections of the Torah so as not to discourage lenders from making loans. But no matter how hard we work, much of what we own—or don't own—is a result of circumstances we played no role in orchestrating. And whether we think it's God who did the orchestrating, or the universe, or other people, there's something to be said for holding the idea of ownership a little more lightly.

The Jewish approach to the poor is informed not just by Judaism's conception of ownership, but also by its understanding of the nature of poverty itself. In Jewish tradition, poverty is generally viewed as something that, with a little bad luck, could happen to any of us, rather than as the result of some moral failing or lack of aptitude or initiative. For example, the Talmud notes that Rabbi Ḥiyya told his wife: "When a poor person comes to the house, be quick to give him bread so that they will be quick to give bread to your children." The Rabbis explain that Rabbi Ḥiyya meant that there is "a wheel that continuously turns in the world," such that his children could one day be poor as well.

As Rabbi Jill Jacobs points out, this conception of poverty "is consistent with the reality of an agricultural society, in which a bad crop or an insect infestation might destroy a person's livelihood for an entire year." It is also consistent with the reality of life in America today, when many people live just one accident, illness, or missed paycheck away from falling into poverty.

In Jewish tradition, poverty is not something that happens to "other people." Rather, the Torah tells us:

If there is among you a needy person, one of your brethren, within any of your gates, in your land which Adonai your God gives you, you shall not harden your heart, nor shut your hand from your needy brother; but you shall surely open your hand unto him, and shall surely lend him sufficient for his need in that which he wants.

"The overarching Jewish attitude toward the poor," writes Jacobs, "is best summed up by a single word of the biblical text: *achikha* (your brother)." The poor are not random people with whom we have nothing in common—they are our brothers and sisters.

And Judaism is concerned not just with the amount of tzedakah we give to them, but with *how* we give it, insisting that we do so in a way that respects the recipient's dignity. The Torah doesn't tell people to take their harvest gleanings and leftover grapes, wrap them up in a gift basket, and hand them to someone in need with a note reading, "I'm so sorry you're poor!" Rather, we should let the poor come and harvest the remnants of the crops for themselves. And in Maimonides' frequently cited list of eight levels of tzedakah—ordered from the best to worst ways to give—the highest level is the most empowering to the recipient:

- Providing a loan or job
- Giving in such a way that the donor and the beneficiary are both anonymous
- Giving in such a way that the donor knows who the beneficiary is, but the beneficiary doesn't know the identity of the donor
- Giving in such a way that the beneficiary knows who the donor is, but the donor doesn't know who the beneficiary is
- Giving before you've been asked
- Giving after you've been asked
- Giving less than you should, but doing so kindly
- Giving resentfully

Note also the emphasis on anonymity. Jewish law is adamant about not humiliating recipients of tzedakah. To that end, the Talmud instructs that if you have given someone a loan, and you know they're not currently able to repay it, you should avoid running into them so as not to embarrass them or cause them stress. The Rabbis even urged rich people to stop bringing food to the homes of mourners in silver and gold baskets. Doing so made the poor feel ashamed since they could only afford wooden baskets for their mourning offerings. Everyone, declared the Rabbis, should use wooden baskets.

The poor are even expected to give tzedakah to other poor people. That may seem silly—why give people money and then require them to give some of it away? But again, it's about dignity, ensuring that no one feels only like a taker. Like everyone else, the poor must be givers too.

Interestingly, there appears to be little concern about fraud or free-loading. The poor are obligated to do everything they can to avoid needing tzedakah—from working at an unpleasant job to living as frugally as possible. But rather than worrying about people taking advantage of the system, the thinking was more along the lines of a midrash that imagines a poor man asking a wealthy man for charity. The wealthy man responds, "Why don't you go out and work at a job and get food to eat? . . . Look at those legs! Look at that belly! Look at that brawn!" God then chastises the rich man: "Is it not enough for you that you give him nothing of yours? Must you also begrudge what I gave him?"

You could argue that this approach is naïve, or suited only to small, tightly knit Jewish communities centuries ago, in which people all knew each other and could keep a close eye on how tzedakah money was spent by recipients. But I would point out that today, in the United States, a country of nearly 330 million people, the Supplemental Nutrition Assistance Program (SNAP), often referred to as "food stamps," serves tens of millions of low-income Americans. According to one measure, the rate of fraud in this program is less than 1.5 percent.

Hesed

"Hesed" is often translated as "loving-kindness," but it's not just an emotion; it's a kind of action we take to help those who are physically or emotionally in need. While tzedakah is offered as a matter of basic justice, ḥesed is a more personal form of assistance offered out of feelings of love and concern. Doing an act of ḥesed generally involves more than simply writing a check. It's often about showing up for people, particularly when things aren't going well—when they're ill, or lonely, or struggling with a life crisis. Traditional examples of ḥesed include visiting the sick, comforting mourners, and burying the dead.

In these moments when people are at their most vulnerable, Jewish law instructs us to lovingly—and sensitively—respond to their needs. For example, when we visit those who are sick, Maimonides urges us to be thoughtful about how and where we sit. If the sick person is lying on the floor (more likely in the twelfth century than in hospitals today), we shouldn't sit on a chair looming above them, which might humiliate them, but get down on the ground with them (though if the person is in bed, it's fine to sit on a chair by their bedside). And we shouldn't just visit once and feel like we've checked the box. We should visit multiple times so the person doesn't feel forgotten (though not so many that we become a burden). There is also a well-developed etiquette for how to care for mourners, which we'll discuss in Chapter 9.

The Rabbis viewed acts of ḥesed as a form of "imitatio Dei," imitating God, citing examples in the Torah of when God comforts mourners and visits the sick. This is the "I will be there with you" aspect of Divinity—the "ministry of presence." When others are suffering—when they're at their weakest and most afraid—Judaism doesn't tell us, "Awkwardly avoid them because they make you uncomfortable, and maybe just send flowers or something." We're told, "Show up for them, and do whatever you can to make them feel loved."

This means that no matter how busy we are, we find time to visit our friend who's in the hospital, sit by her bedside and talk for as long as she'd like, and then visit again a week later. We wake up early to volunteer at our local soup kitchen, and we take the time to get to know the regulars, learning their names and remembering their favorite dishes. We invite the elderly widower in our neighborhood to our home for dinner and treat him as an honored guest. We jump on the red-eye and fly across the country to stand with our college roommate as he shovels dirt into his mother's grave, and we sit with him and his family at their home after the funeral as they begin to process their loss.

No matter the time, logistics, or expense involved, I have never once regretted doing an act of ḥesed—and I very much regret moments when I chose not to. When I've been unsure whether I'm close enough to someone to show up for them, I've always been glad I erred on the side of ḥesed. Even with friends I do not see regularly, or people with whom I had a professional rather than personal relationship, in times of crisis, barriers of social convention have quickly disappeared. And I have found myself unexpectedly holding people in long embraces, shedding tears with them, or just sitting quietly beside them, being there for whatever they may need.

I have also been a recipient of ḥesed—comforted by friends in times of sadness, supported by mentors and colleagues in difficult professional moments. These experiences have often reminded me of a story in the Talmud about a Rabbi named Ḥiyya bar Abba, who becomes ill. His teacher, Rabbi Yoḥanan, comes to visit him, takes his hand, and heals him. Then Rabbi Yoḥanan himself gets sick, and another Rabbi, Rabbi Ḥanina, visits him, takes his hand, and heals him. The Rabbis wonder: If Rabbi Yoḥanan had the power to heal people, why didn't he just heal himself? Why did he need someone else to come heal him? They answer: "A prisoner cannot free himself from prison."

Our suffering can feel like a kind of prison, and sometimes, we just can't get ourselves out. In moments when I've felt like a prisoner of my own anxiety, loneliness, or limited perspective, I have needed others to take my hand and show me a way out.

Acts of ḥesed can also be done for complete strangers. One example occurred on September 11, 2001, in a tiny town called Gander located next to the airport in Newfoundland, Canada. In the hours after the terrorist attacks, planes were grounded, and thirty-eight flights carrying about 6,700 people from ninety-five countries landed at this airport.

Gander had a population of just 9,000 people, so it would have been understandable if they had responded with fear to this flood of strangers, or with irritation at this unexpected burden. They could have said, "This isn't our problem," and locked their doors.

Instead, as planes started to arrive, the people of Gander and the surrounding communities rushed to convert schools, churches, and community centers into shelters and lined up to donate linens, toiletries, and clothes. They transformed a hockey rink into a massive walk-in refrigerator and cooked thousands of meals for their unexpected guests. Pharmacists stayed up all night making phone calls across the globe to fill passengers' prescriptions; a veterinarian cared for passengers' pets; and bus drivers abandoned their strike to drive people around.

When their guests didn't speak English, the people of Gander found a way to communicate with them. Seeking to comfort a group of particularly anxious passengers, they paged through a Bible and pointed to what they hoped would be a familiar and reassuring verse— Philippians 4:6—which reads, "Be anxious for nothing."

Do not be afraid, they told their stranded brothers and sisters. We are here with you.

CASE STUDY ON SELF-RESTRAINT AND SELF-TRANSCENDENCE: THE TREATMENT OF ANIMALS

The Jewish ethics of self-restraint and self-transcendence often overlap. Giving tzedakah requires me to both curb my own greed *and* think about the needs of others. When I refrain from spreading rumors, I both suppress my urge to gossip *and* consider other people's feelings and reputations. And were I to fully observe the Jewish dietary laws known as the kosher laws, I would have to restrain my appetite for certain animal products *and* consider how the animals I'm consuming were slaughtered.

I find many of the Jewish laws concerning how animals are treated to be surprisingly humane, especially for such an ancient religion, and

I want to explore some of the Jewish thinking on this topic as a case study.

The Torah clearly gives human beings dominion over animals. In the first creation story, God commands people to "be fruitful and multiply, fill the earth and master it; and rule the fish of the sea, the birds of the sky, and all the living things that creep on earth."

But by "rule," God does not initially appear to mean "eat." In fact, in the next two verses, God declares: "See, I give you every seed-bearing plant that is upon all the earth, and every tree that has seed-bearing fruit; they shall be yours for food." God also dictates this vegetarian diet in the other creation story: After creating Adam, placing him in the Garden of Eden, and filling the garden with "every tree that was pleasing to the sight and good for food," God tells him, "Of every tree of the garden you are free to eat" (except for that one tree, of which Adam and Eve did eat, leading to their expulsion).

But then, seven chapters later, after people behave terribly and God wipes them out with a flood, God seems to reevaluate. And in a biblical do-over, God tries a new approach, declaring: "Every creature that lives shall be yours to eat; as with the green grasses, I give you all these."

Some commentators have interpreted this decision to allow meat eating as a compromise. Vegetarianism was the ideal, the argument goes, but humans turned out to be prone to violence and bloodshed, and God realized they needed some kind of outlet. So God decided to let them kill and eat animals.

However, God imposes a number of restraints on this new privilege. God first instructs humans not to "eat flesh with its life-blood in it." God later tells the Israelites that they may eat only a limited number of species, including fowl, fish that have fins and scales, and animals with split hooves that chew cud (cows, goats). All other animals—including pigs, birds of prey (hawks, vultures), shellfish, rabbits, and reptiles—are off-limits. God then further prohibits boiling a baby goat in its mother's milk and killing a baby animal from our flock or herd on the same day we kill its mother. And God insists that if we're going to take eggs or baby birds from a nest, we must shoo away the mother bird first.*

This concern with how we treat animals isn't limited to those we intend to eat. We're also told not to yoke an ox and a donkey together to plow a field (which would cause them discomfort because one is so much bigger than the other) and not to muzzle an ox while it works in our fields (which would prevent the ox from eating when hungry). We must also let all our animals rest on Shabbat, and if we see our enemy's donkey struggling under its load, we're required to go over and help relieve the animal of its burden (which is obviously a profound law for nonanimal-rights-related reasons as well).

The Torah does not offer any clear reasons for these commandments. The anti-pork rules, contrary to popular belief, were likely not an effort to avoid trichinosis. Eating meat from goats, cows, and chickens that isn't properly refrigerated in the desert can also make you very sick. But after studying all these limits, the Rabbis seem to have concluded that the Torah prohibits us from causing animals unnecessary pain, a value that has become enshrined in Jewish tradition. We are not allowed to be indifferent to the suffering of animals. This is why Jewish law requires that animals be killed in a way that minimizes the pain they feel, and kosher slaughterers use a very sharp knife and make a cut designed to kill the animal as quickly as possible.

Nor can we take animals' lives without a legitimate reason. So while it is acceptable to hunt for the purpose of making a living, such as selling animal hides, hunting purely for sport is considered unethical. In one well-known Jewish text about hunting, an eighteenth-century rabbi named Yehezkel Landau asks, "How can a man of Israel actively kill beasts needlessly, simply to pass his leisure time by engaging in hunting?" He concludes, "One who does not need [to hunt] for

---

* Note that Jews who keep kosher still observe these rules today. Kosher slaughterers drain animals' blood after killing them, and kosher butchers salt the meat to remove any trace of blood that's left. And to honor the commandment not to boil a baby goat in its mother's milk, observant Jews won't eat meat and milk products at the same meal and even have separate sets of dishes for meat and dairy foods.

his livelihood, and whose main intent is not at all for the sake of earning a living, this is cruelty."

But I don't want to get carried away. Judaism is serious about the idea of dominion: We are not animals' equals, we are their masters. Jewish tradition clearly permits us to use animals for things like food and clothing. And while we cannot cause animals *unnecessary* pain, we *are* permitted to cause them pain if doing so will provide a benefit to us, such as helping us plow our fields or discover and test medical treatments, though we must do everything possible to minimize the pain we cause.

But Judaism is also serious about treating animals with compassion, urging a self-transcending concern for their suffering. Take, for example, the verse in the Torah that prohibits killing a baby animal and its mother on the same day. Maimonides interprets this commandment as a way of ensuring that the mother won't have to witness the death of her baby (he seems to be assuming the animals would be rounded up and killed one by one in front of each other), and he notes: "For there is no difference between the pain of humans and the pain of other animals in this case, for the love of a mother and her compassion upon a child does not depend on the intellect, but rather upon the power of emotion, which is found with most animals, just as it is found in man."

The second rationale for treating animals humanely has to do with *us*. How we treat animals—whether we exercise restraint in how we kill and use them—affects *our* character. The rule against consuming blood has thus been understood by some as a way to prevent *us* from becoming accustomed—and desensitized—to bloodshed. Further, the renowned medieval Spanish commentator Rabbi Moses ben Naḥman (known as "The Ramban") stated that the commandments to shoo the mother bird from the nest and not kill animals and their young on the same day "teach us the trait of mercy and that we may not become cruel." Maimonides weighed in as well, noting, "If the Law provides that such grief should not be caused to cattle or birds, how much more careful must we be that we should not cause grief to our fellowmen."

TRANSLATING JEWISH ETHICS INTO ACTION
THROUGH STUDY

While Judaism is an action-oriented religion, I find it interesting that Hillel did not say, "That which is hateful to you, do not do unto another . . . now get out there and act with great ethical sensitivity toward others" (though he surely meant that too). Rather, he ended with "Now go study." And at one point in the Talmud, the Rabbis debated about which is more important: studying the mitzvot, or actually *performing* them. They concluded, "Study is greater, as study leads to action."

For a long time, this made no sense to me. If the end goal is action, then why not just say that action—rather than the step that leads to it—is more important?

But I think I get it now. On one level, what the Rabbis were saying is obvious: We have to study the law because if we don't know what it says, we can't follow it. But I think the use of the word "study" is significant. In Judaism, studying means questioning, wrestling, and debating. And as Rabbi Jonathan Sacks points out, while the Torah dictates 613 commandments for the Israelites to follow, biblical Hebrew doesn't have a word for "obey." Rather, the Torah uses the word "shema," which means "to listen, to hear, to understand, to internalize, and to respond."

The Rabbis seem to be saying that only through this kind of active, personal engagement can the laws have their effect, penetrating our consciences, sensitizing us to the needs of others, and making us aware of the moral implications of our actions. Only then can we truly comprehend and follow the laws in a meaningful way.

Even with just the small amount of study I have done, I can see what they were getting at. Many times in my life, I have felt the uncomfortable truth of words attributed to Father Daniel Berrigan, an activist priest, who once stated that he was "in danger of verbalizing my moral impulses out of existence." I too have slipped into this kind of self-justification—talking over the quiet voice of conscience in my head as it strains to be heard, drowning it out with convincing-sounding arguments for why it's fine for me to do this or that self-serving thing despite the harm I might cause others.

But my study of Jewish ethics has given some substance and structure to previously vague and intermittent moral impulses, making it harder for me to verbalize them away. And I appreciate that the specificity of Jewish law does not leave much wiggle room for my rationalizations and attempts to cut corners. It doesn't just say "don't gossip" and leave it to me to figure out what that means. If it did, I could easily decide that saying something true about someone doesn't count as gossip, or that it's not gossip if I tell it to just one person and swear that person to secrecy. Jewish law seems to anticipate my attempts to evade it, contemplating one hypothetical scenario after another in which I might be tempted to behave badly, and informing me: No, that is not okay either.

Jewish law demands greater self-discipline and sensitivity to the needs of others than I would summon if left to my own devices—and it demands far greater discipline and sensitivity than our secular laws and cultural norms. As Hillel urges us (and please forgive the gendered language): "In a place where there are no men, strive to be a man." When those around you have given in to their worst impulses, we're told, do not follow their lead. Resist the easy cruelty of indifference. Retain your humanity even when everyone else has lost theirs.

In the battles between my conscience and my callousness, laziness, impatience, and selfishness, Jewish study has given my conscience some ammunition. In revealing to me the harm I cause when I choose the paths of self-indulgence and indifference, it has made those paths less appealing to me, less of an easy way out than they used to be. And while the paths of self-restraint and self-transcendence are often more challenging, I like myself better when I walk in those ways.

CHAPTER 6

Prayer and More: Finding the Primal in Jewish Spiritual Practice

Rabbi Zalman Schachter-Shalomi once wrote: "The problem is that our ancient faiths have become ververbalized and underexperienced. We talk too much and feel too little." This is a good description of how I have often felt about Jewish prayer.

Over the years, when I've found myself in a synagogue, I have tried a variety of strategies to connect with the liturgy—none of them particularly successful. I've tried reading the commentaries and quotations that are in the margins of many modern prayer books, but I would find myself falling behind, unable to finish before the service had moved on to the next prayer. I've tried meditating, but the din of prayers and music was too distracting. I've tried just letting the Hebrew words wash over me, using them as a kind of mantra. But I felt like I was missing out on something. As Rabbi Jeff Roth notes, "If you say *'Modeh ani,'* and you don't know it means, 'I am thankful,' it may take you somewhere, but not necessarily to thankfulness."

So I would show up for services twice a year, at Rosh Hashanah and Yom Kippur, and while these holidays are supposed to be our "spiritual Super Bowl"—powerful moments of self-reflection during which we come face-to-face with our own mortality and perform an unflinching examination of our souls—I was mainly just bored.

I don't think I'm alone in this. As Rabbi Abraham Joshua Heschel once stated, too often, "in our synagogues, people who are otherwise sensitive, vibrant, arresting, sit there aloof, listless, lazy."

Many of us simply have no idea what's going on. Our liturgy isn't exactly accessible to the average Jew. The Jewish prayer book, known as the "siddur," which means "order,"* is written mainly in ancient Hebrew (which is to modern Hebrew what Shakespearean English is to modern English), which many of us do not understand. Saying such words can feel like "wrapping your tongue around a fossil," as the writer Judith Shulevitz memorably observed. And the English translations provided can be stilted to the point of being distracting, such as "Praised are You, Adonai our God, Ruler of the universe, who speaks the evening into being, skillfully opens the gates, thoughtfully alters the time and changes the seasons, and arranges the stars in their heavenly courses according to plan." I feel like this makes God sound like a cross between an emcee, an experienced doorperson, and a professional event planner.

In addition, these services aren't exactly concise. The liturgy has expanded quite a bit over the centuries as we've continued to add new prayers, and today, Shabbat morning services can go on for several hours, and services on Rosh Hashanah and Yom Kippur are even longer. One rabbi I know told me, "By the time we get to the third repetition of the Kaddish,† even the mourners are looking at me like, 'Seriously? Again?'"

Further, many High Holy Day services include numerous lines of

---

* The prayer book we use on the High Holy Days is called the "maḥzor," which means "cycle."

† The Kaddish is, among other things, a prayer recited by those who have recently lost a loved one or are marking the anniversary of a loved one's death.

responsive reading between the rabbi and congregation, a practice I find both awkward and stultifying. As Rabbi Mike Comins describes it: "I read to them, and they read to me in robust, earnest voices. They think I like this and apparently want to appear as if they enjoy it, too. In reality, of course, I know that we are all suffering and far from God, but I don't know what else to do."

Sitting in a synagogue year after year, halfheartedly reciting our lines on cue in that old-timey language, I felt like we were all just bit players in a low-budget historical reenactment, and I had no idea what we were reenacting. I remember the moment when, as a fully grown adult, I suddenly realized: Wait, are we actually supposed to be connecting with God here? It honestly had never occurred to me that this was supposed to be a form of meaningful engagement with the Divine.

And the style of the prayers isn't even the biggest challenge for me. Far more problematic is the siddur's content.

I want to be clear that when I say "the siddur," I'm not referring to one particular book. Throughout history, numerous versions of the prayer book have been published, reflecting the customs and sensibilities of the people who created them. And while they generally include the same core prayers in the same basic order, many modern versions of the siddur take great pains to meet today's Jews where they are, doing away with gender-specific language, including prayers that affirm gay couples, and adding essays and poems for people not engaged by the liturgy.

But even the most progressive prayer books seem to depict a particular kind of God: an all-powerful ruler who created the world, rescued the Israelites from slavery in Egypt, and rewards and punishes us according to our merit. And we praise this God constantly throughout our services, prompting the non-Jewish husband of a friend of mine to lean over and whisper to her, "Why is your God so needy?"

In a moment of frustration, I once complained to a rabbi that I found the whole thing distasteful—that the endless, repetitive groveling to this all-powerful deity seemed primitive to me.

"I hear you," he responded. "But it's important to remember that there's a difference between primitive and primal."

And therein lies the problem. Jewish prayer is supposed to touch some elemental human part of us, cutting through our everyday callousness and helping us express our deepest yearnings. It's supposed to draw us closer to the Divine and transform us into people who embody Judaism's core teachings in our lives. But too often, that's all lost in translation—literally. And many of us don't even realize that scripted communal prayer in a synagogue is not the only Jewish spiritual practice. Judaism includes a variety of tools and techniques for engagement with the Divine—from unscripted personal prayer, to meditation, to study (yes, study is considered a spiritual practice in Judaism).

In this chapter, we'll explore these practices and see what we can do to find the primal within the many, many—like really so many—words of our prayer book.

The "Why" of Jewish Spiritual Practice

Before we delve into the "what" of Jewish spiritual practice, I want to spend some time on the "why," because I had quite a few misconceptions about the purpose of Jewish prayer.

For starters, asking God for things is actually *not* the main purpose of Jewish prayer. Jewish prayers can generally be broken down into three categories: request, thanks, and praise—or as Anne Lamott put it in the title of her book about prayer, "Help, Thanks, Wow"—and the percentage of prayers in the request/help category is relatively small.

As for whether such petitions are even effective, many rabbis I know would likely echo Rabbi Lawrence Hoffman's response: "Does God answer prayer? I truly do not know." Or as the old Yiddish saying goes, "If praying was reliable, they'd be hiring people to pray!"

Instead, a commonly held view in Judaism is that we pray not so much to please or change *God,* but to change *ourselves*—not because God needs our prayers, but because *we* do.

We all go through times—maybe even most or all of the time—when, as Rabbi Shefa Gold puts it, we're "asleep to some extent, lulled by the constant din of media and commerce . . . constricted by past disappointments, habituated to a narrow version of reality, blind to the unexpected."

We might be numb—not feeling much of anything, good or bad—or feel as if we're living life through a veil, and there's a dimness and dullness about the whole enterprise.

Or we may feel a bit lost, as if the life we're living—while objectively fine, or even quite impressive—isn't really ours, but rather the product of other people's expectations, or of our own ideas about the kind of person we "should" be.

Life might feel safe and manageable this way, but it can also be empty and isolating—like an affirmative answer to the poet Mary Oliver's devastating question, "Listen, are you breathing just a little, and calling it a life?"

To me, this feels like being far from the Divine.

Judaism does not want us to be far away like this, sleepwalking through our days in an unfeeling kingdom of one. And a key purpose of Jewish spiritual practice is, to borrow a phrase from Franz Kafka, to be "the axe for the frozen sea inside us." It's designed to wake us up—to show us how far we've wandered from the Divine (or if that doesn't work for you, from your truest self, your soul, the universe, etc.)—and to help us return.

The word "return," or "teshuvah" in Hebrew, is one we use a lot during the High Holy Days, when we focus on atoning for our sins. But it's actually a key point of prayer all year round—to bring us back into sacred intimacy. In fact, the Hebrew word meaning "to sacrifice"—what Jews did at the Temple in ancient times to worship God—is "korban," which is derived from a root that means "to bring close" or "to come close." Prayer, which took the place of sacrifices once the Temple was destroyed, serves the same function.

So how, exactly, does Jewish spiritual practice wake us up and bring us closer to the Divine? I think it does so by connecting us more deeply to others and to ourselves; helping us cultivate gratitude, awe, and humility; and spurring us to take action.

CONNECTING US TO OTHERS

Jewish prayer, which often takes place in community, seems designed to bring us into each other's presence. Much of our liturgy is written in the "we" rather than the "I" voice, and there are certain prayers we're not supposed to say by ourselves—we need a "minyan," meaning a group of at least ten Jewish adults.

No matter what's going on in our lives—whether we're grieving the loss of a loved one, worrying about someone who's sick, entering Jewish adulthood, or getting married—Judaism wants us to be seen and supported in our grief, anxiety, and elation. And it wants us to witness and share in the struggles and celebrations of others, adding our "amen"s to their mourning and healing prayers, and blessing their life cycle ceremonies with our presence.

The message here is clear: We're not supposed to be doing this alone ("this" being life). We are part of, and obligated to, something bigger. And not just the community of people sitting around us, but those sitting in synagogues across the globe reciting the same prayers and chanting the same portion of the Torah that week—as well as all those who have done so for many generations before us.

In fact, if you open up a siddur, you'll find prayers drawn from the Hebrew Bible and recited by priests in the Temple two thousand years ago, along with those composed by Rabbis, medieval liturgical poets, and Kabbalists, and even a prayer based on the writings of Maimonides. As Rabbi Lawrence Hoffman puts it, the siddur is a "Jewish diary of the centuries," connecting us to Jews who lived centuries before us. And in the anguish, joy, and yearning for the Divine presence that our ancestors recorded there, I can sometimes recognize my own.

CONNECTING US TO OURSELVES

The Hebrew word that means "to pray"—"l'hitpalel"—is thought to derive from a word that means "to judge." The tense of this verb is reflexive, meaning that its subject is performing the action on themself. So Jewish prayer involves facing and evaluating one's self. As Rabbi

Aryeh Ben David describes it: "I call out to God from the deepest inner chamber of my being, expressing my greatest fears, disappointments, failures, worries, anxieties—not in order to have my problems solved, not in order to receive something, but in order to fully encounter myself."

This is what happened for me during that first hitbodedut session on the retreat I wrote about in Chapter 3. If you had asked me how I felt five minutes before I hiked out to the woods that night, I would not have replied that I felt lost or alone. I would have just said that I felt anxious. But once I started talking, those deeper truths emerged.

This kind of self-encounter isn't just facilitated through practices like hitbodedut. Communal prayer services also contain moments during which we each address the Divine (or whatever) individually and express what is in our hearts. And as I discovered that night in the woods—and in many moments since then—doing so is not always easy or comforting. But again, as Rabbi Jay Michaelson notes, the point of spiritual practice "is not to feel good, but to feel, period."

CULTIVATING GRATITUDE, AWE, AND HUMILITY

Jewish liturgy is also designed to evoke certain feelings and mind states, like gratitude, awe, and humility.

While gratitude has become trendy, with studies showing its impact on mental health and people undertaking various daily gratitude rituals, Jews have been embracing gratitude as a spiritual practice for centuries. In fact, the first two words of the first prayer Jews traditionally say upon waking up in the morning—a prayer that expresses gratitude for being alive—are "modeh ani." While this phrase is often rendered as "I am thankful" in English, I prefer the more literal translation, which is "thankful am I." The thankfulness comes first, before the self. We do not start our day focused on ourselves and what we lack—on our needs, worries, and wants. Rather, as Rabbi Shai Held observes, we start with gratitude to something far bigger than ourselves, which we believe is responsible for our existence.

As for awe, I think that's the goal of the verses of praise for God in the liturgy, such as this one:

Even if our mouths were full of song as the sea, and our tongues full of joy in countless waves, and our lips full of praise as wide as the sky's expanse, and were our eyes to shine like sun and moon; if our hands were spread out like heaven's eagles and our feet swift like young deer, we could never thank You adequately, Adonai.

Yes, the language is a bit flowery and over-the-top. But as Anne Lamott writes: "Poetry is the official palace language of Wow." And if this liturgical language doesn't do it for you, just consider the following: At every moment, trillions of cells in our bodies are engaging in trillions of interactions that allow us to breathe, eat, walk, talk, cry, and laugh. The plant on my desk is currently—through an intricate process I learned about in high school and have long since forgotten—transforming sun into food for itself. And what about big things like ecosystems—oceans, rain forests, deserts—with all their plants, trees, and creatures? And all of outer space too—with planets, black holes, and galaxies?

Can we just take a moment to acknowledge how breathtakingly, jaw-droppingly extraordinary all of this is? What would our lives be like if we walked around all day in a state of awe at the miracles that surround us at every moment?

In the rare times when I'm able to slip into this mindset, I find that a kind of humility naturally follows. I did not do anything to deserve my life or my wondrous surroundings, and much as I'd like to convince myself otherwise, I am not fully in control of how it all unfolds. And that's what we seem to be saying to God in traditional Jewish prayer—that ultimately, my life is yours, God, not mine. We're acknowledging that we can work as hard as we can, and worry as much as we want, but in the end, we're not in control of everything—God is. And even if, like me, you don't necessarily buy the "God is" part of that last sentence, what comes before it is still undeniably true. So I've sometimes found comfort in saying to myself, "I'm not in charge, and no amount of worrying is going to change the outcome here, so why don't I just let it go."

SPURRING US TO ACT

The end goal of prayer is not just to connect us to ourselves and others and cultivate certain states of mind—I would argue that those are the *means* to the end goal, which is to take Godly action in the world. Piety is good, but not the point. The point is good deeds.

The prophets of the Hebrew Bible were adamant about this, condemning those who engage in acts of ceremonial worship but then turn around and oppress their fellow human beings. For example, in the Yom Kippur service, after we've spent considerable time droning on with our prayers and feeling proud of ourselves for fasting, suddenly there's this fierce public service announcement in the form of a passage from the prophet Isaiah speaking on behalf of God: "Is such the fast I desire, a day for men to starve their bodies?" he asks. The answer is a resounding no. What God desires, Isaiah declares, is that we feed the hungry, clothe the naked, and free the oppressed. God doesn't just want our prayers—God also wants us to actually do some good in the world.

This traditional Jewish story makes a similar point:

A famous Ḥasidic master . . . was walking along a cobbled street in Eastern Europe some two hundred years ago, when he heard the cry of a baby coming from his student's house—a cry that pierced the night. He rushed into the house and saw his student enraptured in prayer, swaying in pious devotion. The rabbi walked over to the baby, took her into his arms, sat down, and rocked her to sleep. When the student emerged from his prayers, he was shocked and embarrassed to find his master in his house, holding his baby. "Master," he said, "what are you doing? Why are you here?"

"I was walking in the street when I heard crying," he responded, "so I followed it and found her alone."

"Master," the student replied, "I was so engrossed in my prayers that I did not hear her."

The master replied, "My dear student, if praying makes one deaf to the cries of a child, there is something flawed in the prayer."

Or as Rabbi Heschel put it, "Prayer is meaningless unless it is subversive, unless it seeks to overthrow and to ruin the pyramids of callousness, hatred, opportunism, falsehoods." With his work to advocate for civil rights and protest the Vietnam War, Rabbi Heschel very much walked this walk. In fact, when he returned from marching with Dr. Martin Luther King, Jr., in Selma, Alabama, he declared, "Even without words, our march was worship. I felt my legs were praying."

The "What" of Jewish Spiritual Practice

How can we cultivate this kind of spiritual practice—the kind that wakes us up, transforms us, and inspires us to do what we're supposed to be doing in the world?

While many of us are only familiar with synagogue prayer, Judaism offers a number of different spiritual practices, five of which I will cover in this chapter: unscripted personal prayer, scripted communal prayer, blessing practice, meditation, and study. Some of them may speak to you, others may not. But I've found that I can't know what effect these practices will have on me until I actually try them (see, e.g., me out in the woods), so I think it's worth experimenting with all of them.

UNSCRIPTED PERSONAL PRAYER

I recommend starting with unscripted personal prayer, like hitbodedut. If you've never tried praying alone in your own words, chances are you won't have much luck doing so in a synagogue with someone else's words—especially those in an ancient language you don't understand.

And lest you think unscripted personal prayer is not authentically Jewish, I would point out that this is precisely how our biblical ancestors prayed. Jacob cried out to God for protection before his reunion with Esau, fearing that his brother sought to kill him. Moses had a running conversation with God that spans much of the Torah, at one point asking God to heal his sister, Miriam; at another, lamenting to God about the challenges of leading the Israelites; and even making a touching request to see God face-to-face. And perhaps the most famous biblical example of unscripted prayer is that uttered by a woman named Hannah, who pleads with God to become pregnant.

When people in the Hebrew Bible wanted to communicate with God, they didn't find a synagogue and whip out a prayer book written in a foreign language. Instead, they just opened their mouths and started talking. As Rabbi Ariel Burger notes, hitbodedut "is the indigenous Jewish practice," and it's worth trying. Just be sure to follow the rules issued by that teacher on my first meditation retreat: Go somewhere you can't be heard (out in nature at night is ideal, but a quiet room works too), and speak out loud to God without pausing, whether or not you believe in God.

If you've never done this before, it will likely be awkward. If you have trouble getting started, I would offer the same advice I give about speechwriting: Just say something true. Even better, say something deeply true, uncomfortably true, painfully true. I think Anne Lamott is onto something in asserting: "When you're telling the truth, you're close to God." Or if you prefer a Jewish source, try this from the Talmud: "The seal of God is truth."

If you don't believe in God, I would make that clear right up front. If you're furious at God, definitely let God know that. If you just feel like an idiot, then say so—simple truths are meaningful too; you don't have to start with your biggest, darkest secrets. And if you feel like you have nothing to say, then tell God, "I have nothing to say to you" over and over again to fill the time. It's all good. Just keep talking.

Rebbe Naḥman (the rabbi who developed this practice) recommended doing hitbodedut for an hour each day, which is a little intense. But he was also clear that even short sessions are worthwhile. I'd recommend starting with thirty minutes and seeing what happens. As I discovered on that retreat, you never know what you might wind up saying.

SCRIPTED COMMUNAL PRAYER

After that initial experience with hitbodedut, I had a sense of what "primal" prayer could feel like and where it could lead me. And I have tried to bring that same energy and commitment to scripted, communal prayer. But I'm not going to lie: Even after many hours spent learning about Jewish liturgy, I still do not find the siddur to be the most user-friendly text. It turns out that there is nothing primitive about it. It is a mind-bogglingly complex and sophisticated work, starting with the individual words of the prayers.

Hebrew, as Rabbi Marcia Prager put it, is a " 'depth' language"—it conveys a great deal of meaning with each word, such that some Hebrew words require multiple sentences of English to translate properly. One of the reasons for this is that each Hebrew word has a three-letter root that it shares with other words and that informs its meaning. For example, explains Prager, the word "barukh," with which we start many prayers, is translated as "blessed"—as in "Blessed are you, Adonai." But it has the same root—BRK—as the word "breikha," which means "pool" or "fountain," and "berekh," which means "knee." Given its connections to these other words, Rabbi Prager translates "barukh" as "a fountain of blessings," and she asks, "Has there ever been an experience of awe so overwhelming to you that it took your breath away and brought you 'to your knees'?"

It turns out that this one word contains an entire spiritual universe—evoking humility, awe, and gratitude for the abundance of blessings we have in our lives. And this is just one of thousands of words in the siddur! You can see what the poet Hayim Nahman Bialik meant when he said that reading Jewish texts in translation is like kissing "through a veil."

In addition, as Rabbi Reuven Kimelman notes, many of the words of Jewish prayers are drawn straight from the Hebrew Bible, and their meaning is found "in the interaction between the liturgical text and the biblical intertext."

Let's take a look at a few examples—all of which come from Rabbi Elie Kaunfer—that appear in a prayer known as the "Amidah" (which means "standing," and this prayer is indeed said while standing). The Amidah is a central Jewish prayer—so central that it's often simply referred to as "The Prayer"—and it consists of a series of blessings.

The Amidah is preceded by the following line: "O Lord, open my lips, so that my mouth may declare Your praise."

As Kaunfer notes, this verse is a quote from the Book of Psalms (which is in the third section of the Hebrew Bible) that references the biblical story of how King David falls in love with a married woman named Bathsheba and gets her pregnant. He then summons her husband, a soldier named Uriah, home from battle so that Uriah will sleep with her and believe he is the father. Things don't go as planned, and David sends Uriah to the front lines in the hope that he will be killed, which he is. David then marries Bathsheba.

The prophet Natan confronts David about what he has done, and David has a moment of truth when he recognizes the gravity of his sins. That line from Psalms—"O Lord, open my lips, so that my mouth may declare Your praise"—represents David's plea to God for forgiveness.

So as we begin reciting the Amidah, the biblical echo of its preamble informs us that we should commit to confronting the most difficult truths about ourselves.

We then start the first blessing of the Amidah by addressing God as "Our God and God of our ancestors, the God of Abraham, the God of Isaac, and the God of Jacob" (many modern versions of the Amidah add the matriarchs—Sarah, Rebekah, Rachel, and Leah).

Why the redundancy (saying "ancestors" and also listing them out by name) and repetition (saying "God of" before every name)? Was the author of this blessing not familiar with the concept of editing?

Actually, Kaunfer points out, this line also comes straight from the Hebrew Bible: God introduces God's self to Moses at the burning bush as "the God of your father, the God of Abraham, the God of Isaac, and the God of Jacob." At this point, Moses might not even know he's an Israelite (remember, he was raised by Pharaoh's daughter), and this is the moment when God tells him who he really is and where he came from.

As for the repetition of "God of"—instead of just saying "God of

Abraham, Isaac, and Jacob"—many have understood this as a reminder that each of these patriarchs had his own unique relationship with the Divine.

So from the first line of the prayer, we're insisting that even though we may feel like outsiders, strangers in our own tradition, we each have a place in Judaism—and like our ancestors, we can each have a personal relationship with the Divine.

Next, we address God as "great, mighty, and awesome God." Wouldn't one or two of these adjectives suffice? Why the repetitive praise?

Again, this phrase is from the Hebrew Bible—and, Kaunfer tells us, it's part of a longer section: "**the great, the mighty, and the awesome God** who shows no favor and takes no bribe, but upholds the cause of the fatherless and the widow, and befriends the stranger, providing him with food and clothing. You too must befriend the stranger, for you were strangers in the land of Egypt."

With this line, we're reminding ourselves of our core mission as Jews: to create a society that is the opposite of Egypt, one in which we honor the Divine image in everyone, particularly the most vulnerable.

The blessing concludes, "Blessed are You, God, shield of Abraham" (many modern versions add something along the lines of "and guardian of Sarah"). This is yet another biblical reference—to the moment in the Torah when God appears to Abraham* and tells him, "I am a shield to you," and assures him that he will inherit the Promised Land. Abraham responds not by saying, "Wonderful—thanks, God!" but by asking: "How shall I know that I am to possess it?"

So, Kaunfer observes, we close the blessing by alluding to a moment when one of our greatest ancestors doubted God, as might we.

Not exactly primitive, or simply groveling praise for God, right? But there is no way you would know all of this without some background. As Rabbi Bradley Shavit Artson explains, the siddur is a "classic," like the works of Shakespeare. We don't expect to be able to open

---

* Technically "Abram," since, at this point, God has not yet changed his name to Abraham.

King Lear and *Macbeth* and immediately understand them with no prior knowledge or study. It's the same with the siddur.

But what if you're not planning to devote yourself to liturgical study and still want to get something from your time with the siddur, even if it's just at a couple of holiday services each year? I feel you on this, and I can offer four pieces of advice that I've found helpful in my own experience:

First, you cannot read the siddur literally like a textbook designed to relay facts to you. The siddur's purpose is not to convey information. As Rabbi Zalman Schachter-Shalomi noted, reading the siddur solely for content is like hearing your spouse tell you "I love you," and replying, "Yes, dear, I know, you told me that yesterday." You would never respond that way, because you understand that your spouse is not communicating data to you, but rather expressing a feeling of affection in the hope of connecting with you. Same with the siddur—it's supposed to help us connect with the Divine. It is more like a love letter than a shopping list.

The siddur is also not meant to be read literally, but more like a poem. You would never read a line of poetry like "O my luve's like a red, red rose,/That's newly sprung in June" and declare, "That's ridiculous! Love is an emotion, a rose is a flower—they are nothing alike!" Same with the language in the siddur.

Take these lines from the prayer known as the "Kedusha" (meaning "holiness"), which is part of the Amidah: "And they [the angels] call to one another saying: 'Holy, holy, holy is the Lord of hosts, the whole world is filled with His glory.'" You could read this and declare, "That's crazy! Angels don't exist!" But reading this line as an angelology proof text is missing the point—it's better understood as a poem that's trying to evoke feelings of transcendence and awe.

Or how about the Shema (which means "listen" or "hear"), a key Jewish prayer in which we assert, "The Lord is our God, the Lord is one." Instead of reading this prayer as describing a being in the sky, why not understand it as a nondualist affirmation that God is everything and everything is one?

Or let's take the Torah excerpt that is part of the Shema in which Moses tells the Israelites that if they worship God, God will give them "rain in your land in its season" which will lead to an excellent harvest and well-fed cattle. But if they worship other gods, "the Lord's anger will flare against you and He will close the heavens so that there will be no rain. The land will not yield its crops, and you will perish swiftly from the good land that the Lord is giving you."

Why not read this passage as a metaphor? We certainly have plenty of false gods in our own time—status, wealth, beauty, likes, retweets—that we seek to appease and that make us utterly miserable. When we obsessively chase after such things, our lives really can become barren, and we can feel like we're losing ourselves. But when we strive for things like friendship, love, justice, compassion, and integrity, we're more likely to experience growth and the satisfaction that comes from serving something bigger than ourselves.

None of these interpretations tracks with the original meaning of these prayers, which seem to assume an all-powerful, reward-and-punishment God. But I think Rabbi Lawrence Hoffman is right that "the first step to prayer is overcoming the sense that the words are empty because the kind of God they seem to presuppose does not exist."

Some of the conceptions of God in the siddur—as a father, king, ruler of the universe—simply don't resonate for many of us anymore. *So my second piece of advice is to avoid getting hung up on the concepts of God the liturgy suggests, and instead focus on the experience of God it evokes and the human experience it reflects.*

A Jewish community known as Lab/Shul in New York seeks to make this shift through creative translations, replacing language like "King" and "Lord" with a variety of other names for God—"the Divine," "the Infinite," "the Source of Life." And rather than focusing on God as subject, they instead emphasize the manifestations of the Divine in the world. This verse: "Creator of day and night, rolling light from darkness and darkness before light" becomes "Notice the endless process of creation: Day becomes night, light rolls from darkness."

They're pivoting from a *concept* of God ("Creator") to an *experience* of God (as felt in the workings of the natural world).

Also, as Rabbi Jordan Bendat-Appell once pointed out to me, the concepts of God in the liturgy don't just express certain theological beliefs, they also reflect core human experiences. He recommends reading the liturgy "descriptively," as a depiction of our ancestors' hopes, fears, and longings—rather than "prescriptively," as statements of theology to accept or reject.

Take that example from the Shema about God granting/withholding rain depending on how faithful we are. Instead of reading these verses as *prescribing* a certain theology (i.e., that God is all-powerful and rewards and punishes us based on our loyalty), we can read it as *describing* a human experience: the terror our ancestors must have felt at being so vulnerable to circumstances beyond their control.

Can we empathize with their fear and their longing for power over their lives—their hope that if they just worshipped hard enough, the rain would finally come? We may not agree with the theology of these prayers, but many of us share the yearning that led so many people to recite them.

That said, I realize it's not always feasible to real-time interpret and absorb the stream of verbiage to which one is subjected at many Jewish prayer services. *So my third piece of advice is that if you're particularly struck by a word, phrase, or line from a prayer, then just stay with it for a while.* Turn it over in your mind, see how it feels when you hold it in your heart.

Verses I've lingered with include one stating that God "counts the number of the stars, calling each by name." While I don't believe in a bearded guy taking account of the firmament, I'm moved by the solicitousness this image suggests, the sense of loving concern for each tiny detail and being in the universe.

I also sometimes sit with a line from a prayer known as the "Hashkiveinu" (which means "lay us down"), in the evening liturgy. Centuries ago, when people lacked electric lights, long hours of darkness were a vulnerable time. As Rabbi Lawrence Hoffman writes, "Night brings out predators, both animal and human; it harbors ghosts like Hamlet's father; it reminds us of mortality." In addition, people back then believed sleep was associated with death, and they weren't certain they would wake up in the morning. So the Hashkiveinu prayer asks God to "spread over us Your canopy of peace."

But as Rabbi Sheila Peltz Weinberg once pointed out, the word "canopy" is a translation of the Hebrew word "sukkah," which makes this an odd request. A sukkah is a fragile, open-air structure (one that we build for the holiday of Sukkot—see Chapter 8) in which we're entirely at the mercy of the elements. We don't ask for a "fortified castle of peace" or a "heavily guarded underground cave of peace." It's not a prayer for total safety, but to somehow find peace even amidst the storms that blow through our fragile lives.

Don't worry if everyone else moves ahead while you're dwelling with your little piece of prayer. I've found that it's better to say fewer prayers with greater intention than to mindlessly rattle through the whole liturgy. As the old story goes: A man tells his rabbi, "I've been through the Talmud three times." The rabbi responds, "How much of the Talmud has been through you?"

Prayer works best when it really goes through you. But for that to happen, you have to open yourself up to it. *And that is my final piece of advice: to bring some vulnerability to your communal prayer experience.*

That starts, I believe, with surrender—as Rabbi Jay Michaelson writes: "At first, the mundane surrender of the pretension that I am too sophisticated for prayer, or too intelligent; then, the surrender of the attempt to make it all work out theologically."

If you are reading this book, you're probably someone for whom it will not all work out theologically. So maybe cut the whole process some slack. Maybe just try to follow Anne Lamott's advice: "Let's not get bogged down on whom or what we pray to. Let's just say prayer is communication from our hearts to the great mystery, or Goodness . . . to the animating energy of love we are sometimes bold enough to believe in; to something unimaginably big, and not us."

The point is to let go of whatever is getting in the way of being fully present, and to really own our prayer experience. Despite appearances to the contrary, a synagogue service is not supposed to be like a concert or lecture where we're the audience, the rabbi and cantor are the performers, and they pray and chant while we listen and occasionally sing or mutter along.

We cannot delegate our praying to others like that. Doing so is like attending a spin class and expecting the instructor to pedal for us while we sit passively on the bike, checking our phones and chatting with our neighbors. There's nothing wrong with spending forty-five minutes this way, but we can't expect results.

I've found that if I want results, I have to be open to being moved. Prayer—including scripted, communal prayer—is supposed to make us feel something (other than boredom). In fact, one midrash lists the following ten words to characterize prayer: "Cry, lament, groan, sing, encounter, trouble, call, fall, pray, and supplicate."

I find this kind of emotional prayer easy to do during hitbodedut and very hard to do in many of the synagogues where I've prayed. I might feel like crying, or singing really loudly (and I've found that good music is essential to a meaningful prayer experience—it can move me and open my heart in ways that sermons and prayers often can't). But doing so is awkward when the people around me are sitting silent and stone-faced with their arms crossed, or are absorbed in their phones.

In the rare services I've attended—often on Jewish meditation retreats—where people were fully present and engaged, I could feel the difference. I was particularly struck during that first retreat by how unselfconscious people were—eyes closed, rocking back and forth while they prayed (a practice known as "shuckling," which comes from the Yiddish word that means "shaking").

On one retreat I attended, one of the rabbis even encouraged us to pray fully prostrate. Jews sometimes prayed this way in Temple, Talmudic, and medieval times, and many Jewish communities do so during part of the Yom Kippur service today. But even in the supportive retreat environment, I was hesitant to do this. You can take the girl out of Washington, D.C., but Washington, D.C., is still in there, reminding the girl of how weird she's going to look and asking her what the people around her will think.

I went ahead and did it anyway, and let me tell you, that is a very real prayer experience. When you're bowed down that low with nothing between your forehead and the cold floor except a very thin blanket, there is no pretense about what is happening. You will wind up telling God some things, whether or not you believe in God.

It's not easy to find spaces for this kind of prayer in the mainstream Jewish world, and even very religious communities struggle to create meaningful prayer experiences. I love the story Rabbi Elie Kaunfer tells about the time he wound up praying with a group of ultra-Orthodox Jews one Shabbat. And as they were singing together, the lights went out. No one seemed troubled, so Elie assumed that someone had accidentally bumped the switch. It turned out that they actually had a custom of setting a timer to turn the lights off. Their leader had realized that people often feel intense emotion during prayer but are embarrassed to express it, and he figured the darkness would give them some privacy.

I often wish for this kind of darkness in the places where I pray.

BLESSING PRACTICE

Jewish prayer isn't limited to certain places, like a synagogue, or done only at certain times. It's supposed to be more of an all-the-time/anytime activity—a way of life really. Hence the Jewish blessing practice.

Blessings are brief scripted prayers of praise and gratitude traditionally addressed to God (but I think you can direct them to whomever or whatever you think is appropriate), and they are supposed to be said anytime something worthy of blessing crosses our path. According to Jewish tradition, that would be quite often—at least one hundred times a day!

Blessings traditionally begin with the words "Blessed are you Lord, our God, ruler of the universe, who . . ." But you can play with the language if words like "God" and "ruler" don't work for you. Lab/Shul offers one alternative: "A blessing: in the Presence of the Infinite, we pause with gratitude for . . ."

The siddur contains many blessings, so the prayers traditionally observant Jews say three times a day cover quite a few of the one hundred. There are also blessings for everything from witnessing the beauty of the natural world ("who has such things in the universe!"), to drinking wine ("creator of the fruit of the vine"), to encountering a renowned scholar ("who has imparted Godly wisdom to human beings"), to seeing an unusual-looking person or animal ("who makes varied creatures"). I particularly love this last one: At a moment when we may be inclined to recoil or judge, we're instead called to notice the Divine imprint on another.

There is also a well-known blessing called the "Sheheḥeyanu" (meaning "who has given us life"), which marks the first time something occurs, either in a year (we say it on the first night of many Jewish holidays) or in our life: "who has given us life, sustained us, and brought us to this time."

There's even a blessing to say after we go to the bathroom, in which we thank God for "fashioning the human body in wisdom, creating openings, arteries, glands, and organs, marvelous in structure, intricate in design," and we acknowledge that "should but one of them fail to function by being blocked or opened, it would be impossible to survive and to serve You. Praised are you, Adonai, healer of all flesh, sustaining our bodies in wondrous ways."

Laugh if you want, but I think this is a profound prayer. Just one tiny thing going wrong can wreak havoc on our health. And how often, when we're actually healthy, do we stop and feel grateful that our bodies are working properly?

In our tendency to take what we have for granted, we're like the two characters in a midrash about God parting the Sea of Reeds who became preoccupied with the muddiness of the sea floor:

Reuven stepped into it and curled his lip. "What is this muck?"

Shimon scowled, "There's mud all over the place!"

"This is just like the slime pits of Egypt!" replied Reuven.

"What's the difference?" complained Shimon. "Mud here, mud there; it's all the same."

Because Reuven and Shimon didn't bother to look up, they missed the miracle happening all around them. This is an apt description of how I often approach my life. I grumble about the line at the grocery store while failing to appreciate that I am surrounded by every kind of food I could ever want—an abundance that, for most of human history, and for most people on this planet today, would appear outright miraculous. Or I get annoyed by the forms I have to fill out at my doctor's office, while failing to appreciate the miracle of being cured of illnesses that would have killed my great-grandparents.

The blessing practice is calling us to wake up again and again to these kinds of miracles. Rabbi Max Kadushin deemed this approach "normal mysticism"—the habit of infusing daily life with a sense of the sacred, and transforming it from a succession of unremarkable acts we mindlessly perform to a series of wonders in which we delight.

In the rare moments when I embrace this mindset, the shift is dramatic. It's amazing what I start to notice and appreciate, from the taste of my food, to the comfort of my sneakers, to the kindness of my friends. If I lived this way all the time, I imagine it would feel like the world was constantly giving me gifts.

The official scripted blessings are quite old—many were composed during Talmudic times. Some Jews today compose their own blessings, which I think is lovely. But plenty of the traditional ones are quite good—filled with unexpected wisdom and insight—and they're worth considering before striking out on your own.

MEDITATION

Another Jewish spiritual practice—one which I'm obviously fond of—is meditation. That's right, there is a Jewish tradition of meditation. It appears to date back to biblical times as a technique used by prophets to foster connection with the Divine. The sages who came before the Rabbis also seemed to meditate: These previous generations, the Rabbis claimed, would "wait one hour and then pray, in order to direct their hearts toward the Omnipresent [God]." There are also Jewish texts about meditation from the Talmudic era and the Middle Ages, and meditation was an important practice for the Kabbalists and Ḥasids. In recent years, as meditation has become more mainstream, it has become increasingly popular in synagogues.

There are many kinds of meditation, but the one that I do—and that is commonly done in Jewish contexts—is mindfulness meditation. The point of mindfulness meditation, teachers of the practice will tell you, is to learn to be more present. But what does that mean? And why is it valuable?

Well, for starters, think about how often you drive to work or to the grocery store, and when you arrive, you have no recollection of how you got there. Or you're having dinner with a friend, and all of the sudden, they ask you, "So what do you think about that?"—and you have no idea how to answer because you were spaced out and didn't hear a thing they said.

In these situations, you simply weren't present. Your mind was either in the past (rehashing an argument you had with your mother last week, or wishing you'd bought that shirt when it was on sale yesterday) or in the future (planning your next vacation, or spinning a frightening story about the pain in your leg turning out to be cancer). Or maybe you were just caught up in some kind of fantasy (imagining a fire breaking out at work and how grateful your colleagues will be when you heroically save them all from a smoky death).

There's nothing wrong with not being present sometimes. It's important to reflect on the past and plan for the future. But when reflection devolves into obsessive rumination about a past that you can't change, or planning spirals into terrifying yourself with stories about a future that doesn't exist, that's just suffering, and it isn't all that useful.

This is where mindfulness meditation can help. This kind of meditation isn't about clearing your mind and having no thoughts, but rather, about noticing the thoughts you do have, instead of being swept away by them.

Typically, you close your eyes and try to focus on your breath—

how it sounds, how it feels going in and out of your body. You do this because your breath is an anchor to the present—it's always (hopefully!) there, happening in real time.

Within seconds, your mind will wander—to the past, or future, or some random fantasy. At some point, you'll notice that you're lost in thought—caught up in that argument/shirt, vacation/potentially cancerous leg pain, or firefighting fantasy—no longer in the present moment. That's great! You've woken up! Now just return to your breath.

This process of wandering, noticing, and returning isn't a failure of meditation—it's the *point* of meditation. This is how you train your mind to be present, in touch with what's actually happening, rather than constantly tangled up in stories and thoughts. And that moment when you realize you're not present and return to your breath happens to be the very moment when your body receives the stress-relieving benefits of meditation.

How this practice lines up with what Jews were doing two thousand years ago, I have no idea. And it is definitely informed by Buddhist meditation traditions and techniques. But the context in which I do it—in classes and retreats led by rabbis, which include Jewish prayer and lectures on Jewish texts—is unmistakably Jewish. As is one of the primary goals of the practice, which is to be more aware of, and connect more deeply to, the Divine. The idea is that if everything is a manifestation of the Divine, then being radically present in each moment, attuned to yourself and everything around you, is a way of being close to God.

Rabbi Alan Lew offered a taste of the effects meditation can have when he wrote:

> We inhabit the most basic elements of our present-tense reality— our breath and our body—and we fill these things with consciousness until they glow, until they become vibrant, radiant. Then this vibrancy fills us body and mind, and we walk through the world with it, awakening every moment from the dimly lit fantasy we have been caught in until now, to a luminous, sacred world, a world suffused with the presence of God.

This is a bit more intense than what I typically experience. But on weeklong meditation retreats, as my brain quiets down, and I'm more present from moment to moment, the world around me takes on a different quality. I find myself captivated by natural beauty—mist rising from a pond in the morning, bare tree branches intertwined overhead. I'm more sensitive to myself—able to discern feelings that had been obscured by distracting thoughts—and I have moments of insight and clarity about my life (as one of my friends put it, "A meditation retreat is like seven years of therapy in seven days"). I'm more sensitive to others as well, deeply moved by what my fellow retreatants say during the rare moments when we're allowed to ask questions or share our experiences. And when I return to my normal life, I feel more awake and openhearted; better able to be present with whatever is happening in the moment; and more focused and attentive, quicker to notice when my mind has wandered and to bring it back.

I've done many retreats since that first one, and the Jewish meditation world is where I've met many of the rabbis and teachers who have most influenced my understanding and practice of Judaism. I would not be writing this book today had the Internet not led me to that first meditation retreat, and I give thanks for the algorithm that set me on this path.

STUDY

When I first learned that in Jewish tradition, study is understood as a form of worship and that one school of thought even views study as more important than prayer, I was confused. An intellectual experience, sure, but studying as a spiritual experience? Really?

But as I've studied, I've come to see why this is. I'm often moved by the humanity of Jewish law and by the human stories in Jewish texts—the accounts of my ancestors wrestling with themselves, each other, and the Divine. Learning about their struggles often helps me better understand my own. So I see what Rabbi Louis Finkelstein meant when he said: "When I pray I talk to God. When I study, God talks to me."

I feel this way particularly when I study in ḥavruta, poring over texts with a partner via video chat, uncovering deeper and deeper layers of meaning—far more than either of us would find on our own.

During one recent session, my partner and I studied the biblical Book of Jonah, pondering questions like: What does it mean to try to run from a Divine calling? Why does the only Jew in this story come off looking terrible, while the non-Jews are all righteous? What is the text telling us about how we should regard the "other"? Why do we read this book on Yom Kippur?

At one point, in the midst of our back-and-forth, my partner happily declared, "Man, for me, *this* is going to shul!"*

The more I've studied, the more I've begun to question the idea that prayer, unlike study, is a totally noncognitive experience—that it's not supposed to be about analyzing or intellectualizing, but about feeling and connecting. While I think that's largely true, I also think Rabbi Jeff Roth is right that when reciting "modeh ani," you're not going to have the spiritual experience of thankfulness if you don't also have the intellectual experience of learning that "modeh ani" means "thankful am I." And after studying the first blessing of the Amidah with Rabbi Kaunfer, I no longer regard its verses merely as Hebrew syllables to be intoned, but as words with meanings that have the power to take me on a particular spiritual journey. My "cognitive" study of the prayer transformed the "noncognitive" experience I have when reciting it. For me, study is a prerequisite for meaningful prayer, and the two are very much intertwined.

But as much as I love practices like hitbodedut, meditation, and study, and as frustrating as I often find Jewish liturgy, it is important to me to say the same prayers that my grandmother said, and that her grandmother said, and that other Jews around the world are saying today. These prayers have traveled a journey over thousands of years, echoing through ancient stone Temples, teeming synagogues, and boister-

---

* "Shul" is a Yiddish word that's used to refer to a synagogue.

ous Shabbat tables; spoken under wedding canopies and over squirming babies, on deathbeds and during dark nights of the soul. And they have been the last words on the lips of many people who lost their lives because they refused to give up their right to utter them.

Even if these words do not always resonate with me today, I cannot deny that they are holy, sanctified by the joy, heartbreak, terror, sacrifice, and hope of the millions who have said them before me, and I do not feel that I can casually disregard them.

I also think practices like hitbodedut alone are insufficient. Unbridled self-expression can quickly morph into self-indulgence and self-absorption, isolating us in what Rabbi Heschel refers to as "the pitiful prison of the platitudes of self."

So I continue to show up to services each year on Rosh Hashanah and Yom Kippur and occasionally on Shabbat, and I do the best I can with the liturgy. I accept that engaging meaningfully with these prayers requires me to read them descriptively, intertextually, and with imagination and knowledge. And in moments of frustration and doubt, there are two Ḥasidic teachings that I try to recall.

The first is from Rabbi Menachem Mendel of Kotzk. He asks why the Shema prayer states that God's commandments to us should be "*on* your heart" rather than "*in* your heart." His answer: Often, our hearts simply aren't open, but if we place these words *on* our hearts, then the moment our hearts do open, the words can fall *in*.

The second teaching is in the form of an old Ḥasidic story:

A young, uneducated shepherd comes to the synagogue to pray. Not knowing the prayers of the established liturgy, he sits in the back row and sings the alphabet over and over. The men of the synagogue confront him: "Why do you disturb our prayers with your gibberish?"

The boy explains, "I do not know the prayers. But I wish to thank God for my sheep and the stream, for the warmth of the sun and the silver moon that keeps me company as I sleep. I am singing the alphabet, and surely God can put the letters in the correct order to make the prayers."

Sometimes the best I can do is to just carry prayers I don't understand on my heart in the hope that at some later point, in some moment of openness, they will find their way in. And when my Hebrew reading skills simply aren't sufficient to keep up in a synagogue, I try to just mouth the words I do know with as much intention as I can in the hope that they will somehow be heard and lovingly woven together into whatever it is I needed to say.

That said, while the siddur has a great many words, and they are deep, and meaningful, and beautifully crafted, my truest prayers are still the ones I uttered on that first meditation retreat and on others since: "I don't know." "Stay with me." They're clearly nothing fancy, but they're the prayers to which I return again and again, the ones that most open my heart so that the other prayers that have piled up there can fall in.

And for those of us who try to pray, but simply can't, I think those attempts too are holy. As Rabbi Heschel so beautifully put it:

Those who honestly search, those who yearn and fail, we did not presume to judge. Let them pray to be able to pray, and if they do not succeed, if they have no tears to shed, let them yearn for tears, let them try to discover their heart and let them take strength from the certainty that this too is a high form of prayer.

CHAPTER 7

Giving Shabbat a Chance

used to be a bit judgmental about the way traditionally observant Jews celebrate Shabbat. All those rules! No turning lights on or off or pressing the button to call an elevator. No watching TV or using a computer or phone. No driving or cooking.

Shabbat is supposed to be a day of rest from Friday evening to Saturday evening. But how is it restful to trudge up multiple flights of stairs rather than taking the elevator? And what if catching up on TV or spending time on social media is how you rest and relax? Why can't you do that?

It all seemed so rigid and oppressive, like something from olden times intruding into the modern world. But as with many Jewish practices, I had rushed to judge too quickly. And I definitely got this one wrong, starting with the very meaning of the word "Shabbat." It actually doesn't mean "rest," though rest is certainly an important part of Shabbat. Rather, it comes from a Hebrew verb that means "to pause" or "to cease."

This word first appears at the beginning of the Torah, when, after creating the world in six days, "God finished the work that He had been doing, and He ceased on the seventh day from all the work that He had done." This verse seems to be saying that on day seven, God did nothing because God was done creating. But the renowned medieval rabbi Rashi has a different take, arguing that God's work stoppage was actually part of creation. By pausing on the seventh day, God created Shabbat—by the power of Divine example, God created this break from creating. Only then was the world complete.

I now understand that this is what people who take Shabbat seriously are doing each week: Like God, they're seeking to make the world whole. And I no longer regard Shabbat as backward or reactionary. I see it as one of the most radical, subversive, countercultural parts of Judaism.

But getting to that point was a bit of a journey.

When I first started learning about Shabbat, I was struck by how important it seemed in Judaism—disproportionately so, to my mind. As one of the Ten Commandments, observing Shabbat is right up there with refraining from murdering, lying, and stealing. It is also the longest and most detailed commandment:

> Remember the sabbath day and keep it holy. Six days you shall labor and do all your work, but the seventh day is a sabbath of the Lord your God: you shall not do any work—you, your son or daughter, your male or female slave, or your cattle, or the stranger who is within your settlements. For in six days the Lord made heaven and earth and sea, and all that is in them, and He rested on the seventh day; therefore the Lord blessed the sabbath day and hallowed it.

This day is so important that even animals get to experience it. And it's the only day of the week that has its own Hebrew name—the others are named around it. Sunday is "the first day" after Shabbat, Monday is "the second day," and so on. Every day leads up to Shabbat—it is the last day of the week, not the first. It's not a day to rest up so we can work as hard as possible the next six days. It's the other way around: We work as hard as possible for six days so we can finally have Shabbat. Shabbat is the climax of the week.

The Rabbis even went so far as to claim that Shabbat is a taste of the World to Come. This seemed a bit much to me. How is a daylong pause from working supposed to simulate the messianic dream fulfilled?

But despite my skepticism, I had to admit that the overall concept had merit. Modern life is almost defined by its relentlessness. Much as Pharaoh insisted that the Israelites produce more and more bricks in less and less time, argues Christian theologian Walter Brueggemann, our modern market economy demands ever-increasing productivity and ever-higher profits.

To convince us to purchase all the items they're producing, Brueggemann explains, companies subject us to a barrage of advertising pointing out our many deficits and flaws. If we just buy this product, we're told, then we'll feel beautiful/thin/secure/powerful/loved/healthy. Whatever hole we have in our lives will finally be filled. But of course, there is always another hole. And social media just piles on with its continuous loop of other people living their best lives, eating nicer meals and taking fancier vacations than we do.

To keep up, we need a job that pays enough, and today's high-paying jobs require higher education. In some communities, notes Brueggemann, the result is a college admissions rat race that entails its own cycle of spending (test prep classes, lessons, activities) and work (late nights doing homework, endless carpools).

If we manage to get that education and secure that job, the race continues, as we're expected to work long hours and be available after hours and on weekends too. Or maybe we have to work more than one job to make ends meet. And while technology has given us unprecedented workplace flexibility, it has also blurred, if not outright erased, the line between work time and family and leisure time. The more reachable we are, the more available we're expected to be. When we live like this, there's little difference between weekdays and weekends.

I lived an extreme version of this lifestyle while working on presidential campaigns and at times in the White House. When I was putting in eighteen-hour days on Hillary Clinton's 2008 presidential campaign, I dropped a glass in my kitchen one night. And as I stared at the shards scattered across my floor, I felt overwhelmed. I just didn't have the time or energy to clean up this mess. So I left it. For three weeks. And I wore flip-flops in my kitchen.

I have pulled all-nighters, slept on campaign office floors, and wrestled with printers on multiple continents at all hours. I have answered work emails at weddings, baby showers, birthday parties (including my own), and in the basement of a building where I was attending a Yom Kippur service one year. I once even took my phone into the shower in a plastic bag because I was afraid of missing a call.

So I had to admit that the Torah's insistence on letting servants, animals, and strangers rest on Shabbat spoke to me. They don't call my line of work "public *service*" for nothing. At the end of the day, that's what you are, a *servant*—to the American people and your boss (in that order). And during particularly busy times, I started to feel a little bit like an animal—a proverbial workhorse, vision narrowed by blinders, focused only on trudging ahead. When those times stretched on for weeks or months—of getting in early, coming home late, going to bed, and doing the same thing the next day—I began to feel disoriented and unmoored, like a stranger in my own life.

Living this way, "without pause, without space or rest," Rabbi Sheila Peltz Weinberg writes, "there is no place for the new to enter." At times, I felt stuck, almost suffocated. But unable to stop and take stock, I just kept going.

. . .

While I don't want to romanticize the past, I can't help thinking back to my childhood in the 1980s and how my father, who worked long hours at his job, could always carve out uninterrupted time to spend with me and my brother. When we were with him—bowling, hiking, fishing—there was no way for anyone to reach him, and no expectation that he be reachable. His attention undivided by any device, he would cheer us on as our balls hit the pins, point out landmarks from the summit of the trail, and stand quietly by our side as we waited for the fish to bite, attentive to whatever childhood musings we felt compelled to share.

I miss those days when I took for granted this kind of uninterrupted time with the people I love. And if this is what Shabbat is about, I thought, maybe there's something to it.

But then I started looking into the details.

The Torah lists very few rules for Shabbat: don't work or make others work, don't kindle fire, don't "leave [your] place" (whatever that means).

But then the Rabbis got ahold of Shabbat and seem to have lost their collective minds.

Hundreds of pages of the Talmud are devoted to the do's and don'ts of observing Shabbat. And to say that the Rabbis got into the weeds would be quite the understatement. Questions they pondered include: If you poke holes in an eggshell placed over a lamp and fill it with oil such that the oil drips down and keeps the lamp lit after Shabbat has started, does that constitute kindling fire? If a deer happens to enter your home and you lock it inside, does that count as doing the work of animal trapping on Shabbat? What about a lion? What should you do if a bird flies under your clothing on Shabbat and cannot get out? Would keeping the bird there count as the work of trapping an animal?

These debates led to numerous laws, and plenty of additional rules and customs have been layered on since Talmudic times.

To be fair, the do's of Shabbat are generally delightful. Do take a break from work and rest. Do prepare a special dinner on Friday night—serve your favorite foods, use your nicest dishes, put fresh flowers on the table. Do light candles before Shabbat begins,* and say a blessing over them. Do serve, and say blessings over, wine or grape juice and bread known as "ḥallah" (a delicious, braided loaf is often used).† Do perform a ritual hand washing before blessing the ḥallah and sprinkle salt on it to symbolically reenact the purification rituals and salting of sacrifices done by priests at the ancient Temple. Do sing songs, tell stories, and have pleasant conversation.

If you're a parent, do say blessings over your children.‡ And if you have a partner, later that night, do have sex with that person. That's right, having sex on Shabbat is a well-established Jewish tradition.

In addition to the meal, do take part in a special prayer service on Friday night known as "Kabbalat Shabbat," meaning "Receiving Shabbat" or "Welcoming Shabbat," which includes spirited (ideally) singing and a special liturgy, some of which was drafted by Kabbalists back in the sixteenth century. There are also services on Saturday during which the weekly portion of the Torah is read out loud in front of the entire congregation.

---

* Shabbat starts at sunset. While the Torah prohibits lighting fires on Shabbat, back in the days before electricity, fire was the only source of light at night. A total ban on fire would have made for a depressing Shabbat—cold and dark—and Shabbat is supposed to be delightful. Fortunately, the Rabbis interpreted the no-fire verse to mean that we can't light fire *during* Shabbat, but it is fine to do so beforehand and leave it burning. It is customary to light candles eighteen minutes before Shabbat starts, just to be safe.

† We're actually supposed to serve two ḥallahs to recall the story in the Torah of how God gives the Israelites a double portion of manna (the special food God provides for them during their desert wanderings) on Friday so that they won't have to work to collect it on Saturday. And we're supposed to cover the ḥallah to symbolize how, in the Torah, the manna from God is covered with dew. There is also an adorable interpretation of this ritual that says we cover the ḥallah because we don't want it to feel rejected when it sees the wine get blessed first.

‡ Some people use this ancient blessing from the Torah, which was recited by Priests in the Temple: "May God bless you and keep you. May God shine God's face upon you and be gracious to you. May God favor you and grant you peace." Others use this modern blessing written by Rabbi Marcia Falk: "Be who you are—and may you be blessed in all that you are."

Finally, about twenty-five hours* after it began, do mark the ending of Shabbat with a brief but lovely ceremony known as "Havdalah," meaning "separation," which separates Shabbat from the rest of the week. Havdalah is typically done at home and has its own associated blessings and songs.

This all seemed lovely to me, and more or less reasonable.

But then came the don'ts.

What exactly does the Torah mean, the Rabbis wondered, when it says that on Shabbat, "you shall do no labor"? To answer this question, they turned to the sections of the Torah describing the building of the Tabernacle (the portable sanctuary the Israelites constructed so that God could dwell in their midst when they were in the desert),† which are insanely detailed, right down to the type of wood for the altar (acacia) and the kind of cloth for the wall hangings (blue, purple, and crimson twisted linen with a cherub design).

The Rabbis counted thirty-nine different activities associated with constructing the Tabernacle, including sowing, plowing, baking, weaving, tearing, writing, shearing, building, and animal trapping and slaughtering.

They then got to work determining which activities fell into these categories. They decided that getting a haircut is forbidden (presumably since it's a form of shearing). Watering and fertilizing plants are forbidden, since those activities are considered sowing or plowing.

They even put restrictions on *handling* objects that one was prohibited from using on Shabbat, because doing so might lead one to

---

* Shabbat ends when three stars have appeared in the sky. Many traditionally observant American Jews wait forty-two minutes after sunset to end Shabbat. And when you add that extra time to the eighteen minutes from the night before, Shabbat winds up being twenty-five hours long, not twenty-four.

† They did so in part because in the Book of Exodus, Moses relays God's instructions for building the Tabernacle immediately after telling the Israelites to observe Shabbat. The Torah also uses the same Hebrew word—"melakha," meaning "creative activity"—to describe the work of building the Tabernacle and the work from which the Israelites must refrain on Shabbat. So the Rabbis figured there must be a connection.

perform a prohibited act. So no picking up pens (which could lead to writing) or tools (which could lead to construction). They also forbade activities even *associated* with the weekday, such as gathering fruit fallen from trees in a basket or box (though picking it up and eating it immediately is fine, as long as it fell from the tree before Shabbat).

So today, in addition to not driving (a car's internal combustion engine kindles fire) or switching on or off lights (also considered kindling fire or even building since you complete a circuit when you turn on a light),* on Shabbat, many traditionally observant Jews will refrain from cooking (no baking or kindling fire with an oven or stove)†; placing freshly cut flowers in a vase of water (no sowing); and using computers or household appliances (even if they're turned on before Shabbat, they're too associated with the weekday world); and on and on.‡ People even pre-tear toilet paper before Shabbat (no tearing).

All this and so much more just from don't work/light a fire/leave your place! At one point, the Rabbis themselves admitted that the Shabbat laws they were developing were "mountains hanging by a hair."

At best, this approach seemed a little nutty. Not tearing toilet paper? At worst, it seemed like the result of untreated OCD and a depressing example of missing the forest for the trees.

It also seemed totally unrealistic, as least for me. When you work on a presidential campaign or in the White House, telling your colleagues that you're not going to answer their emails or calls for twenty-five hours each week is like telling them you're not going to wear clothes in the office. It's absurd and socially inappropriate. In most of my jobs, I couldn't imagine being offline for an hour or two, let alone twenty-five.

---

* Though it's fine to switch lights on before Shabbat and leave them on, or to connect them to a timer that switches them on and off automatically.
† They cook Shabbat food before sunset on Friday night and keep it warm on a special metal tray on top of the stove.
‡ Though any of the rules of Shabbat can be broken to save a life—and that exception is interpreted liberally. If someone requires urgent medical attention, you can do whatever needs to be done to get that person help.

. . .

But then, in 2016, I decided to actually try doing Shabbat. Or at least a decent approximation of it.

I fretted about how I was going to inform my colleagues about this experiment, worried they would think I had become some kind of religious fanatic. I settled on a matter-of-fact email explaining that I was going to be observing Shabbat, which is a Jewish thing that I'd be happy to explain further. And while I wouldn't be checking email, I would keep my phone on at all times, would take calls, and could attend to urgent work matters if necessary.

Within minutes, I received a series of supportive messages along the lines of "good for you!" and "don't worry, we won't bother you." It probably didn't hurt that it was year eight of the Obama administration, and by this point, we were all very tired and had considerably mellowed out.

Thus began a routine that would start early Friday evening, as I scrambled to get through unanswered emails before finally setting an "out of office" message and dashing out the door. I would then speed-walk to either a Friday night service or a Shabbat dinner with friends, anxiously eyeing my phone the whole way and hoping nothing crazy would happen before I went offline.

For the first hour or two, work thoughts would be swirling through my head: *Did I double-check to ensure I had made all the First Lady's edits to the latest draft of the speech before sending it back to her? Is it possible I had missed one? What about that comment my colleague made about how the ending of the speech felt weak? Maybe it is weak. Does Mrs. Obama think it's weak? She hasn't said anything yet. Maybe I should find a good story for the ending. Would finding the story on Sunday be too late? Or maybe the ending is okay as it is . . .*

While it was easy to power down my computer, it was hard to power down my brain. But as I joined in the singing and prayers or the banter around the dinner table, the work thoughts needling my mind would grow quieter and begin to dissipate, and the impulse to reach for my phone would become less frequent.

By the time I went to bed that night, the shift from workday mind to Shabbat mind would be complete. And when I woke up the next morning, I was often struck by how *quiet* everything was—no buzzing devices, whirring appliances, or blaring headlines. And unlike the rest of the week, there was nowhere I had to be and nothing I had to do. I might just read for pleasure and take a nap, or go for a meandering walk with a friend.

Occasionally, I would attend Shabbat lunches at the homes of traditionally observant friends I had met through Jewish classes or events, and I would spend the afternoon with their families and guests. After the meal was finished and the kids headed off to play, the adults would linger at the table, chatting as the hours unfolded and the light faded. No one had to rush out to soccer practice or to do errands. No one ever stepped away to take a call or check email. None of that was permitted.

Sometimes I would catch a glimpse of the kids messing around outside, and I would be reminded of my own childhood, before smartphones and helicopter parenting, when we would spend endless afternoons entertaining ourselves—riding bikes, playing board games, romping around in the yard.

It turns out that when time isn't carved up into tiny slices for meetings and calls, or constantly interrupted by tweets and texts, it takes on a different texture. When I slowed down, time seemed to slow down as well, languidly stretching itself out ahead of me.

But this shift didn't just happen on its own. So while we can quibble with the details of the rules—and I certainly don't think it's necessary to follow all of them—they reflect an important Rabbinic insight: Like God in the Torah, we have to *create* Shabbat.

On day seven of creation, the Torah states, "God blessed the seventh day and declared it holy, because on it God ceased from all the work of creation that He had done." That's what we do to the hours between Friday and Saturday nights to create Shabbat—we make those hours holy, separate from all the other hours in the week. We sanctify time. We yield to ancient wisdom that tells us to live our lives differently for one day each week. We build, in the words of Rabbi Abraham Joshua Heschel, a "sanctuary in time" in which "the goal is not to have but to be, not to own but to give, not to control but to share, not to subdue but to be in accord." On Shabbat, we create and dwell in that sanctuary.

It now makes perfect sense to me that the Rabbis connected Shabbat to the Israelites' creation of the Tabernacle for God. Like the Israelites, we are lovingly, painstakingly creating the most beautiful, durable space possible for the sacred in our midst.

This is no easy task, especially today, when the workday world is so determined to intrude on our time—and so adept at doing so. The more technologically advanced we become—going from immovable desktop computers, to portable laptops, to smartphones that fit in our pockets—the harder it is to rope off Shabbat.

So like them or not, I have to give credit to the Shabbat rules. By being so thorough and detailed, they help us plug up the many nooks and crannies through which the everyday world threatens to seep. And when a group of people all decide to observe these rules together, they can create something remarkable, not just in one home, but in an entire community.

One Shabbat a few years ago, I visited the town of Safed up in the north of Israel with several Israeli friends. Centuries ago, Safed became a world center for the study and practice of Kabbalah, and many people who live there today are quite traditionally observant. As the four of us strolled through town, I couldn't get over the quiet. There were no cars on the road, no shops open to sell us anything, no one using any kind of device. It felt as if the world had stopped, as if we were walking around a city where everything was frozen in time except for the people. I thought about all the moments during campaigns and in the White House when I desperately needed a break and wished I could just press pause for a day. These people were actually doing it.

. . .

Observing Shabbat in a serious way may seem like an extreme measure just to get a real day off once a week. But Shabbat is more than just a regular minivacation. It's a way to reorient our lives—not just for one day a week, but for the other six as well:

First, Shabbat can help us stop being such control freaks and just let go for a change. Six days a week, we're creators—in charge, bending the world around us to our will: shaping pages of disorganized notes into a memo, carefully cultivating a certain image on social media, scrubbing and vacuuming until our home meets our standards for cleanliness.

But we have no control over when Shabbat starts. And when it does, even if we're midsentence, or about to post an amazing photo, or there's some dust we haven't quite reached, we cease. We step away. We exhale. Whatever we're working on, for twenty-five hours, we let it go. We let things remain unfinished.

As Brueggemann points out, after creating the world for six days, "God rested on the seventh day. God did not show up to do more. God absented God's self from the office. God did not come and check on creation in anxiety to be sure it was all working."

On Shabbat, we do the same. We shift our perspective: Instead of seeing the world as an object to manipulate and exploit, we view it as something to experience and appreciate. On Shabbat, we exist "not as creators but creations," writes Rabbi Jonathan Sacks. We live in what Rabbi Zalman Schachter-Shalomi refers to as "organic time" rather than the "commodity time" we impose upon the other six days. Shabbat doesn't begin at midnight, like days in commodity time, but at sunset. So by celebrating Shabbat, we submit to the natural world, escaping our undifferentiated, fluorescent-lit existence and noticing the days growing longer, then shorter, then longer again.

Shabbat is our weekly reminder that ultimately, we are not in charge. We do not run or own the world. And whether or not we think there is a God who does, we are not that God. Much as I sometimes worried about being offline, I found that when I got back online Saturday night, work had been just fine without me. The White House was still standing. The speeches had not devolved into gibberish in my absence. I was not quite as important as I thought I was.

Second, Shabbat can help us fight consumerism, materialism, and workaholism. In the Torah, in addition to being associated with the creation of the world, Shabbat is connected to the liberation of the Israelites from slavery. When Moses reviews the Ten Commandments in his final speech to the Israelites, he adds this line to the end of the commandment about Shabbat: "Remember that you were a slave in the land of Egypt and the Lord your God freed you from there with a mighty hand and an outstretched arm; therefore the Lord your God has commanded you to observe the sabbath day."

Shabbat is thus a pointed reminder: We must not subject ourselves to, or impose upon others, another version of Egypt. While the Torah clearly exalts work—the Shabbat commandment explicitly states, "Six days you shall labor and do all your work"—by mandating a day off each week, Shabbat reminds us that we are not slaves. No one else owns us, nor do we own others. And for twenty-five hours, we refuse to be captive to the "Earn more! Spend more!" demands of modern society. We say: No, boss, I will not answer your emails, nor will I send them if I'm the boss. No, TV and social media, you cannot bombard me with endless advertisements about my deficiencies and what I should purchase to remedy them. I will not be making any such purchases today.

Rigorously observing Shabbat like this is not a reactionary act—it is a radical one. Shabbat is wildly countercultural, rejecting the consumerism, materialism, and workaholism in which so many of us are trapped.

On Shabbat, we remind ourselves that some things are more important than profits or professional success, like our physical, mental, and spiritual health and the well-being of our families and communities.

We take a break from the exhausting display of résumé virtues and enjoy a daylong celebration of eulogy virtues.

Third, Shabbat can be a mini-holiday that injects joy into our lives each week. Judaism seems designed to ensure that life doesn't become a dull procession of identical days, each of which feels like a Wednesday. To that end, Shabbat is essentially a mandatory break from the daily grind—a requirement that once a week, we throw a little celebration. No matter what else is going on in our lives, Judaism tells us, stop and rejoice. Eat good food! Sing some songs! Delight in the company of those you love! Be grateful for everything you have!

The Shabbat liturgy actually omits the requests to God made in the weekday Amidah prayer (for health, prosperity, justice, etc.). On Shabbat, there is no wishing for more, or wishing things were different. Instead, we're supposed to act as if we already have everything we want—as if, at least for these twenty-five hours, we have enough.

I initially had some doubts about this approach. I don't love the idea of telling people how they should or shouldn't feel for twenty-five hours. If someone is having a hard time, it seems unkind to instruct them to just act like everything is okay.

But I don't think that's the point. The point is simply to shift—or at least expand—our focus from what is going wrong in our lives to what is going right. Shabbat isn't about forcing ourselves to go from feeling devastated to feeling delighted, but maybe just from devastated to devastated but consoled by the presence of loved ones. Or from being totally caught up in that drama at work to having some distance from it—maybe even enough to laugh at it and feel thankful that we have a job at all.

As leading Orthodox feminist thinker Blu Greenberg puts it: "Those occasional Shabbat dinners when I am just not in the mood? When I don't feel like blessing anyone? Simply, I must be there. Involuntarily, almost against my will, a better mood overtakes me."

Fourth, Shabbat can help us connect with ourselves. In the Torah, when God provides the Israelites with a double portion of manna on the sixth day of the week (so that they won't need to go out and collect it on the seventh), God instructs, "let everyone remain where he is: let no one leave his place on the seventh day."

There is a voluminous body of Jewish law figuring out how far one can travel (on foot, of course) from one's home on Shabbat. But I think this verse also has an important metaphorical meaning, especially today. Many of us constantly use work or technology to "leave our place"—to escape the moment in which we currently find ourselves so that we can avoid the uncomfortable feelings that are arising. Bored? Hop on Twitter! Lonely? Start texting people! Anxious? Unwind with some TV! Doubting your purpose in life? Dive into those work emails!

But on Shabbat, many of the strategies we use to run away from ourselves are prohibited. We can't escape to the office or into a screen. We can't curate our life for others' consumption on social media, focusing on how our life looks, rather than how it feels. Instead, for twenty-five hours, we actually have to live it.

And when the clamoring voices of the weekday world finally go silent—all those likes and retweets, headlines and ads, grades and performance reviews—suddenly, with nothing to drown it out or crowd it out, we may be able to hear another voice: our own.

We might hear those little whispers at the edge of our consciousness that ask questions like "This is a respectable, even impressive career path you're on, but is it really yours?" Or "Do you really love this person you're with, or are you in this relationship because you're too afraid to leave?"

When we finally have some time and space to hear ourselves think, we get some perspective. As Rabbi Alan Lew wrote, "We can't see the picture as long as we are in it." On Shabbat, "we step out of the picture."*

In her book, *The Sabbath World,* the writer Judith Shulevitz asks, "Why *did* God stop, anyway?" She offers an answer from a renowned eighteenth-century rabbi known as the Vilna Gaon: "God stopped to

---

* Lew was writing about meditation, not Shabbat, but I think the metaphor works here as well.

show us that what we create becomes meaningful only once we stop creating it and start remembering why it was worth creating in the first place. Or—if this is the thought to which our critical impulses lead us—why it *wasn't* worth creating."

On Shabbat, when I sat in deep conversation with a friend, or strolled through my neighborhood, I had some distance from the White House—both physically and mentally—and I found my thoughts starting to shift from what Michelle Obama needed to what *I* needed. I began to think about how, once the Administration ended, I might want to use my own voice for a change rather than continuing to help others use theirs. Thoughts and feelings for which I had no room during the week found space to emerge on Shabbat, so I can understand what Rabbi Yitz Greenberg meant when he wrote, "The Shabbat is more than a day of being, it is a day of becoming. Rest is more than leisure from work, it is a state of inner discovery, tranquility, and unfolding."

The Torah tells us that God stopped working on the seventh day and "vayinafash," which has been translated as "was refreshed" or "was ensouled"—or, as Rabbi Harold Kushner renders it, "He got His soul back." According to Jewish tradition, so do we. One ancient Jewish teaching even claims that on Shabbat, we're given an extra soul. Rabbi Zalman Schachter-Shalomi explains that this isn't a quantitative statement that for twenty-five hours, we have two souls. Rather, it's a qualitative claim that on Shabbat, we're given "a superabundance of soul, an overflowing."

Or maybe it's not so much that we're given extra soul, but that on Shabbat, we have access to more of our soul, and it just feels like extra.

Fifth, Shabbat can help us connect with others. In her book about Shabbat, Judith Shulevitz describes an experiment conducted by social psychologists in the 1970s. Students at the Princeton Theological Seminary were told to walk, one by one, to another building to give a talk. On their way, each of the students encountered a man—who, unbeknownst to them, was part of the study—hunched over in an alleyway, clearly in distress. Some of the students stopped to assist the man, some did not.

The psychologists studied three variables that may have influenced whether a student stopped: the student's personality traits (each was given a personality test in advance); the topic of their talk (half were told to speak about their future careers as ministers, while the other half were instructed to talk about the biblical parable of the Good Samaritan, the moral of which is that we should stop to help those in need); and the time pressure the student was under (some students were told they were late and should walk quickly, some were told they were right on time, and some were told they had several minutes to spare).

The study found that the only factor that really correlated with whether or not students stopped to help the man was how much of a hurry they were in. The less time they had to get to the other building, the less likely they were to stop: 63 percent of "low hurry" students stopped to help as opposed to just 10 percent of "high hurry" students.

The results of this study are not shocking. When we're in a rush, we tend to have less empathy and patience for others. And we do not like to be interrupted when we're trying to get somewhere or get something done.

On Shabbat, we take away both the rush and the to-do list. No scrambling to get the kids off to school and get to work on time. No gazing anxiously at our watch as our lunch partner talks, worried that we'll be late for an upcoming meeting or that we're missing important emails.

One of my traditionally observant friends told me that his kids look forward to Shabbat because they know they'll have his undivided attention since he can't check his phone. I look forward to Shabbat meals with friends for the same reason: Everyone is fully present, fully engaged in whatever is happening at the moment.

And as Shulevitz points out, there is something powerful about spending time with people in the noncommodity contexts in which Shabbat unfolds. We're not running into them in a workplace, where they perform a certain function and fit into a certain hierarchy; or in a store, where we can see how much money they're spending. We're not looking to each other to provide any services or obtain any goods.

Shabbat thus seems to increase the chances of I-Thou—rather than I-It—encounters with others, when we see them for who they are, rather than what they can do for us. It gives us some time and space to experience the Divinity between us.

Sixth, Shabbat offers a vision of the world as it should be, inspiring us to improve the world as it is. I initially thought (and still think) it was a bit much for the Rabbis to claim that Shabbat was a taste of the messianic era, when all would be right and good in the world. But I now see what they were getting at. On his 2008 campaign and in the White House, President Obama spoke about the difference between the "world as it is" and the "world as it should be," and he urged people to do their part to bridge the gap between the two. Shabbat is a once-a-week enactment of a Jewish idea of the world as it should be.

On Shabbat, we are all equal. The Torah is very clear that everyone rests on Shabbat: masters, servants, strangers, even animals. We are all entitled to Shabbat, and we don't get more or less of it depending on how much we earn or how accomplished we are.*

On Shabbat, we're (ideally) supposed to be at peace with each other. Some commentators have interpreted the prohibition on lighting fires not just literally but metaphorically as well, advising us not to kindle or fan the flames of anger or discord. If we have a beef with someone, for twenty-five hours we should let it go. We can get into it again during the week, but for now, let's just all get along.

Finally, on Shabbat, we seek to be in harmony with nature. We cease from exploiting the earth's resources for our gain, or at least reduce the extent to which we do so. Instead, we act as if everything is

---

* Of course, in reality this is not true—some people may not have the workplace flexibility or financial security to take a day off. Though traditionally, Jewish communities have taken pains to ensure that poor families have food and provisions to celebrate Shabbat and that people who have nowhere to go for Shabbat meals are invited as guests.

perfect the way it is. This is the point of a midrash about the verse in the Torah that says, "Six days you shall labor and do all your work." The midrash asks: How can we do all our work in just six days? The answer: "We should rest *as though* [emphasis mine] all our work were finished."

Is this just wishful thinking? An elaborate twenty-five-hour game of make-believe? You could see it that way. But even so, I think there's value in making a special effort to live out our ideals this way. Having experienced how good life can be on Shabbat, we may well be inspired to try to make the other six days more like it.

While I'm obviously a fan of Shabbat, my experiment with a serious Shabbat practice was short-lived. Work became increasingly hectic during my final year in the White House, and it became harder and harder to be out of pocket for twenty-five hours each week. I'm sure my colleagues would have found a way to accommodate me, but insisting on observing Shabbat during such a busy time would have felt like holding myself out as more traditionally observant than I really am, and I wasn't comfortable with that.

This is one of the reasons why I think there's real value to having an unshakeable commitment to a rigorous Shabbat practice. My friends who view Shabbat as mandatory do not decide whether, or to what extent, to observe it each week based on what else is happening in their lives. They arrange their lives around observing Shabbat, often working extra hours during the rest of the week, and getting back online Saturday night to catch up on anything they've missed. And many of them have jobs that are just as busy and intense—if not more so—than my job in the White House.

Without the sense of obligation they feel, I found it easy to let Shabbat slip—to tell myself I would work just this one Shabbat—and then slowly fall out of the habit. There is a story in the Talmud along these lines, claiming that on Shabbat, two angels—one good and one bad—visit the homes of Jewish families. When the angels find the table beautifully set, with everyone ready to celebrate, the good angel says, "May the next Shabbat be just as beautiful as this one," and the bad angel must say "Amen." But in homes that are not prepared for Shabbat, the bad angel says, "May the next Shabbat be just as awful as this one," and the good angel must say "Amen."

I find this story to be slightly creepy, but also in some way true. When I first stopped observing Shabbat I could feel the difference. My life became less spacious, almost a little claustrophobic, as work seemed to press in on me at every moment. But after a while, this just became my new normal, as if the bad angel's curse had come true, with Shabbat passing unobserved week after week, and the good angel growing ever more despondent. Once I left the White House, I immediately transitioned to a fellowship and rushed to draft a proposal in the hope of getting a publishing contract for this book. Once I got the contract, I found myself scrambling to meet the deadline I had agreed to and working through most weekends.

But while I think Shabbat is most impactful when done seriously and regularly, it definitely does not have to be done in the absolute to be meaningful. Even in my most intense efforts at observance, I turned plenty of lights on and off and never pre-tore my toilet paper (though I do appreciate Blu Greenberg's observation: "Look how clever the Rabbis were: even in as mundane a place as a bathroom, one is reminded of the uniqueness of the day"). Many Jews observing Shabbat will drive somewhere to take a hike, or call family members living far away for an afternoon chat.

These days, I try to spend as many Friday nights as I can doing something in the Shabbat spirit. I'm lucky to have a small group of dear friends who take turns hosting Shabbat dinners every three or four weeks. These are highly informal affairs. Some or all of us are usually running late. The host may or may not have had time to clean their house. And no one ever dresses up. But we do our best to cook (or order) a good meal and set a beautiful table. We always say the prayers. And we have spent many evenings sprawled out on each other's couches over dessert, laughing like maniacs, talking way too late into the night about the most ridiculous things.

When I picture Shabbat, these dinners are what come to mind—the feeling that I have of stepping out of my weekday skin and settling into myself, knowing there is no one here to impress, that these are "come as you are" friends, who, on Shabbat, feel like my family.

At some point, I may ramp my Shabbat practice back up to a full twenty-five hours, or maybe to Friday night and Saturday morning. Whatever I choose to do, the key for me will be to make those hours feel special, totally separate from and unlike the other six days. And I know that for Shabbat to work its magic on me, I will once again have to submit to it. I've found that Shabbat is like getting a massage. If I tense up against it, it's painful. But if I relax into it, trusting that it will be good for me, I walk away feeling amazing.

It is counterintuitive that accepting so many constraints can make us more free. But if we cannot bear to miss the latest tweet or breaking news update, and if we feel compelled to record and post our every waking activity on social media seven days a week and keep up with everyone else's too, then I'm not sure we're all that free in the first place.

But if each week, we could step away from it all and build a sanctuary in time where we could just *be*—away from the demands of work and media; more fully present and connected to ourselves, others, and the Divine; at peace and content with what we have—I think that would feel like a kind of freedom many of us don't have right now, maybe even like a small taste of the World to Come.

CHAPTER 8

Jewish Holidays and the Power of a Well-Placed Banana

When I first caught sight of the banana on the seder plate at a Passover seder I attended a few years ago, it took considerable self-restraint to keep from rolling my eyes.

I've had mixed experiences at seders. I appreciate the point of them, which is to gather with loved ones over a meal and retell the story of the ancient Israelites' journey from slavery in Egypt to liberation. I also appreciate how the script we use to tell that story, the Haggadah*—which dates back to the third or fourth century—includes all kinds of texts and rituals to make the story come alive: songs to sing, questions to ask, and symbolic foods to eat, which are set out on a special seder plate.†

---

* Note that like with the siddur (prayer book), there is not just one version of the Haggadah, but many.

† We dip a vegetable, often parsley, in salt water, which represents the tears of the Israelite slaves. We eat a paste made of fruit and nuts known as "ḥaroset" to represent the mortar the enslaved Israelites used in their labor. And for all eight days of Passover, we refrain from consuming leavened bread products. Instead, we eat large crackers known as "matzah," both to remind ourselves of the hard "bread of affliction" the Israelites ate when they were enslaved, and to recall that when they fled slavery, they didn't have time to let their bread rise.

And I appreciate the effort many Jews put into creating memorable seder experiences. I know of one couple who had their guests reenact the Exodus story, complete with elaborate costumes and an attempt to transform the avocado tree in their yard into a burning bush. Another friend spends months each year preparing special effects for her family's seder, including setting up a bubble machine to reenact the splitting of the sea and hanging plastic locusts from her ceiling fan, which, when switched on, creates a swarm during the part of the seder where we list the ten plagues.

But while I have nothing against seder innovation—recent trends have included adding an orange to the seder plate to represent the struggles of women and LGBTQ people, or an olive to symbolize aspirations for peace in the Middle East—at some point, things can get out of hand. I suspected the banana might be that point.

This seder, however, turned out to be lovely. The hosts had created their own Haggadah, filled with moving poetry and thoughtful quotes. The guests were from a fascinating array of backgrounds and faiths. And the whole thing was proceeding along at a heartening clip as we went around the table, each reading a section of the Haggadah . . . until we reached a page entitled "The Banana on the Seder Plate: A Ritual to Reflect on the Refugee Crisis During the Passover Seder," and the guy whose turn it was started reading:

The world was awakened and shattered by the images of a little boy whose body lay lifeless amidst the gentle surf of a Turkish beach . . . Another nameless victim amongst thousands in the Syrian Refugee Crisis, the greatest refugee crisis since WWII. But this little boy, like every little boy, had a name. His name was Aylan Kurdi (age 3), he drowned along with his older brother, Galip (age 5), and their mother, Rihan, on their own exodus to freedom's distant shore.

As he came to the next paragraph, his voice grew tight:

Aylan and Galip's father, Abdullah, survived the harrowing journey—though how does a parent survive the death of their children? In teaching the world about his sons, he shared that they both loved bananas, a luxury in their native war-torn Syria. Every day after work, Abdullah . . . would bring home a banana for his sons to share, a sweet little treat, a sign of his enduring love for them. Tonight we place a banana on our seder table and tell this story to remind us of Aylan, Galip and children everywhere who are caught up in this modern day exodus.

The previously boisterous table had fallen silent save for the rustling of people reaching for their napkins to wipe their eyes. We had all seen the photograph of that little boy's lifeless body, facedown on the beach. It had been in the news for days, along with other stories of people fleeing Syria in rickety boats.

At that moment, I finally understood: *This* is the kind of heartbreak and outrage that the bitter herbs and ḥaroset are supposed to make us feel. *This* is the kind of terror and desperation the Haggadah is trying to conjure with its imminent, personal language: telling us not that "your *ancestors* were slaves in Egypt," but that "*you* were slaves in Egypt."

It's hard to evoke the suffering caused by events that may have taken place thousands of years ago with symbolic vegetables. But this Haggadah and that banana had nailed it. Ironically, the object that least belonged on the seder plate had breathed life into all the others, helping those traditional items fulfill their intended purpose. It had even rendered the salt water unnecessary; there were real tears at this seder table.

This is what Jewish holidays are supposed to do: move us, inspire us, challenge us, and shake us up. But all too often, they're just kind of boring. Or pleasant, but not particularly meaningful. Or a bit confusing.

To start with, there are a lot of them—way more than I had expected. Who knew there were four separate fast days to mourn the destruction of the ancient Temples in Jerusalem? Some Jewish holidays originate in the Torah, some were created by the Rabbis, and some were developed more recently in response to events like the Holocaust and the founding of the State of Israel. And the timing of when the holidays fall changes each year—they're always in the same season, but not on the same day.*

Jewish holidays also operate at a number of different levels, marking historical and biblical events, teaching moral and spiritual lessons, and calling our attention to the cycles of nature. Passover, for example, is simultaneously a commemoration of the Exodus, a celebration of freedom, and an ancient harvest festival welcoming the arrival of spring. As Blu Greenberg has noted, "One could, in fact, teach all of Jewish history and dogma through the Jewish calendar, and it would be quite an exhaustive lesson at that."

So in this chapter, I'm not going to try to cover all of the holidays (sorry, Shemini Atzeret!), nor will I get into the nuts and bolts of how to observe them (between the Internet and the numerous Jewish holiday how-to books out there, you're covered). Instead, I'm going to focus on the two major holiday seasons of the year—the springtime Passover to Shavuot season and the autumn Days of Awe season—and share what I think are some of their banana-on-the-seder-plate themes and lessons.

---

* Jewish holidays are regulated by a separate Jewish calendar. Unlike the secular calendar, which is based solely on the sun (which takes 365.25 days to circle the earth), the Jewish calendar is based on both the moon and the sun. Jewish months are measured by the cycles of the moon, which are 29 or 30 days. But that leads to only 354 days in a year. The Jewish calendar therefore inserts a leap month every few years, which keeps it roughly in line with the secular calendar and ensures that holidays are in the same season each year. So we have celebrated Ḥanukkah on Thanksgiving and on New Year's Eve, but we'll never celebrate it in spring or summer. Also note that some holidays (including Passover) are celebrated for an extra day outside of Israel. The reason for this is that centuries ago, there were often delays in informing far-flung Jewish communities that the new moon had appeared in Israel, which signaled the start of a new month and determined when holidays would begin and end. Diaspora communities added an extra day to certain holidays just to be sure they were celebrating them on the correct days.

The Passover to Shavuot Season:
The Journey and Mission of the Jewish People

I had always thought of Passover as a one-off holiday, along the lines of "We were slaves, then God liberated us, the end." And until I started learning about Judaism as an adult, I hadn't even heard of Shavuot, which marks the anniversary of when God gave—and the Israelites accepted—the Torah at Mount Sinai, with its instructions to build an opposite-of-Egypt, In-the-Divine-Image kind of society.

But I now realize that Passover and Shavuot don't just represent major plot points in the Torah's account of the Israelites' journey from oppression to freedom thousands of years ago. These holidays are also yearly reminders of who we are and our mission in the world as Jews *today*. They are two parts of a single story we are called to retell, two compass poles for a journey we must continue.

PASSOVER

The Torah's account of the Israelites' escape from Egypt is considered the founding story of the Jewish people. As Rabbi Jonathan Sacks points out, the Book of Exodus is the first time the Torah refers to the Israelites as an "Am," meaning "a people," or "a nation." Passover, the holiday dedicated to retelling this Exodus story, is "the festival of Jewish identity," Sacks writes. "It is the night on which we tell our children who they are."

We tell them the following: You were a stranger and a slave in Egypt, and you must always retain that sensibility; you must always identify with the outsider, the other, the abused and oppressed.

At moments in history when Jews faced daily, unrelenting persecution, I imagine it didn't take much to evoke these feelings of subjugation and exclusion. But while American Jews today are increasingly unsettled and fearful in this time of rising antisemitism, we still live in relative security and prosperity when compared to our ancestors. And a surface read of a traditional Haggadah doesn't inspire confidence that it will leave us feeling like strangers and slaves.

While the word "Haggadah" means "to tell," and "seder" means "order," the Haggadah is by no means an orderly retelling of the Exodus story. Instead, it is a mishmash of Torah verses, Talmud passages, medieval poetry, and even children's songs. One commentator, comparing the Haggadah to "a cubist composition," writes, "Rejecting standard narrative, it presents us with an ensemble of interlocking facet-like passages and ritual acts. Each one refers to an important aspect of the story but relates to adjacent sections in a seemingly disjointed fashion." If you didn't already know the plot of the Exodus story, I'm not sure you would be able to piece it together by reading through a traditional Haggadah.

But at a recent seder, I started to wonder whether the Haggadah's approach to retelling this story is less about content and more about style. As I leafed through it, I was struck by how the Haggadah feels like a kind of trauma narrative. Aspects of it remind me of my experience years ago as a volunteer counselor on a rape crisis hotline. During my shifts, I spoke with many survivors of sexual assault, and I don't recall any of them ever telling me their story as a clear, linear narrative. Instead, they spoke of having flashbacks that made them feel as if they were reliving the assault, which had sometimes happened years or decades ago. And they would share heartbreaking snippets, along the lines of "I wanted to scream, but I was frozen," "I could hear people talking downstairs," "He was so much stronger than me."

Who is he? Where are they? What happened leading up to the assault? I hardly ever found out. Traumatic experiences do not lend themselves to orderly recountings. And when you hear a story that is stripped down to just a few wrenching facts like this, without any of the particular details that make it specific to someone else, you begin to feel that it could happen to you—even, in some very faint way, that it *has* happened to you. After a few months on the hotline, I felt less safe walking down the street. Wolf whistles and crude comments that I would have previously brushed off now filled me with fear and rage.

I think this is what the seder is supposed to do to us. It's not so

much about ensuring that we *know* the story,* but that we *feel* it—that we're left with a visceral, lingering sense of how it feels to be on the wrong end of oppressive power. The Haggadah seems almost designed to achieve this effect with a narrative style that careens between

- Poignant details: "The children of Israel groaned under the burden of work, and they *cried out*."
- Varied sensory experiences: instructions to sing songs, read and hear sacred texts, and taste and touch specific foods to evoke particular historical memories—as if to flood our senses.
- Unexpected detours into intellectual discourse: random accounts of debates between ancient Rabbis, as if we're suddenly dissociating, spinning off into intellectualization because remembering has become too painful.
- Present-tense language that tells the story as if we are currently in it, experiencing a flashback: "Now we are here; next year in the land of Israel. Now—slaves; next year we shall be free."
- Passages insisting that each of us actually experienced this story for ourselves: "The Lord acted for me when I came out of Egypt" (not "for my *ancestors*," but "for *me*") and "It was not only our ancestors whom the Holy One redeemed; He redeemed us too along with them."

In theory, this is powerful stuff. In practice, between the traditional Haggadah's archaic language and the sheer length of many seders, which can go on for five or six hours, the Exodus can feel distant, shrouded in the mists of ancient history. It can be hard to identify with the plight of people living three thousand years ago.

This is why that banana was so important—it helped translate this ancient trauma story into a language modern people could understand.

---

* The Haggadah itself makes this point, stating, "Even were we all wise, all intelligent, all aged and all knowledgeable in the Torah, still the command would be upon us to tell of the coming out of Egypt." Even if we already know the story, we are required to retell it.

That is what the seder is supposed to do for us. The Haggadah itself declares, "Everyone who elaborates on discussing the story is praised." So while the Haggadah is a helpful jumping-off point, we're responsible for retelling this story in our own words, in a way that inscribes its trauma on our souls.

My friends who host those creative seders aren't abandoning the tradition, they're honoring it. So are countless other Jews who over the years have published thousands of different Haggadot (plural of Haggadah)—from those that are Zionist-, pacifist-, and feminist-themed to LGBTQ, vegetarian, and environmentalist ones—with all kinds of commentary seeking to bring the Exodus story to life. Families often further customize these versions, editing them and creating new rituals of their own. And many people, like my friends who hosted that banana-on-the-seder-plate seder, use online resources to create their own Haggadot.

But even with all these creative efforts, for me, the Haggadah's approach still doesn't quite resonate. I find it to be an oddly edited version of the Torah's account of the Exodus story.

The Haggadah focuses on the all-powerful, supernatural God who hears the Israelites' cries, sends the plagues, and splits the sea. But that is not an accurate reflection of the biblical narrative, which also features a number of *human* characters who choose—at great risk—to protest the values of Egypt and identify with the stranger: the midwives, who refuse to follow Pharaoh's order to drown all newborn Israelite boys in the Nile. Moses' mother, Yokheved, who follows the letter of Pharaoh's order but subverts its purpose by placing Moses in a protective basket that keeps him from drowning. Pharaoh's daughter, who knows full well that Moses is an Israelite and has the audacity to rescue him and raise him in her father's household, defying his law right under his nose. Miriam, who has the gumption to approach this Egyptian princess and convince her to hire Moses' own mother as a wet nurse. And Moses himself, who was raised as Egyptian royalty, yet risks his position of privilege to defend an Israelite slave.

It wasn't just God's actions that led to the Israelites' liberation, but the courageous acts of these human characters as well. Yet, other than one mention of Moses in some versions, not a single one of these people appears in a traditional Haggadah.

While the traditional Haggadah's version of the story, which emphasizes the role of an almighty interventionist God, may have resonated for previous generations, many Jews today identify less with that theology and more with the human characters in the story—and not just the Israelites.

Like Yokheved and Miriam, we're defiant, continuing to attend our services and celebrate our holidays despite our fears of violence in the wake of the synagogue attacks. Like the midwives, Pharaoh's daughter, and Moses, many Jews have stepped forward to stand up for strangers and confront abusive power, often at great risk. A Jewish organization called HIAS, which assists immigrants and refugees, continues its work despite being the target of antisemitic conspiracy theorists, including the Pittsburgh gunman. And Jewish journalists continue to report on corruption and injustice, undeterred by the barrage of antisemitic death threats they receive.

The Torah repeatedly instructs us to tell our children about the Exodus, to embed this story firmly at the core of their Jewish identity, teaching them that no matter how economically secure we may become, no matter how close to the inner circles of power we may get, our ancient plight as strangers and slaves must still form the basis of our moral orientation today.

But I think we also need to remind our children that even in conditions of crushing oppression, some of the Israelites resisted, and there were righteous people who helped them. That too is our story. That too is part of who we are and who we must we aspire to be.

SHAVUOT

While Shavuot is a major Jewish holiday, in modern times it has become the "Hey guys, wait up!" of holidays, lagging far behind the others in name recognition and attention.

According to the Torah, Shavuot is simply an agricultural festival marking the beginning of the wheat harvest, and it takes place seven weeks after the second day of Passover (Shavuot means "weeks" in Hebrew). But the Rabbis noticed that in the Torah, seven weeks elapse between when the Israelites were freed from Egypt and when they encountered God at Mount Sinai. They therefore decided that Shavuot is the anniversary of the moment when God gave the Israelites the Torah.

Today, people celebrate Shavuot by staying up all night studying the Torah and other sacred texts and attending synagogue services during which the Ten Commandments and the biblical Book of Ruth are read.* People also eat dairy foods, particularly cheesecake (there are various explanations for this tradition, including that the Torah was sometimes compared to milk and honey).

It is unfortunate that Shavuot isn't better known, because this holiday marks the moment when we operationalized the lessons of the Exodus, translating them into a set of laws by which we committed to live. Just as the Passover Haggadah tells us that we were all slaves in Egypt, the Rabbis claimed that all Jews who have ever lived—including those alive today—were present at Mount Sinai when the Jewish people were given their mission as articulated in the laws of the Torah. And these two events—the Exodus from Egypt and the revelation at Mount Sinai—are linked. Through the Exodus, we were granted our freedom; at Mount Sinai, we were given laws that told us what we should do with that freedom—laws that made clear that our purpose in the world is to resist Egypt wherever we may find it. The former event is the very basis

---

* The Book of Ruth is about a Jewish woman named Naomi, who travels from Judah to Moab with her family. Both her sons marry Moabite women, but then both men die, along with Naomi's husband. Naomi decides to head back to Judah alone, but her Moabite daughter-in-law Ruth insists on accompanying her, declaring, "Wherever you go, I will go; wherever you lodge, I will lodge; your people shall be my people, and your God my God." This sums up what it means to be a Jew by choice: It is an act of love and conviction. And once you convert, the Rabbis insisted, you're considered to have been present at Mount Sinai along with every other Jew. Furthermore, Ruth's great-grandson was none other than ancient Israel's greatest king, King David, and Jewish tradition holds that the Messiah will be one of David's descendants. This gives you a sense of the esteem in which Jews by choice should be held. Ruth is considered a model for those who convert, so Shavuot is often associated with Jews by choice.

for the latter, and the laws God dictates are explicit in making this connection:

> You shall not subvert the rights of the stranger or the fatherless; you shall not take a widow's garment in pawn. Remember that you were a slave in Egypt.

> When you gather the grapes of your vineyard, do not pick it over again; that shall go to the stranger, the fatherless, and the widow. Always remember that you were a slave in the land of Egypt.

> Remember that you were a slave in the land of Egypt . . . therefore the Lord your God has commanded you to observe the sabbath day.

"Remembering 'that you were once slaves in Egypt'," Rabbi Jonathan Sacks observes, is the Torah's most often cited rationale for the commandments, and he argues that "the Exodus . . . forms an essential part of the logic of Jewish law." This logic seems to have two parts: (1) You know what it feels like to be a stranger; (2) That feeling should heighten your sense of obligation to those who are strangers today. Part two is not possible without part one.

The logic of the Exodus, I think, is best encapsulated in this line from the Torah: "You shall not oppress a stranger, for you know the feelings of the stranger, having yourselves been strangers in the land of Egypt." As Rabbi Shai Held points out, in biblical Hebrew, the word "nefesh," translated in this verse as "feelings,"* literally means "throat," "gullet," or "life." So the Torah is essentially saying this: Do not oppress the stranger, for you know the very life-breath of the stranger, the place from which they cry out in agony, joy, or fear. Passover is

---

* While "nefesh" later came to mean "soul," the Torah does not ascribe to the belief that human beings have souls that are separate from their bodies. We'll discuss further in Chapter 9.

about reinforcing part one of the logic (knowing how it feels to be a stranger) by ensuring we retain that visceral, bodily sense of being vulnerable. Shavuot is about part two (feeling obligated to care for strangers today), reminding us that our experience of oppression in Egypt is the lens through which we must see the world, and that the laws dictated at Mount Sinai are our instructions for how to act on what we see.

As the political theorist Michael Walzer once wrote, "Wherever you live, it is probably Egypt." Wherever we are is Egypt for someone, and even if that someone is not us, as Jews, we cannot turn away from their plight. This core Jewish belief likely explains the disproportionate role Jews have played in American social justice movements. Jews have been at the forefront of the labor movement, leading major American unions. Jews helped create the NAACP, traveled south to support African Americans in the Freedom Rides and Freedom Summer (two-thirds of the white people who participated in the Freedom Rides in the summer of 1961 were Jewish), and played an important role in drafting the Civil Rights Acts and Voting Rights Act. Jews like Gloria Steinem and Betty Friedan played seminal roles in the feminist movement, and a Jew named Harvey Milk is a gay rights icon.

Today, leaders and employees in numerous antipoverty, criminal justice reform, human rights, and immigrant and refugee assistance organizations are Jewish. And in a recent survey, a majority of American Jews said that "working for justice and equality" is "an essential part of what being Jewish means to them."

This Jewish concern for others is what prompted former Governor of Texas Ann Richards to serve as a visiting professor at Brandeis University. In a tribute written after her death in 2006, one of her students recounted:

When a classmate of mine once asked Ms. Richards why a Christian Texan and Baylor University graduate would come to teach a course at a predominantly Jewish school in Massachusetts (and, later, join its board of trustees), she responded that from the day she took office as governor of the Lone Star State, people appeared outside her house every day demanding something. The Jewish community in Texas, she observed, was always there demanding something that would benefit people other than themselves. "I decided," she drawled, "that I wanted to do a *mitzvah*."

Now, are there Jews who seem to have missed some of the key points of our sacred texts? Jews who haven't exactly lived up to the highest ideals of these texts? Of course. And have they occasionally done so in serious and high-profile ways? Unfortunately, yes, causing no small amount of distress to the rest of us, who fret that they make all Jews look bad. But fortunately, most American Jews seem to have concluded that to be Jewish is to take the story of the stranger personally, knowing, and more important, *feeling* in our gut that it is our story too and that a core part of being Jewish is "working for justice and equality."

The folks at HIAS offer a good example. This organization was originally known as the "Hebrew Immigrant Aid Society." From its founding in 1881, HIAS has assisted generations of Jewish refugees fleeing persecution, up through the wave of Russian Jews who arrived in the United States in the 1990s. As the flood of Jewish immigrants ended, rather than closing their doors, HIAS decided to shift their mission to helping other refugees fleeing persecution in Africa, Asia, the Middle East, and elsewhere across the globe.

As the CEO of HIAS put it, "We assist refugees today not because *they* are Jewish, but because *we* are Jewish."

The Days of Awe Season: From Tisha B'Av, to Rosh Hashanah and Yom Kippur, to Sukkot

Years ago, when I found myself asking big questions about my life—Who am I? Why am I here? What is this all about?—I turned to philosophy classes, meditation, therapy, other religious traditions, and books of all kinds. But those Rosh Hashanah and Yom Kippur services that I attended each fall? Not so much.

For me, these two holidays felt a lot like the name we often use for them: "the High Holy Days." Formal. Stiff. Ponderous.

That's unfortunate, because this is not in any way how these holidays are supposed to feel. Another name for them is "the Days of Awe," which refers not just to Rosh Hashanah and Yom Kippur, but to the ten days between them. *That's* how they're supposed to feel: awesome, in the being-in-touch-with-something-transcendent sense of the word. And as Rabbi Alan Lew notes in his remarkable book *This Is Real and You Are Completely Unprepared,*[*] these ten days are situated within an entire season of reflection and transformation, one that he believes starts with the late summer holiday of Tisha B'Av and ends with the fall holiday of Sukkot.

The holidays that take place during this period are supposed to break our hearts wide open, prompt a wrenching examination of our souls, and force us to come face-to-face with our own mortality. During this season, we step back and ask ourselves: How's it going? Not in the meaningless small-talk sense of that question, when the response is always "Fine," but in the big existential sense that requires an honest answer and prompts further questions, like "Am I a good person?" and "Am I living a good life?"

To that end, the month leading up to the Days of Awe—the Hebrew month of Elul—is a time of spiritual preparation. During morning services in Elul, Jews traditionally have someone blow a shofar, a ram's horn that was sounded in ancient times as a call to battle, at the coronation of kings, and to herald other significant events. The sound of a shofar is both primitive and primal—like a cross between sobbing, wailing, and a panicked plea for help. It is a sound you cannot ignore. Maimonides viewed it as a wake-up call, a kind of spiritual alarm clock set to go off in the fall of each year.

What, exactly, are we waking up to? One answer can be found in this line from the Days of Awe liturgy: "A great shofar sounds, and a

---

[*] I have read this book—which is about the Days of Awe season—multiple times, and it informs my thinking throughout this section.

still small voice is heard." This is a verse from the biblical story of the prophet Elijah, who encountered God on a mountaintop:

> There was a great and mighty wind, splitting mountains and shattering rocks by the power of the Lord; but the Lord was not in the wind. After the wind—an earthquake; but the Lord was not in the earthquake. After the earthquake—fire; but the Lord was not in the fire. And after the fire—a still small voice.

God was not in the powerful forces of nature, but in that still, small voice. And that's what we're trying to wake up to during this Days of Awe season—that quiet voice of conscience that says, "What you did wasn't right"; that voice of truth that says, "This isn't who you are or who you want to be." I've heard it described as the voice in which our souls speak to us, and some call it the voice of the Divine.

To help ourselves awaken to this voice, we do what is known as "heshbon hanefesh," meaning "accounting of the soul"—a searching examination of how we have acted and who we have become over the past year. A fundamental assumption underlying this process is that each of us has a pure soul (some refer to it as our truest self, or as the spark of the Divine within us). But sometimes we give in to our bad impulse (the yetzer hara) and commit sins—we miss the mark/go astray by being cruel, selfish, dishonest, etc. In doing so, we wander from, and become distant from, our pure souls/truest selves/the Divine.

Fortunately, it is always possible to come back through a process known as "teshuvah," which is sometimes translated as "repentance," but really means "return." Blu Greenberg, drawing from the writings of Maimonides, describes this process as "the four Rs": "Recognition of having done wrong. Regret. Resolution not to repeat. Restraining oneself in the face of the same temptation or opportunity that previously led to wrongdoing."

When your wrongdoing has harmed someone else, doing teshuvah requires you to approach that person, acknowledge what you have done, and ask for forgiveness. No amount of prayer, fasting, and self-reflection will suffice. According to Jewish tradition, you cannot receive Divine forgiveness for something you did to another person until you have sought to make amends with that person.

Once you have completed the process of doing teshuvah, there is no lingering stigma. Jewish law actually forbids us from reminding others of sins they have previously committed.

During the month of Elul, Jews undertake all kinds of practices to facilitate their soul accounting and teshuvah making. My friend Abby Pogrebin describes one in her wonderful book *My Jewish Year: 18 Holidays, One Wondering Jew.* Each day, she and a friend reflected on a particular trait (anger, gratitude, regret, loving-kindness) and then shared their reflections with each other over email. Doing this exercise, Abby wrote, pushed her "to zero in on pockets of myself I rarely turn inside out."

So the work of this season doesn't just happen over a few days in a synagogue. It stretches for weeks, with each of the holidays serving as another step in the process. And it starts with Tisha B'Av.

TISHA B'AV

The late summer holiday of Tisha B'Av, which literally means the ninth day of the Hebrew month of Av, is a day of mourning that commemorates the loss of the First and Second Temples, both of which are said to have been destroyed on this day. This holiday is also associated with the First Crusade, the expulsions of Jews from England and Spain, major events during the Holocaust, and other tragic moments in Jewish history, all of which also occurred on or near the ninth of Av. Jews have traditionally marked Tisha B'Av with a daylong fast and somber prayer services.

Some commentators regard Tisha B'Av not just as a historical commemoration but in more spiritual terms. The Temple was, after all, Jews' main conduit to God. Postdestruction, especially the first time around, when they had not yet developed synagogues for worship outside the Temple, their distress at feeling cut off from the Divine must have been acute. Rabbi Alan Lew described Tisha B'Av as "the beginning of Teshuvah, the point of turning toward this process by turning toward a recognition of our estrangement from God, from ourselves, and from others." It is the moment, he writes, "when the walls come tumbling down."

I do not love this moment of recognition when I dredge up memories of all the times over the past year that I've been impatient, unkind, selfish, callous, ungenerous . . . honestly, it's a long list, and just typing it out is dispiriting. So I have certainly built my share of defensive, self-justifying walls: "Whatever, he deserved it," "I just didn't have time to help her," "It wasn't my fault, I was tired/stressed/busy," "If I acknowledge this truth about myself, I'll have to make some serious life changes, and that would be scary, so let's not go there."

I've found that meaningful soul accounting requires some amount of demolition, or at least the courage to stop frantically trying to hold up so many walls and to step back and let them fall of their own accord. And it can be uncomfortable, even painful, to come face-to-face with what is on the other side—truths I've been hiding from, transgressions I'd like to forget I committed.

But I find it heartening that the destruction of the Second Temple, horrific as it was, led to an era of renewal when Jews left behind their sacrifice-based practices and transitioned to the kind of Judaism we're still practicing today, two thousand years later. Without this transition, Judaism likely would not have survived and flourished as it did.

We too must let our old walls crumble.

ROSH HASHANAH

For me, Rosh Hashanah, which takes place seven weeks after Tisha B'Av and is considered the Jewish New Year, is where the Days of Awe season takes a challenging turn. I am all for the rituals associated with this holiday: eating apples dipped in honey to usher in a sweet new year and blowing the shofar during services (it's traditionally blown one hundred times, so if you missed the wake-up calls during Elul, you will definitely hear them now).

But when it comes to the themes of the day as described in the liturgy, I've struggled. The Rosh Hashanah prayers are filled with images of the Divine as a "King" who remembers everything we've done over the past year, rewards and punishes us accordingly, but really doesn't want to punish us and hopes we'll do teshuvah so that "He" can forgive us. For so many reasons (gendered imagery, anthropomorphic depictions of God, reward-and-punishment theology), this is not my cup of tea.

But I also appreciate Rabbi Harold Kushner's warning that "the worst thing you can do to a poetic metaphor is to take it literally." So I want to use some of the interpretive techniques from Chapter 6 to explore a few of the themes of Rosh Hashanah—Divine sovereignty, remembrance, and forgiveness—particularly as they appear in a prayer known as "Unetaneh Tokef," which has been a central part of both the Rosh Hashanah and Yom Kippur liturgies since the Middle Ages.

Kingship

Unetaneh Tokef begins, "And so let holiness rise up to you, for you are our God, King," and it describes God sitting on a throne. The prayer then informs us that we will all pass before this Divine sovereign like sheep passing before a shepherd, and God will decide "who will live and who will die." According to Jewish tradition, on Rosh Hashanah, God inscribes thoroughly evil people in the book of death (meaning they will die this year) and thoroughly good people in the book of life (meaning they will live) . . . and the rest of us (which I assume is really everyone, since who is completely good or evil?) have to sweat it out until Yom Kippur, when a final judgment is made and our fate is sealed. If we ultimately wind up in the book of death, the prayer states, God will decide how we die: "who by water and who by fire; who by sword and who by beast; who of hunger and who of thirst; who by earthquake and who by plague," and so on.

As I said, none of this works for me theologically, so I think this prayer is a good candidate for Rabbi Jordan Bendat-Appell's prescriptive/descriptive technique. Read that way, it's not so much *prescribing* a certain theology (i.e., a reward-and-punishment God who controls everything), but rather *describing* the unavoidable reality that our fate is not entirely in our hands. We generally do not decide how or when we die. The prayer doesn't say "who by eating poorly and not exercising, and who by driving drunk" or whatever the medieval equivalents of those behaviors would be. Instead, it highlights causes of death that are largely not within our control.

That we are not 100 percent in charge of what happens in our lives is not exactly a novel insight. But as true as it obviously is, I can never quite seem to accept it. I instead tend to think that I can prevent misfortune by worrying a lot about it in advance. After I've endured so much preemptive suffering, my thinking goes, it's only fair for bad things not to happen to me. If I don't obsess about everything that could go wrong, on the other hand, I'm begging for bad things to happen. I'm unreasonably trying to have my cake (not worrying) and eat it too (nothing bad happening).

This is, of course, absurd. I know the world does not work that way. But this kind of reasoning gives me the illusion of being in charge. And I think Unetaneh Tokef is telling me: Drop the illusion. While it's fine to plan, strive, save, and get yearly checkups, it's time to "resign as general manager of the universe," as the Methodist pastor Larry Eisenberg put it. That job was never really mine to begin with.

Remembrance

Once settled on that kingly throne, God immediately starts judging us. Unetaneh Tokef declares, "You [God] will remember everything that has been forgotten and You will open the book of memories and it will be read from: Everyone's signature is in it."

Rabbi Alan Lew recounts a story that I think perfectly explains what these verses are getting at. A man invites his rabbi to his house for the very first family viewing of the video of his daughter's wedding, which the rabbi had performed. Everyone gathers around the TV:

> As the tape begins, the rabbi and the cantor are seen standing alone under the wedding canopy blissfully unaware that the videotape is running. They can be heard making fun of both fami-

lies . . . the cantor makes a disparaging remark about the bride's mother's dress . . . Then the rabbi himself can be heard uttering a profane assessment of the groom's uncle.

This is the "book of memories." Not just what we post on social media for others' consumption, but also everything we would never dream of posting: the stingy tip we left for the waiter after we took that beautiful picture of our meal. The nasty remark we made to our spouse right after we stopped recording that smiley video of our vacation. All the times we trash-talked our friends behind their backs, or lied to our bosses to cover up our mistakes.

Unetaneh Tokef is informing us that in some cosmic sense, all of that has been recorded, along with every other moment of our lives over the past year. And this prayer insists that we sit down, watch these tapes, and ask ourselves: What parts do I wish I could edit out? When would I have acted differently if I had known I was being watched? What moments do I never, ever want to repeat?

Forgiveness

Lest we be alarmed by the judgment/remembrance imagery in Unetaneh Tokef, the prayer reassures us that God is "slow to anger, quick to forgive." In fact, God really doesn't want to inscribe us in the book of death: "For You [God] do not desire the condemned man's death, but that he may come back from his ways, and live. To the very day he dies, You wait for him; and if he comes back: You welcome him at once."

"This is how God is different from Big Brother, who also knows everything we do and say, but who uses it against us," explains Rabbi Lew. "God watches the whole video with a boundless, heartbreaking compassion." As Unetaneh Tokef puts it, "Truly, it was You [God] who formed them [human beings], You know the forces moving them: they are but flesh and blood."

Even as I write this, I find myself resisting it. All this talk about what God feels, knows, and does makes me uneasy. But I'm also thinking back to when I was in law school, and my professors would sometimes pose outlandish legal hypotheticals—situations that would never actually happen in an American courtroom but that were designed to highlight some aspect of the law or reveal some flaw in its logic. Occasionally, one of my classmates would point out that the scenario described was unrealistic, and the professor would respond, "Yes, I know, but don't fight the hypothetical." The hypothetical was not a depiction of reality, but rather a thought experiment, a pedagogical tool.

What if I viewed the liturgy in a similar light? What if I stopped fighting the hypothetical and imagined that there actually *is* a boundlessly loving God who knows me inside and out—better than I know myself—and understands exactly why I do what I do.

What would it feel like to stand before such a God and say, "Yes, I did these things, and yes, I feel awful about that, and I don't ever want to act this way again." What would this God say to me? I imagine it might go something like "Dearest,* I know. Those things you did are not you. And I feel quite confident of that because I created you, and I am intimately familiar with your pure soul. So really, sweetheart, stop tormenting yourself and just focus on doing whatever reflecting/apologizing/resolving-to-be-better that you need to do to come back to me and return to your pure soul/truest self."

I imagine that coming before such a God would make it a lot easier for me to confront what's on those tapes. And maybe that is the point Unetaneh Tokef is trying to make.

Even when I read Unetaneh Tokef as a poetic metaphor or a pedagogical hypothetical, I found it hard to get around the reward-and-punishment framework upon which it seems to be based. But as I've learned more about this prayer, I've come to understand that rather than fully embracing this approach, Unetaneh Tokef actually calls it into question.

Like many other prayers, Unetaneh Tokef includes a number of quotes from the Hebrew Bible—and guess which book it draws most

---

* I think this God would use many terms of endearment.

heavily from? Believe it or not, it's the Book of Job, in which God unfairly punishes a righteous man named Job—an extreme example of bad things happening to good people. When Job confronts God, God basically replies, "You have no idea what it's like to create and rule the universe, so back off." Not exactly the biblical book I would advise quoting from if you're trying to promote a clear-cut reward-and-punishment theology.

In addition, after Unetaneh Tokef insists that God will decide who lives and dies and how, it declares that teshuvah, prayer, and tzedakah* "help the hardship of the decree pass." This line is based in part on a passage from the Talmud that clearly states that if we do such activities, God's decree will be *torn up*. But it seems that whoever wrote Unetaneh Tokef realized that the Talmud's version simply wasn't true. Each year, plenty of people who did all three things still died. So the prayer was edited in a way that seems to *reject* reward-and-punishment theology, telling us: You can repent, pray, and donate as much as you want, but that won't change what happens to you—it won't lead God to tear up the decree. It *will,* however, "help the hardship of the decree pass," meaning that it will make it more bearable.

Now this I can get behind. I agree that we can't always control what happens to us, but we do have some control over how we react. When bad things happen, we can cultivate a spiritual practice so that we feel less isolated. We can engage in self-reflection, and do teshuvah if necessary, to help us grow. And we can get some perspective by helping others who are worse off. These actions may not change our circumstances, but they may change *us,* giving us what we need to cope and even thrive.

YOM KIPPUR

Yom Kippur, which occurs ten days after Rosh Hashanah, is when things get very real.

On this "Day of Atonement," the Torah tells us, "you shall practice self-denial . . . you shall do no work . . . It shall be a sabbath of complete

---

* As we discussed in Chapter 5, tzedakah is about giving financial support to those in need.

rest for you." In addition to requiring us to observe the constraints of Shabbat on Yom Kippur, the Rabbis established a number of "self-denial" rules: no eating or drinking (though children and people for whom fasting would be unhealthy are not expected to fast), no sex, no bathing or wearing makeup, no leather shoes. It also became customary to wear a "kittel," which is a white robe in which Jews are traditionally buried when they die.

That's right, on Yom Kippur, we dress like a corpse and refrain from all life-sustaining activities—we act out our own death. We embody the words of Unetaneh Tokef that warn us that we may well die this year. Yom Kippur is Judaism's annual daylong death meditation.

A sermon given back in the 1980s by a rabbi named Kenneth Berger vividly highlights this aspect of Yom Kippur. Rabbi Berger delivered this sermon just eight months after the *Challenger* spaceship had exploded soon after takeoff, killing all seven astronauts on board, including one who was a schoolteacher. The whole thing had been captured on national television, to the horror of children across America who had gathered in their classrooms to watch it.

In his sermon, Rabbi Berger noted that scientists who investigated the crash concluded that the astronauts may not have died when the shuttle exploded midair, but rather, moments later when their capsule smashed into the water below. And he said:

> For perhaps as much as five minutes, the astronauts were alive and conscious and yet knew that death was certain . . . Can you imagine knowing that in a few moments death was imminent? What would we think of? If God forbid, you and I were in such circumstances? What would go through our mind? . . . I know it is not pleasant, but I want you to consider on this Yom Kippur, what if? What if I had five minutes to live?*

---

* This sermon is especially poignant because three years after Rabbi Berger delivered it, he, his wife, and two of his three children were on a plane when one of its engines exploded. For forty minutes, everyone braced for an emergency landing. The plane caught fire upon landing, and both Rabbi Berger and his wife were killed.

This is the point of Yom Kippur: "to bring us to the point of existential crisis," as Rabbi Lew put it, to remind us that at every moment, we are plummeting to our deaths, whether in five minutes or five decades. Yom Kippur is a wrenching reminder of our own very fragile mortality. As Unetaneh Tokef states: "Man is founded in dust and ends in dust. He lays down his soul to bring home bread. He is like a broken shard, like grass dried up, like a faded flower, like a fleeting shadow, like a passing cloud, like a breath of wind, like whirling dust, like a dream that slips away."

Yom Kippur is Judaism's way of telling us: Do not wait for a nose-diving airplane or your final days in hospice to take your life seriously. Have a near-death experience at least once a year (ideally much more frequently*) during which your life passes before your eyes, and you ask yourself, "Is this the life I want to have lived? If my life ended five minutes from now, what would I wish I had done differently?"

To that end, the Yom Kippur liturgy pushes us to take a final look at those tapes—an even closer, more honest look. The liturgy seems to anticipate that, even after all those weeks of soul accounting, there may be some parts of the tapes that we still cannot see clearly, or that we simply refuse to watch. And with its extensive confessional prayers, in which the entire congregation confesses out loud, in unison, to various sins, the liturgy seems to almost be forcing us to reckon with those tapes—to admit to ourselves (and the Divine, if that works for you) what they reveal about how we have acted and who we have been over the past year.

We might walk into Yom Kippur services thinking: "Nothing on those tapes is that bad. I haven't committed any crimes. I'm generally a good person. Why do I need to spend all this time atoning?"

But we would quickly discover that the sins listed in the confessional prayers are generally not the big "thou shalt not kill" sins, but the

---

* One of the Rabbis in the Talmud urges people to do teshuvah one day before their death. But since none of us knows when we're going to die, this means we should do teshuvah every day, just to be safe.

ones that many of us commit on a daily basis. About a quarter of the transgressions listed in one of the prayers have to do with speech, including foul language, foolish speech, mockery, deception, gossip, and slander. We also admit to hard-heartedness, ignorance, arrogance, envy, sexual impropriety, and pride.

Much like when I study Jewish ethics, I have a feeling of being found out when I read these prayers. I am definitely guilty of many of these transgressions. And even worse, I'm often guilty of not even considering them "sins" in the first place and not feeling particularly bad when I commit them.

Another defense we might try to employ is something like: But I'm so diligent about my ritual observance—the tapes show it!—no one is more stringent about keeping kosher and observing Shabbat than I am!

But the response of the confessional prayers seems to be something along the lines of "So what?" Hardly any of the sins specifically named in these prayers involve a ritual law. We are not asked to admit that we worked on Shabbat or failed to pray regularly. Furthermore, as mentioned in Chapter 6, on Yom Kippur, we read a passage from the Book of Isaiah that makes very clear that ritual piety is meaningless—if not downright offensive to God—unless accompanied by moral righteousness. It starts with the Israelites asking God, "Why, when we fasted, did You not see? When we starved our bodies, did You pay no heed?" The prophet Isaiah responds:

> Because on your fast day you see to your business and oppress all your laborers! Because you fast in strife and contention, and you strike with a wicked fist! . . . Is such the fast I desire, a day for men to starve their bodies? No, this is the fast I desire: . . . to let the oppressed go free; to break off every yoke. It is to share your bread with the hungry, and to take the wretched poor into your home; when you see the naked, to clothe him . . .

Yet another defense we might employ—albeit unconsciously—is to deny, block out, or simply forget about the transgressions we have committed. The confessional prayers address this as well, mainly through endless repetition. There are five services on Yom Kippur, some of them quite long, and if you attend all of them, you will say the confessional prayers no fewer than ten times. And when you are tired, hungry, and dressed for your own funeral, repeating these prayers hour after hour can be an effective way of prompting a journey from "I'm sure I've never done X," to "Hmmm, maybe I have done X," to "Okay, I've definitely done X, and I regret it, and I don't want to do X anymore."

But I don't want to make Yom Kippur sound like some kind of prison interrogation with each of us cowering alone before the Divine/our conscience in our own windowless cells. That is not what it's supposed to feel like. The Yom Kippur confessional prayers are very much a communal experience. I have often felt a sense of relief when reciting the lists of sins in these prayers, thinking to myself, "Other people do that too—I'm not the only one!" And note that the prayers are phrased in the "we" voice: not "I" did X, but "*we*" did X. Regardless of whether or not you personally committed a sin, you're still supposed to join in the chorus of voices saying, "We committed this sin."

I find this to be deeply humane, allowing us to acknowledge where we've missed the mark while protecting our privacy. It also reflects a deep truth, one that is a core theme in Judaism: We are all responsible for each other. We may not have mocked or slandered anyone, or committed sexual impropriety, but did we fail to confront others who did? Every community—whether it's a congregation, school, or workplace—has a moral atmosphere, and that atmosphere influences how we act. When I've been part of gossipy communities in which people curse a lot (these are known as political campaigns), I have definitely gossiped and cursed more. None of us is alone in our sinning—we're all in some way implicated in how others behave.

In addition, on Yom Kippur, we soften the harshness of the atonement theme by doubling down on the theme of forgiveness, which is all over the day's liturgy, particularly in the selection from the Hebrew Bible that is read during the afternoon service, the Book of Jonah.

In this book, God instructs a man named Jonah to travel to the city of Nineveh and tell people there to renounce their sinful ways or risk Divine punishment. After refusing to perform this mission and instead running away and winding up in the belly of a large fish, Jonah finally does what God asked. The people of Nineveh repent—fasting, donning sackcloth, crying out to God—and God quickly forgives them. When Jonah protests, believing God let them off too easy, God makes clear that God cares deeply about the people of Nineveh, and that they are entirely worthy of Divine mercy.

I'm moved by this story for many reasons, one of which is that Nineveh was the capital of Assyria, which, you'll recall, conquered the northern Israelite kingdom and is responsible for those "lost tribes" of Jews. The message here seems to be that if even your worst enemies can be forgiven for their sins, then so can you.

Also, the Talmud points out that in the Book of Jonah, the people of Nineveh were forgiven not because "God saw their sackcloth and their fasting." But rather they were forgiven because "God saw their deeds, that they had turned from their evil way." We win no Divine points for self-flagellation, but rather for doing the work of teshuvah.

Doing teshuvah is not so much about beating yourself up over what you've done in the past, but about changing yourself so that you act differently in the future. When done well, I think it is a self-affirming rather than self-denigrating process, and I appreciate this advice from the Baal Shem Tov (the founder of Ḥasidism): "It is necessary to find the root of love in evil so as to sweeten evil and turn it into love." I interpret this to mean that if you dig down to the root of any sin, you generally discover some perfectly good or legitimate yearning.

Why do I sometimes gossip? Probably because it makes me feel better about myself and is a way to connect with others. And there's nothing wrong with my desire for self-esteem and intimacy. Those are good things. I'm simply seeking them in the wrong way. Now that I realize this, I can focus on finding other ways to meet those needs. As Rabbi Lew notes, "Even that behavior we took to be wrongful, we now realize, has a holy spark at its center waiting to be released."

There can be deep joy in excavating and releasing these holy sparks, which is why Yom Kippur is traditionally regarded as a joyful day. Notes Blu Greenberg, "The thought of starting with a clean slate, or of having an opportunity to continue to build up one's life, can be exhilarating." Some congregations even dance and sing at the end of the day.

I want to be clear, however, that "clean slate" is not synonymous with "the slate you had before you committed the sin." That is not how teshuvah works. Rather, it's more like the account in the Torah of how, after the golden calf incident, Moses became so enraged that he smashed the stone tablets on which God had inscribed the Ten Commandments. He then hiked back up Mount Sinai and begged God to forgive the Israelites. God eventually did so, and God and Moses created a new set of tablets. Jewish tradition has it that Moses returned with these new tablets on Yom Kippur. And the Talmud claims that the Israelites saved the broken pieces of the old tablets, placing them alongside the new ones in the Ark at the heart of the Tabernacle, and carrying those shards with them on their journey through the desert.

I love that the Israelites seemed to believe that those shattered pieces were also somehow holy and necessary for the process of teshuvah. This has been the case in my own life as well. I can recall moments in which I have been presented with the opportunity to repeat a sin, and as I feel the pull of temptation, I've found myself reaching back and running my mind over the jagged edges of those old fragments, reminding myself of the pain I caused that first time around. That is generally enough to keep me from transgressing again. According to Jewish tradition, this is the moment when you know you have truly repented—the moment when you're presented with the opportunity to repeat a past sin, and you choose not to, because you have changed.

We try our best to live by those new tablets, but we still carry our broken parts around with us to remind us not of who we *are,* but of who we *aren't*—of who we do not wish to be. And I find it heartening that the Rabbis actually regarded someone who committed a sin and then did teshuvah to be in a better position than one who never committed that sin in the first place. "In the place where penitents stand," they declared, "even the completely righteous do not stand."

SUKKOT

Sukkot is a seven-day holiday that starts four days after Yom Kippur. Like Passover and Shavuot, it is a harvest festival, so I could have included it in the Passover-Shavuot section of this chapter. But in addition to its temporal proximity to the Days of Awe, Sukkot seems to have a spiritual proximity to these holidays. We have just spent Rosh Hashanah and Yom Kippur acknowledging that we're all going to die and have little control over how and when that happens. On Sukkot, we ask ourselves: If this is true—if we're just fragile, mortal beings hurtling to our deaths—how are we supposed to live?

The answer Sukkot offers is embedded in one of the Torah's instructions for how this holiday should be observed: "You shall live in booths seven days . . . in order that future generations may know that I made the Israelite people live in booths when I brought them out of the land of Egypt, I the Lord your God."

On Sukkot, the Torah is telling us, we should reenact how the Israelites lived when they wandered in the desert after being freed from Egypt. But what, exactly, is a "booth"? The Hebrew word for booth is "sukkah" (hence the name of the holiday, "Sukkot," the plural form of the word), and it seems to mean some kind of temporary dwelling.

The Rabbis developed highly specific rules for how to construct a sukkah such that it is a fragile structure, like a tent or yurt, but also sturdy enough for families and their guests to eat and live in. It has to be erected outdoors, and people often build their sukkah in their backyard or on their rooftop, porch, or balcony. The roof must be made of plant or tree branches (bamboo, pine tree boughs, cornstalks, etc.), and it should provide shade from sunlight but be open enough for its inhabitants to see the stars. Traditionally, during Sukkot, Jews eat their meals in their sukkah, and it is customary to invite guests. Some Jews even sleep there.

What does all of this tell us about how to live our lives?

On Tisha B'Av, we are reminded that we can build all the Temples we want—all the fancy houses, fat bank accounts, and impressive résumés; all the barriers and defenses against confronting the reality of how we're living our lives—but those walls offer far less protection than we think.

On Sukkot, we're told to construct a visibly fragile, temporary structure—one that offers little protection from the wind, rain, heat, and cold, but affords a clear view of the heavens. It is a house that "gives us no shelter . . . a parody of a house," Rabbi Alan Lew observes, "it exposes the idea of a house as an illusion."

Sukkot seems to be telling us that being written in the Book of Life is an all-inclusive kind of deal. It is not "The Book of the Pleasant Things in Life" or "The Book of the Easy Things in Life." It is "The Book of Life"—all of it. If you try to keep out all the rain, you'll be unable to see any stars. If you refuse to bear the heat, you'll never feel the sun on your skin. Either you get the whole package—pleasure *and* pain, joy *and* sorrow—or you get a numb, closed-off, sleepwalking existence that might seem safe and manageable, but isn't much of a life. That kind of existence offers only the illusion of control, and it's no way to live.

Echoing a theme that runs throughout Judaism, Sukkot urges us: Do this awake. And don't anxiously brace against the uncertainty of an awakened life, or grudgingly endure it. Rejoice in it. As the Torah states in its instructions for how to observe Sukkot, "You shall rejoice before the Lord your God seven days."

After surviving a near-death experience, which is what the Days of Awe are supposed to be, we don't sweat the small stuff—the gust of wind that knocks over the centerpiece, the leaves from the roof fluttering into our soup. Sitting in a shelter that provides hardly any shelter, surrounded by people we care about, we're delighted simply to be alive, and nothing else really matters.

On Sukkot, we acknowledge that we all wander the earth in rickety booths, exposed to the elements, and the key to living a good life is finding peace, joy, and gratitude along the way.

It should by now be clear just how right Blu Greenberg is: You really can teach just about all of Judaism—history, theology, ethics, law, culture—through the holidays. And none of them are meant to be celebrated for just one or two days, or a week, and then forgotten until the following year. They all articulate themes that Judaism emphasizes all year round: caring for those on the margins, living life fully awake, returning to our pure souls/truest selves/the Divine.

And I have covered only a handful of Jewish holidays in this chapter. There are many more: Purim, during which we revel in a story about Persian Jews averting a plot to kill them in the fifth century B.C.E.; Tu B'Shvat, which celebrates trees and has taken on increased significance with the rise of the environmental movement; newer holidays that mark the tragedy of the Holocaust and commemorate Israel's founding. Each has its own important spiritual, moral, and historical lessons to teach us. And as I have learned about them, I've found that they're often far more complex and interesting than the versions I was taught as a child.

Take Ḥanukkah, for example. Growing up, I was told that the story went something like this: The ancient Greeks denied Jews religious freedom and desecrated their Temple. In the second century B.C.E., a group of Jews known as the Maccabees fought back, defeated the Greeks, reclaimed the Temple, and found enough oil to light the Temple lamp for one day, but it lasted for eight days. Miracle!

But the actual story is far more complicated. It appears that the Maccabees were zealots, opposing not just the Greeks but also their more Hellenized Jewish brethren, whose embrace of Greek culture they disdained. And the miracle of the oil? It looks like the Rabbis, uncomfortable with the Maccabees' extremism, made that part up hundreds of years after the fact, possibly hoping to shift the focus of the holiday to something more appealing. Also, Ḥanukkah is a minor holiday in Jewish tradition. It has taken on outsize importance in America mainly because of its proximity to Christmas.

So there's a lot going on with our holidays. And when I read books about them and talk to my more observant friends, I'm moved by the rich experiences and traditions they describe: Yom Kippur services where people openly sob and plead for forgiveness, seders filled with passionate debates about the language in the Haggadah, lively all-night study sessions on Shavuot.

But I worry that for some of us, the traditional rituals don't always serve their intended purpose. For most of my life, I figured that this is just how Judaism is—meaningful in some vague way, occasionally fun, but generally dull and hard to understand. And while there's nothing wrong with the kind of synagogue experience where we just let the music and Hebrew words wash over us and enjoy the time offline, or the seder that's mainly just a chance to catch up with family, I think we deserve more.

I'm certainly not saying we should abandon our holiday traditions. Just the opposite: I think we should assume that each of them has something profound to teach us—something that will touch our souls and transform our lives—but we need to put some effort into finding it. We need to keep digging, learning, and interpreting until we unearth the beating-heart meanings of these holidays. And we need to celebrate them in ways that bring those meanings to life so that their lessons stay with us long after they have ended.

Sometimes, all it takes is a well-placed banana.

CHAPTER 9

Life Cycle Rituals (Well, Mainly Just Death)

A few years ago, at a conference, I took part in a small group exercise in which each participant gave a brief presentation on an issue they cared about. As we went around the table, people spoke about a variety of topics—new technological developments, public policy problems, speechwriting techniques (me, obviously)—and the room buzzed with the back-and-forth between the presenter and the rest of us.

We then got to a man who looked to be in his forties and had been sitting quietly, barely blinking behind his thick-framed glasses. After hesitating for a moment, he took a deep breath and said, "The truth is, my mother passed away about a month ago, and I'm having a really hard time right now."

In an instant, the energy in the room shifted as everyone fell silent and leaned in closer. "I know I have a lot of anger and grief I need to process," he continued, "but I haven't figured out how to do that. So I've just been keeping busy, kind of avoiding it." He continued on in this vein for the rest of his three minutes.

When it was time to offer responses, after saying how sorry I was, I told him about the traditional Jewish mourning rituals—how for seven days after we bury our loved ones, we do something called "sitting shiva." During this time, we don't leave the house, go to work, or do the usual tasks of daily life. Instead, our friends and community come to us and form a loving circle around us, sitting with us as we grieve, helping with cooking and errands, and joining us for daily prayer services as we say the special mourner's prayer called "the Kaddish."

After the shiva is over, we can return to work if we like, but we don't resume normal life. Judaism understands that we need time to transition back into a world that hasn't stopped turning just because our loved one is no longer in it. So for thirty days, we continue to say the Kaddish every day, but we now do so at a synagogue or elsewhere, often with others who have lost loved ones. (If the deceased was a parent, the mourning period lasts an entire year, and we say the Kaddish daily for eleven of those twelve months.) In addition, every year for the rest of our lives, we mark the anniversary of our loved one's death with special rituals to honor their memory.

When someone we love dies, we may feel as if the world as we know it has been shattered and we're suddenly forced to live in a new world of which we want no part. And when everyone is telling us that we need to be strong, and get it together, and act like everything is okay, Judaism says: No, actually, you are *not* okay, and you may feel this way for quite a while. And though you will slowly heal and eventually find your footing, this loss will always be with you. This will always hurt in some way.

The secular world might expect us to act like nothing has happened, but Judaism certainly doesn't. Rather, it lays out a process that gives us the space to fully feel and express our grief and that guides us forward, gradually helping us reenter our life and learn to live it again without the one we love.

The guy's eyes lit up. "That's what I'm missing!" he exclaimed. "That's what I need—some kind of ritual to get me through this."

• • •

The secular world is not great at helping us cope with big life transitions like getting married, starting a family, or losing someone we love. Instead of supporting and comforting us, it often does the opposite, scaring the living daylights out of us and then selling us products it claims will alleviate our fears.

Getting married? Your wedding must be absolutely perfect! And that can only happen if you spend a fortune on a dress you'll wear just once . . . and also on invitations, the venue, food, music, flowers, photography, videography, and a wedding planner to coordinate it all.

Having a baby? That child is in danger from the moment of conception—maybe even before! Be sure to buy exactly the right crib, car seat, baby monitor, carrier, changing table—no, not that one, the more expensive one! Yes, you really should buy a stroller that costs more than your first car.

Someone you love just died? You'd better buy a really fancy casket . . . and if you truly loved that person, you would spring for the most expensive headstone as well. That's how you'll work through your grief, rage, guilt, and anxiety over their death.

Jewish life cycle rituals, on the other hand, are not consumer experiences—at least they're not supposed to be. In fact, as Rabbi Harold Kushner points out, they're often not even necessary to bring about the change in status that they mark. For example, when you turn thirteen,* you automatically become a "bar/bat mitzvah," a "child of the commandments"—meaning you're responsible for observing the mitzvot. No ceremony or party is required.

But while life cycle rituals may not be necessary to mark life transitions, they can help make them more meaningful and manageable, highlighting their sacred dimensions and offering us the support we

---

* In more traditional communities, a boy becomes a bar mitzvah at age thirteen and a girl becomes a bat mitzvah at age twelve. And that is the correct terminology—a child does not "have a bar/bat mitzvah," they "become a bar/bat mitzvah"—but the former phrase is commonly used as well.

need to get through them. And by undertaking these rituals, we situate our personal story in the larger Jewish story as we perform the same actions and utter the same words as our grandparents, their grandparents, and Jews around the world today who are marking these transitions in their own lives.

So I have great respect for Jewish life cycle rituals. And I appreciate how, in recent decades, thanks to the influence of feminism in Judaism, rituals have been developed to help people cope with infertility, pregnancy loss, menopause, and other transitions and struggles that have too often been ignored or given short shrift.

That said, as an unmarried woman who does not have children, I have little personal experience with many of the moments Jewish life cycle rituals mark, and that makes it hard for me to write about them. As a speechwriter, I'm no stranger to writing about topics that don't hold great personal meaning for me. It's part of the job to get yourself jazzed up about roads, bridges, and high-speed rail to write that speech about infrastructure—and I have, at more than one point in my career, written lofty tributes to President Eisenhower and the National Defense and Interstate Highways Act of 1956. But those words were written for someone else, and I've found that when I'm speaking with my own voice, it's best to stick to my own truth. And the truth is, beyond thinking that they're powerful, beautiful, and important, I just don't have much to say about most Jewish life cycle rituals.

There is, however, one set of rituals about which I have a great deal to say, in part because they touch on a topic that has caused me no small amount of anxiety. And those are the Jewish rituals around death.

As a child, I spent many nights lying awake, terrifying myself by imagining what it would be like to be dead, lying all alone underground while the world went on up above without me. My parents repeatedly reassured me that I would not die for a very long time. But they offered no afterlife scenario—no "you'll be up in heaven with the angels and Grandpa" kind of comfort.

At some point, I grew out of this fear, and I can no longer conjure up the visceral hold it once had on me. But I still really do not want to die. I love being alive. I am baffled—and horrified—by people who do things like climbing cliffs without safety gear or walking a tightrope across a canyon without a net. If something went wrong, and they found themselves plummeting to their deaths, would they really be thinking, "Yeah, this was totally worth it"?

I know I'm not the only Jew who's not keen on dying. Nor am I the only Jew who has lost people I love, though I am extraordinarily fortunate in that respect, never having had to endure the death of an immediate family member or very close friend (knock on wood). Yet, like many Jews, beyond being vaguely aware that there are some mourning rituals that involve saying the Kaddish, I had no idea what Judaism says about death. And I had always assumed (wrongly, it turns out) that there is no Jewish conception of an afterlife.

This surprises my friends of other faiths, who wonder how I can not know what my own religion says about something so important. It's a fair question, and I think the answer is largely that Judaism simply isn't a death-focused religion. Just the opposite—we're very big on life. In Moses' final speech to the Israelites in the Torah, he exhorts, "I have put before you life and death, blessing and curse. Choose life." During the Days of Awe, we plead with God to "Remember us for life, Sovereign who delights in life, and inscribe us in the Book of Life." And the best-known Jewish toast—l'ḥaim!—means "To life!"

So this chapter runs deeply counter to the spirit of Judaism. A representative account of Jewish life cycle rituals would include a section on death along with sections on other life transitions like birth, coming of age, and marriage. But given my interest in this topic and the fact that many Jews don't know what Judaism has to say about it, I'm going to focus this entire chapter on death, starting with Jewish burial and mourning rituals and then exploring what Judaism has to say about what happens after we die.

JEWISH BURIAL AND MOURNING RITUALS

According to Jewish tradition, when someone has died, we have two sacred responsibilities—honoring the deceased and caring for the mourners left behind—and Judaism has developed a number of rituals to help us fulfill these obligations. While today, some of these practices are done mainly in traditional communities, they are by no means only for traditionally observant Jews. Jews of all backgrounds can avail themselves of these rituals, and many do, sometimes modifying or personalizing them to meet the needs of their families or honor the wishes of the deceased.

Honoring the Dead: From Death to Burial

Jewish law requires the deceased to be buried within twenty-four hours,* and the first day after death is spent preparing the body for burial and making arrangements for the funeral.

PREPARING THE DECEASED FOR BURIAL

Jewish tradition requires that we treat the body of the deceased as respectfully as possible. To that end, Jewish law prohibits embalming dead bodies, since injecting the deceased with chemicals and applying cosmetics to their face is considered deeply disrespectful. As is putting them on display, so Jews generally do not have open-casket wakes or public viewings. Jewish law also prohibits cremation. Like embalming, it is considered a serious violation of the body, even more so since the Holocaust, with its images of smoke billowing from concentration camp ovens.

Rather than displaying our dead or burning them, Jews in America traditionally bury them unembalmed in simple wooden caskets so that the body can decompose naturally back to the earth.† This practice is

---

* Though it makes exceptions, including for when family members must travel from far away for the funeral.
† In Israel, the deceased are wrapped in a shroud and put straight into the ground, except for fallen soldiers, who are buried in coffins.

rooted in a verse from the Torah, when God creates Adam out of the dust of the earth and informs him, "For dust you are, and to dust you shall return."

For centuries, Jews have prepared the dead for this kind of burial with a ritual known as "Tahara," which means "purity" and involves washing and dressing the body. Tahara is done by specially trained volunteers who are members of their synagogue's or community's "Ḥevra Kadisha," which means "Holy Society." As historian Deborah Lipstadt points out, that name—"*Holy* Society," rather than merely "*Burial* Society"—reflects the high esteem in which members are held. Tending to the deceased is one of the holiest mitzvot we can perform. It is considered the truest act of kindness, one that can never be repaid by the recipient.

When someone dies, a team of Ḥevra Kadisha members is assembled. Men tend to the bodies of men and women to the bodies of women. The team gathers, usually in the funeral home where the body has been sent, puts on protective gear, and says a special prayer for the deceased. They then gently and meticulously wash the body—right down to cleaning the dirt out from under the person's fingernails—and ritually immerse the body in water or pour water over it. Various prayers are said throughout the process.

As I read descriptions of the Tahara ritual, I was struck by the reverence and tenderness that Ḥevra Kadisha members bring to their work. They never turn the body facedown—when they need to wash someone's back, they turn the body on its side. They do not pass anything over the body—if they need to hand something to someone across the table, they walk all the way around. They also take great care to respect the modesty of the deceased, ensuring that the body stays covered at all times, and only uncovering the particular part they are washing and then immediately re-covering it. And once they have finished, they recite a prayer asking the deceased for forgiveness for any inadvertent distress, offense, or embarrassment they may have caused.

Those tending to the body seem to be treating the deceased as if they are somehow still there, aware of what is happening to them. Some Ḥevra Kadisha members even believe the souls of the dead are present, and they see their role as helping those souls transition from this world to the next.* Others speak of the process as being similar to caring for a newborn baby. Just as we lovingly wash, swaddle, and soothe babies when we welcome them to the world, helping them adjust to this new way of being, we do so for the deceased as they depart.

It is "an act that seemed impossibly intimate," said one rabbi about her experience with a Tahara. "I felt an outpouring of tenderness," she recalled, and she found herself thinking, "It's okay, dear. We're here. You're okay."

Once the body has been washed, the deceased is dried and dressed—not in their fanciest or most favorite clothes, but in a simple, hand-sewn outfit consisting of a white cotton or linen shirt and pants without any pockets. Whether the person was rich or poor, renowned or unknown, this has been the Jewish practice for centuries. As one Rabbinic text noted, "When a person enters the world his hands are clenched as though to say 'The whole world is mine, I shall inherit it'; but when he takes leave of it his hands are spread open as though to say 'I have inherited nothing from the world.'" We are all equal in death, and we cannot take anything with us when we go.

GUARDING THE DECEASED UNTIL BURIAL

Once the Tahara is finished, the deceased is not supposed to be left alone. In fact, the body should not be alone at any time before burial. So families arrange for people, ideally friends or fellow congregants, to take turns serving as a "shomer," meaning "guardian," who stays with the body all day and all night long. Centuries ago, the shomer's role probably involved protecting the body from rodents and thieves. Today,

---

* This belief actually has Jewish roots. The Rabbis had a debate about when, exactly, the deceased stopped being able to hear the living. One believed the dead could only hear what was happening until the tomb was closed—another, until the body decomposed.

when we refrigerate bodies securely in funeral homes, the shomer generally just sits quietly near the refrigerator, and the traditional practice is to read from the Book of Psalms.

The role of the shomer took on particular significance in the wake of the September 11th terrorist attacks. Given the magnitude of the destruction, it took workers months to recover the remains of those killed. To ensure that the deceased would not be left alone, Jewish volunteers from across New York City and beyond stepped forward to serve as shomrim (plural of shomer), taking turns sitting in a tent near the refrigerated trucks that housed remains waiting to be identified.

One volunteer, who took the 2:00 A.M. to 6:00 A.M. shift, recalled reading a particular Psalm that is an acrostic—each verse starts with a different letter of the Hebrew alphabet. During cemetery visits, some Jews recite the verses of this Psalm that spell out the name of their loved one. "Since I didn't know whose remains were being brought in," she explained, "I said the whole psalm so as to cover all victims."

Similarly, in the wake of the 2018 terrorist attack at the Tree of Life synagogue in Pittsburgh, the bodies of those who were murdered could not be moved for many hours while the FBI investigated. A group of Jews stayed on-site all night long to guard them and pray for them, ensuring they were never left alone.

These traditions of preparing and guarding the dead are thought of as a mitzvah for the dead. As one of my friends exclaimed when I described the process to him, "It's like an honor guard for every single person!" But these rituals also serve as acts of kindness for the living. Even if the deceased is not aware of the care and respect shown by the Ḥevra Kadisha and the shomrim, the deceased's loved ones certainly are.

THE FUNERAL

Typically, before the funeral starts, mourners will gather together to perform a ritual known as "kriah," which involves making a symbolic tear in one's clothing—ripping a shirt, sweater, or blazer (over the heart if the deceased is a parent, on the other side for other relatives). Kriah can also be done the moment you hear that a loved one has died, or at or after the funeral. The idea is to do it in a moment of intense distress. Kriah is an ancient Jewish practice: In the Torah, when Jacob's sons lead him to think (falsely) that their brother Joseph has been killed, Jacob cries out and rends his garments.

In recent times, finding the ritual of kriah to be unseemly, many Jews began skipping it and instead simply tearing a black ribbon and pinning it to their clothing. But I think this substitution may miss the point. Kriah is *supposed* to be socially outrageous and primal. Mourners are not raising awareness for a cause, they are expressing the sense that their world has been torn apart. Kriah is Judaism's way of providing mourners a controlled outlet for the almost feral despair they may be feeling—the impulse to just shred everything around them.

The point here isn't to try to *protect* mourners from what is happening, but to help them *confront* it. This is also true of the funeral itself, which is not focused on assuaging mourners' anguish by assuring them that their loved one is in a better place. There is no attempt to paper over the magnitude of the loss. Rather, in addition to a handful of prayers and psalms, a Jewish funeral includes a eulogy, the purpose of which is, in the words of the Shulḥan Arukh, the key Jewish law code, "to utter over him [the dead] words which break the heart in order to cause much weeping, and to mention his praise."

When it comes time for the burial, the mourners themselves take turns shoveling dirt into the grave. I did this at my grandmother's funeral, and let me tell you, there is nothing like the hollow sound of hard earth hitting a wooden coffin—a sound that grows duller and duller as the grave is filled. It is the sound of something very real, and very final.

Caring for the Living: The Next Thirty Days or Twelve Months

People often have two unhelpful tendencies in the wake of losing a loved one: to drown in their grief, becoming totally consumed by it . . . or to deny it, stuffing it deep down and keeping busy in the hope of avoiding it.

The Jewish mourning rituals seek to avert both of these impulses, helping mourners face their grief head-on, but also giving them the support they need to keep from being overwhelmed. Judaism provides what author Anita Diamant calls "a kind of itinerary of grief work" consisting of "rituals that give shape to the emotional chaos and break through the terrible isolation of bereavement."

The process Judaism lays out for mourners is intense and time-consuming, so it actually makes sense that Jewish law limits the definition of who is considered a mourner to only immediate family members. It would be cumbersome if we had to undertake all of these obligations for every cousin, aunt, and friend we lost. But some Jews voluntarily perform the mourning rituals even when they're not technically considered mourners. Plenty of people have loved ones with whom they're just as close as their parents, children, spouse, or siblings, and the mourning rituals are available to them as well.

SHIVA

The moment the funeral ends, the process shifts from caring for the dead to caring for the living.

When mourners arrive home from the cemetery, Jewish law instructs them to eat what is known as "the meal of recuperation" prepared by friends or relatives. This is the last thing many mourners want to do. As Rabbi Jack Riemer puts it, "To eat means to live, and you don't really want to live, so the law makes you eat."

Thus begins the shiva, a period of seven days* following the burial when mourners gather daily, generally at the home of the deceased or another family member. During this time, friends and community members visit to offer their condolences, join prayer services with mourners so they can say the Kaddish (which requires a minyan, a group of at least ten Jews), and help create a loving space in which mourners and visitors can share memories of the deceased.

---

* "Shiva" is the Hebrew word for seven, though many Jews shorten the shiva period to three or four days, or even just one day.

The main point of the shiva is to encourage mourners to fully feel and express their emotions. Mourners are not supposed to work, cook, do household chores, have sex, watch TV, study Torah, or even bathe for pleasure (though bathing for hygiene is fine)—all things they might do to distract themselves from their grief. They aren't even supposed to rise to greet visitors or accompany them to the door when they leave, since playing host is another form of distraction. Instead, as Anita Diamant writes, "*Shiva* is for one thing only, and that is exploring the emotional catalog of grief: sorrow, emptiness, regret, relief, guilt, anger, shame, self-pity, remorse."

During shiva, mourners are not expected to put on a brave face, or have a stiff upper lip, or otherwise keep up appearances. It's fine to look exactly as we feel. In fact, the Jewish laws of shiva seem to mandate it, prohibiting shaving, haircutting, wearing freshly washed clothes, and putting on makeup or leather shoes, and instructing mourners to cover mirrors in the house, in part so that they won't be thinking about how they look. Mourners are also supposed to sit on special low stools close to the ground, which is, as Rabbi Maurice Lamm notes in his classic book *The Jewish Way in Death and Mourning,* "an adjustment of one's body to one's emotional state, a lowering of the human frame to the level of his feelings, a symbolic enactment of returning to the earth that swallowed his beloved."

The role of shiva visitors is not to cheer up mourners. "The purpose of the condolence call," Rabbi Lamm explains, "is not to convince the mourner of anything at all." Rather, visitors should simply be fully present with mourners however they are. To that end, Jewish law instructs visitors to wait for mourners to speak first before addressing them. The law seems to anticipate our tendency to say unhelpful things to grieving people—"she's in a better place now" or "you need to be strong for the kids"—and it instructs us to just keep quiet until we're spoken to.

Jewish law even advises visitors not to use the typical "how are you?" kind of greeting to address mourners, preferring something more like "I'm so sorry" and/or a heartfelt hug. After all, how is the mourner supposed to respond to this question? "How am I? Well, let's see, I just lost the love of my life, and I would have thrown myself into the grave with him if my grandkids hadn't been standing there, and I have no idea how I'm going to survive feeling this much pain. And how are *you*?"

In my shiva-attending experience, I've found that it's best to let mourners take the lead. If they don't wish to talk, a long hug or simply sitting quietly beside them can say a great deal. If they wish to speak about the deceased, I listen with great care, ask questions, and if appropriate, share my own memories of their loved ones (families will often put out photos to prompt such sharing). But if mourners wish to speak about something else, that's okay too. Laughing during a shiva is perfectly fine—people sometimes recall happy moments with the deceased—as is numb silence, as is hysterical sobbing. As a visitor, your job is to simply be lovingly present with whatever arises.

SHLOSHIM/THE NEXT TWELVE MONTHS

When the shiva ends, mourners can go back to work. But for the next thirty days, a period known as "shloshim" (which means "thirty"), mourners traditionally continue a number of practices from the shiva, including attending daily prayer services (at a synagogue or elsewhere) where they recite the Kaddish with others (those mourning parents do these practices for twelve months, though they say Kaddish for only eleven of those twelve months). There are three Jewish prayer services a day—in the morning, afternoon, and evening—each of which takes between fifteen and forty-five minutes, and at each of these services, the mourners recite the Kaddish.* Less traditionally observant mourners might say Kaddish just once a week at Shabbat services, or less frequently.

Saying Kaddish regularly is at the heart of Judaism's don't drown/

---

* The latter two are often done together, such that mourners can show up for services twice a day instead of three times.

don't deny approach to mourning. Mourners often find that once they emerge from shiva and return to school, work, and some semblance of regular life, there isn't any space for their grief. It is not appropriate workplace behavior for mourners to stand up in the office each day and announce to everyone that they're still grieving. But that is exactly what we do when we stand up to recite the Kaddish each day in a minyan.

This is a serious time commitment—at least twice a day, we have to stop everything we're doing and find at least nine other Jews to pray with us. By requiring us to acknowledge and create space for our grief like this—whether we want to or not—Judaism makes it hard for us to deny the reality of our loss. It also reminds us that grief does not recede in a linear fashion—we don't say the Kaddish less frequently as the year wears on. Rather, there will be okay days, awful days, and maybe even good days, but every day we will recite the Kaddish with others.

At the same time, saying Kaddish helps keep us from drowning in our grief, both by setting some limits—we can only say it at certain times of day for a certain number of months—and by requiring us to say it in a community that likely understands exactly what we're going through. In fact, when people first show up to a minyan, they're often welcomed by more experienced mourners who show them the ropes. If a mourner doesn't show up for a few days, someone might call to make sure they're okay.

And this support network spans the globe. Just about anywhere you can find Jews, you can usually find a minyan where you can say Kaddish. In a pinch, people have gathered minyans on airplanes, and I've heard of minyans at Grand Central Station in New York and in a trolley car in San Francisco. And when a young lawyer at the law firm where I once worked lost her mother, and her Jewish colleagues realized she was trekking to a synagogue across town each day to say Kaddish, they decided to create a daily minyan for her right in the office.

They weren't a particularly observant bunch, but they collected some prayer books and a mismatched assortment of yarmulkes. And each afternoon, whoever was available would file into a conference room to pray. Much to their surprise, many of them came to look forward to this ritual, finding it a welcome respite from their otherwise hectic days.

At this point, you may be thinking that this Kaddish prayer must be something pretty special, filled with great wisdom about death and the afterlife. But from a surface read, that does not appear to be the case. In fact, this prayer seems to make no sense whatsoever as a liturgy for mourners. That wasn't even its original purpose. Written mainly in Aramaic, the Kaddish was recited during Talmudic times by Rabbis after finishing a study session, and it's not entirely clear how, over the centuries, it came to be associated with mourners.

The text of the prayer is as follows:

Mourner: Magnified and sanctified
may His great name be,
in the world He created by His will.
May He establish His kingdom
in your lifetime and in your days,
and in the lifetime of all the house of Israel,
swiftly and soon—and say: Amen.

All: May His great name be blessed for ever and all time.

Mourner: Blessed and praised, glorified and exalted,
raised and honored, uplifted and lauded
be the name of the Holy One,
blessed be He,
beyond any blessing,
song, praise and consolation
uttered in the world—and say: Amen.
May there be great peace from heaven,
and life for us and all Israel—and say: Amen.
May He who makes peace in His high places,

make peace for us and all Israel—
and say: Amen.

A few things seem to be missing from this prayer . . . like any mention of death, grief, or an afterlife. Instead, this prayer seems to be little more than praise for God, and that is how it has often been understood: as a show of faith in the face of loss.

But I'm not sure this interpretation is necessarily borne out by the text of the prayer. As Rabbi Elie Kaunfer points out, the Kaddish does not say "Magnified and sanctified *is* God's name," but "Magnified and sanctified *may* His great name *be*." Instead of "Blessed and praised, glorified and exalted . . . *is* the name of the Holy One," it's ". . . *be* the name of the Holy one."

So maybe we're not declaring that God's name is *presently* magnified, sanctified, praised, etc.—we're pleading for it to become so. The Kaddish could therefore almost be understood as a challenge to God, a way of saying, "Your name really *isn't* so great and holy to me right now."

This prayer also seems to raise a question: Magnified and sanctified *by whom*? One would assume the mourner, but take another look and you'll see that it actually doesn't specify. So perhaps the Kaddish could be understood as a request for *others* to praise God's name, and thus a declaration by mourners that they are in no place to do so themselves.

Or perhaps the Kaddish isn't a prayer about praising God at all, but rather a prayer to *console* God. This seems to be the point of a moving midrash about Moses' final days in which Moses begs God to let him keep living. Moses' soul also pleads with God, asking not to have to leave Moses' body. But God refuses to relent, and the story concludes, "God kissed Moses on the mouth and drew his soul from him with the kiss. And He [God] wept and said, 'Who will now rise up for me against the evildoers? Who will now stand up for me against the workers of iniquity?'"

With the Kaddish, perhaps we are acknowledging that God is grieved and diminished by the loss of our loved one, just as we are, and we're praying for God to be restored, once again magnified and sanctified. Understood this way, the Kaddish implies that we and God are mourning together.

Or perhaps, as occurred to me when I read the following account from a mourner, the Kaddish actually *is* hyperbolic praise for God, and maybe that's okay. She writes:

> The one thing that had seemed odd was that, in the hours of pain, we were reciting an ode of adoration to God. But one morning, as I was looking at the rising sun, the thought came to me, "How could God be so good to me as to give me such a wonderful mother, this wise and beautiful woman, this living personification of selfless love to her children, and a living example of the saintly person?" And then I understood that the recitation of Kaddish is an ode of Thanksgiving and totally appropriate.

So perhaps the Kaddish is not asking us to praise God *despite* our grief but *because* of our grief, maybe even out of *gratitude* for our grief. Perhaps it's reminding us that, as Queen Elizabeth wrote in a memorial statement about British citizens lost on September 11, "Grief is the price we pay for love." Perhaps with the Kaddish, we're declaring that despite our pain, our love was absolutely worth the price we are now paying, and there is no question that we would do it all over again if we could.

THE REST OF OUR LIVES

Jewish law lays out specific instructions for how those mourning parents should mend the garment they tore when performing kriah: They must do so with a rough stitch such that the tear is still visible. Centuries ago, when people had few articles of clothing, the garment would be worn again, so it would need to be functional. But the fabric could not be mended in a way that made the tear disappear. And as Rabbi David Stern notes, "In time even the rough stitch feels good to the touch, because it has the texture of reality to it—of longing and sorrow and resilience and strength."

This is an apt metaphor for the Jewish approach to the rest of our lives after losing a loved one. After thirty days or eleven months, we stop saying Kaddish every day. But our grief, while hopefully more manageable, does not magically disappear at this point. It will always be with us in some form. Even once the fabric of our life has been sewn back together, the tear is still there.

Many people find the holidays to be especially challenging, with the empty seat at family meals and the feelings of guilt at enjoying celebrations without their loved ones. So I think it's fitting that each year, on four Jewish holidays—Passover, Shavuot, Shemini Atzeret,* and Yom Kippur—there is a special memorial service called "Yizkor," where people gather in synagogues to say prayers honoring the dead.

The word "yizkor" comes from the same Hebrew root as the word "remember," but as Rabbi Immanuel Jakobovits noted, in the Torah, this word isn't just used to mean remembering the past. When God "remembered Noah" and all the animals in the ark, God was moved to end the flood. When God "remembered Abraham," God then rescued his nephew Lot from Sodom. When God "remembered Rachel," God helped her conceive a child. At its best, remembering can be a lifesaving—and life-giving—kind of activity.

In addition to these holiday remembrances, each year, on the anniversary of our loved one's death, we observe their "yahrzeit" (Yiddish for "a year's time") through rituals such as saying Kaddish, giving tzedakah, lighting a twenty-four-hour memorial candle, and visiting their grave.

During cemetery visits, Jews traditionally don't leave flowers, but instead place a small rock on the gravestone. There are many explanations for this, but one that I particularly like is based on an observation made by Rabbi David Wolpe about the traditional Jewish inscription on gravestones: "May his/her soul be bound up in the bond of life." The Hebrew word translated as "bond," Wolpe notes, can also mean "pebble."

---

* Shemini Atzeret is a holiday that occurs at the end of Sukkot.

By putting a pebble on a gravestone, we could be indicating that we take this phrase literally—that as our loved one's body decomposes into the earth, nourishing the plants and animals in the soil, the person is simply becoming a different part of the ecosystem, still very much bound to the world of the living. Or perhaps when we speak of our loved one's soul being "bound up in the bond of life," we're saying that they are still somehow intertwined in our lives, still bound up in the bond of love that connected us, a bond that does not dissolve upon death.

And if none of this works for you, Wolpe also offers the following: "While flowers may be a good metaphor for the brevity of life, stones seem better suited to the permanence of memory. Stones do not die."

WHAT HAPPENS AFTER WE DIE

In my experience, Jews aren't big on talking about the afterlife. I have never once heard a rabbi give a sermon about it. I can't recall ever hearing a Jew say they were behaving a certain way in order to be rewarded, or avoid punishment, after death. And in the books I've read about Judaism, the afterlife is treated as an afterthought, if mentioned at all. That is even true of books about death. Rabbi Lamm's book on death and mourning is about three hundred pages long, and it includes a grand total of eighteen pages on the afterlife.

Judaism is very much a this-world-focused religion. As Rabbi Abraham Joshua Heschel notes, "There is no craving for death in the history of Jewish piety . . . Earthly life, mortal life, is precisely the arena where the covenant between God and man must be fulfilled . . . Life here and now is the task."

It is also true, however, that for thousands of years, Judaism *has* embraced the idea of an afterlife—many ideas, actually. Bodily resurrection? Yup. Immortality of the soul? Check. You live on in other people's memories? Definitely. Reincarnation? Sure, why not? (Seriously.) Yet while Jews seem to be in general agreement about burial and mourning rituals, there isn't much consensus on the details of any of these afterlife ideas, and I often found myself confused.

Here is an attempt to offer brief accounts of a few of the key Jewish conceptions of the afterlife as best as I can understand them:

THE TORAH'S DEPICTION OF THE AFTERLIFE: YOU DIE, YOU'RE BURIED, AND THAT'S ABOUT IT

Judaism's here-on-earth focus is evident in the Torah, where when the Matriarchs, Patriarchs, and Moses die, they are buried and mourned . . . and that's about it. There are allusions to a place called "Sheol," which seems to be some kind of underground pit where people go after death, but the details are hazy. With a few possible exceptions, which became important in later Jewish thought, this view is maintained in the rest of the Hebrew Bible as well. All rewards and punishments from God—rainfall/drought, children/infertility, military victory/defeat—are meted out in this world, not in any kind of afterlife.

The Torah doesn't even conceive of human beings as having spiritual souls that are separate from their physical bodies and that continue on once the body dies. Rather, as Rabbi Neil Gillman explained in *The Death of Death,* a book about the evolution of Jewish thought on the afterlife, each of us is "a single entity" animated by a Divine spark. This spark is a breath of life like that which God breathed into Adam after creating him from the dust. Unlike a "soul," which gives a person their unique personality and consciousness, this Divine spark/breath is entirely impersonal. It is a generic life-giving energy—and when it leaves your body, you die.

A TALMUDIC CONCEPTION OF THE AFTERLIFE: RESURRECTION

The Torah's conception of death makes for a difficult theological row to hoe. Plenty of bad things were happening to good Jews in the centuries after the Torah was canonized. The second century B.C.E. was a particularly rough time, as religious Jews appear to have found themselves in conflict with both their Greek rulers and Jewish reformists who were embracing Greek values and lifestyles. Many were persecuted for their insistence on adhering to Jewish law. While Jews had largely blamed themselves for the destruction of the First Temple, regarding this tragedy as punishment for their sins, Gillman notes, "Now, however, pious Jews were being persecuted, precisely because of their piety." The rewards for good behavior did not seem to be coming in this lifetime.

Two afterlife ideas eventually took hold in Judaism that would help resolve this problem. One was resurrection, the belief that God will one day raise people's bodies from the dead. The other was the immortality of the soul, which likely came from Greek philosophy and holds that we have a mortal, flesh-and-blood body and a nonbodily, immortal soul. When we die, the body disintegrates, never to rise again, but the soul continues on for eternity.

Rabbi Gillman explains that the Rabbis took these two ideas and wove them together into the belief that after we die, our souls survive, and at some point in the future, God will resurrect our bodies and reunite them with our souls. The Rabbis held a variety of views about the logistics of how this would all happen, but it seems to go something along the lines of the following:

1. We die.
2. If we were good, our souls go to a lovely place called Gan Eden, a heavenly Garden of Eden. If we were bad, our souls go to a terrible place called Gehenna, where they are purified through very unpleasant punishments (a process that lasts for a maximum of twelve months*). Once our souls are purified, they go to Gan Eden, where they reside until resurrection.
3. The Messiah comes, God resurrects our bodies and reunites them with our souls, and we all wind up in the Land of Israel.

---

* Note that this timing is actually connected to the length of time Jews say Kaddish for their parents. Jewish tradition held that saying Kaddish for your loved ones could help them complete their purification process in Gehenna more quickly. But because none of us should assume that our parents were bad and went to Gehenna, or that if they did, they were so bad that they required a full twelve months of Kaddish to help them get out, we say Kaddish for only eleven months rather than twelve.

4. There is some kind of judgment by God as to who has a place in the World to Come.

5. We enjoy existence in the World to Come. The Rabbis had a range of opinions as to what this would look like. One Rabbi claimed that in the World to Come, people would have no need for food, sex, and money, and would sit around wearing crowns "enjoying the splendor of the Divine Presence." Others claimed that the World to Come would be a utopia where each grape would produce thirty jugs of wine, and trees would produce new fruit daily—as would people (women would conceive and give birth to babies in the same day).

This new understanding of what happens after death rescued the reward-and-punishment aspect of God, such that Jews who were devout but still suffered greatly during their lives could reassure themselves that they would be rewarded in the World to Come. And this afterlife idea still endures today among many traditionally observant Jews. It is also featured in the siddur in the Amidah prayer, which states that God revives the dead and keeps faith with "those who sleep in the dust."

A KABBALISTIC IDEA OF THE AFTERLIFE: REINCARNATION

Neither the Hebrew Bible nor the Talmud mentions reincarnation, and it's not clear how this idea made its way into Jewish thinking. But by the twelfth century, Kabbalists seem to have embraced it.

There are a variety of Kabbalistic conceptions of reincarnation, some of them quite esoteric. But the basic idea is that our souls aren't perfected during our lifetimes. When we die, God assigns our soul to the body of someone about to be born,* thus giving it a chance to atone

---

* Though in some cases, the Kabbalists believed, souls would enter the bodies of people who are already living. Righteous souls would enter people's bodies and help them achieve something extraordinary, perform a certain mitzvah, or just get through a difficult time. Wicked souls, known as "dybbuks," would enter people's bodies and afflict them with conditions that we would today likely diagnose and treat as mental illness.

for—and be punished for—errors in its past life. Souls continue from body to body, becoming increasingly perfect by performing the mitzvot they neglected in past lives, until the resurrection. Over time, a single soul may inhabit many bodies, and one person may wind up with "soul sparks" from a number of different souls.

Reincarnation thus offers the following answer to the theodicy problem: A person who behaves perfectly may still have a life filled with tragedy and suffering because their soul committed sins in a past life and is now being punished. That is the unfortunate consequence of souls working to perfect themselves: The people they inhabit sometimes pay the price.

MODERN AFTERLIFE CONCEPTIONS: IMMORTALITY OF THE SOUL AND LIVING ON THROUGH OTHER PEOPLE'S MEMORIES AND DEEDS

In the nineteenth and twentieth centuries, many Jews began rejecting traditional beliefs such as resurrection as irrational superstitions, instead embracing the idea of immortality of the soul: We die, our bodies disintegrate, and our disembodied souls live on. Or they rejected the idea of an afterlife entirely, choosing instead to believe that we simply live on in people's memories. When speaking or writing about those who have died, Jews often say, "May his/her memory be a blessing."

This idea used to strike me as a consolation prize afterlife notion, one to which you resigned yourself if you couldn't talk yourself into believing in one of the more reassuring options. But then I learned about the scientific research indicating that recalling a memory is not like looking at a photograph, which is unchanging. Rather, each time we access a memory, our brains actually alter it in some way.

This isn't all that surprising. As we grow and change, so does our understanding of past events. When we were teenagers, our memories of our parents making us go to bed early when we were younger may have been tinged with annoyance. But when we recall those memories as adults who understand that our parents' bedtime rules reflected their loving concern for our well-being, our brains may tweak those memories, transforming them into happy ones, flooded with affection. So while our parents may be deceased, our memories of them aren't just static snapshots that pop up in our brains, but a way of continuing to actively engage with them long after they're gone.

Another modern afterlife idea is that we live on in the deeds of the people we touched, and all those affected by those deeds, who then go on to affect others with their deeds in an endless pay-it-forward chain. This idea is beautifully captured in a Ḥasidic text that asks how we'll be able to recognize our loved ones when we're reunited with them in the World to Come. If they were ill or injured when they died, will they be restored to health? Will they have aged since we knew them? The text responds, "We will recognize them because they will be clothed and cloaked in the good deeds we do in their name."

This belief is implicit in the Jewish tradition of drafting an "ethical will," which is a letter outlining the values we wish to pass on to our heirs. For centuries, Jews have left behind these documents offering advice to their descendants on everything from the number of children they should have to the good deeds they should do.

Rabbi Lamm includes in his book the ethical will of his grandfather Rabbi Yehoshua Baumol, who encourages each of his heirs to be someone who "loves all people, ever judges them leniently, thinking always: 'if I were in their place I would possibly have done as they did, and therefore why should I be angry with them?'" Rabbi Baumol then advises, "The main thing is to be good to all and compassionate to all; at the least, to be unable to tolerate their pain and to rejoice in their welfare and tranquility."

WHAT I MAKE OF ALL OF THIS

There is no such thing as complete closure when someone we love dies. As grief expert Dr. Donna Schuurman writes, "I look at rituals not as closure—I don't think the word closure goes with death—I look at them as punctuation." The best we can do is pause, create space for our loss, and find a way to live our lives without our loved one. And the

Jewish death and mourning rituals seem to do an excellent job of guiding people through that process.

As for Jewish thinking on the afterlife, when I view it prescriptively—as prescribing various conceptions that I can accept or reject—it feels vague and unpersuasive to me (though I appreciate that we've more or less agreed that there's no permanent hell—that idea never caught on in Judaism). I understand that people needed something to rescue the all-powerful, all-knowing, all-good, reward-and-punishment idea of God when it broke down in the face of life's realities. But our attempts to do so with various afterlife conceptions feel like efforts to shore up one idea I don't buy with a bunch of other ideas I don't buy.

When I view our afterlife ideas descriptively, however—as describing what my ancestors yearned for—I'm moved. I can understand why, when facing scourges like hunger and infant mortality, they dreamed of a World to Come with trees bearing fruit and women bearing children on a daily basis. And had I lived in times when so many people were dying untimely deaths from disease and persecution, I too would have wanted to believe that my departed loved ones would get another, better chance at existence.

I once studied with a very traditional Orthodox rabbi, a thoughtful man who had endless patience for my vehement, and not always polite, objections to some of his teachings. He had the misfortune of being the one to teach me about the concept of Gehenna.

"Are you kidding me?" I asked, incredulous. "You're telling me that Judaism has some kind of temporary, twelve-month rehab hell where people go to atone for their sins? And mourners can help their loved ones get out of there more quickly by saying Kaddish? Do you hear how crazy this sounds?"

He tried to respond, but I wouldn't let him, becoming more and more agitated over the sheer absurdity of what he was saying. "This is what Judaism has to offer on the afterlife? Seriously?"

Finally, he interrupted me, his voice uncharacteristically raised. "Sarah, Sarah, all I'm telling you is that Judaism says that when you die, you're not lost. The people you love who have died are not lost."

When it comes to Jewish ideas about the afterlife, I think that what we intuit meets what we need—and that overlap is the feeling that our loved ones are not lost. To get there, we don't have to take any of these ideas literally. Rather, we can understand them as metaphors or as ways to allude to something we sense and yearn for but cannot logically defend. For example, the Talmud claims that when we recall an insight from a deceased scholar, that scholar's lips are moving in the grave. While I don't think a corpse is literally mouthing words, I share the sense that the dead can "speak" to us in this way, continuing to impart their wisdom long after they have left us.

I also appreciate the metaphorical power of the reincarnation idea. A college classmate of mine who was one of the most outstanding people I've ever known—he was awarded a Rhodes Scholarship and spent countless hours volunteering with the Red Cross and other organizations—died of cancer the year after we graduated. One of his many close friends delivered a eulogy at his memorial service in which she said something like "I felt as if our two souls had been plucked from the same basket." This seems to be what the Kabbalistic idea of "soul sparks" is getting at—that feeling of discovering a kindred spirit with whom you share a sacred spark. I'm also moved by the Kabbalistic idea that people who feel called to convert to Judaism have souls that previously resided in the body of a Jew. I definitely know Jews by choice who, long before they converted, already felt like they had a Jewish soul.

And while I don't buy the resurrection idea, I think it gestures at something important. It may be a failure of imagination on my part, but immortality of the soul doesn't do much for me. I'm pretty wedded to my own consciousness, and I don't relish the idea of becoming a disembodied soul. I like having thoughts and feelings, and for that, I need a body. I also appreciate, as many commentators have noted, that resurrection places real value on our bodies, affirming that they are far more than merely sin-prone flesh containers for our souls.

I'm probably most comfortable with the idea that we live on in people's memories and deeds. During my time in the White House, I thought often of my grandmother who died in 2011 at the age of ninety-nine. She cared passionately about social justice and gave so much of her modest income to charity that she once got audited by the IRS. She had always wanted to attend law school and go into politics, but as a woman born in 1912, she never had those opportunities. Just two generations later, I have a law degree, and for eight years I walked through the gates of the White House each morning to get to work. My grandmother didn't live to hear many of the speeches I'm most proud of having written, but I feel that her compassion and righteous indignation somehow live on in their words.

When I write, I also sometimes think of my junior- and senior-year English teacher from high school. A bit of an iconoclast, he had little patience for stilted, five-paragraph-essay prose. He would instead insist that we write in our own authentic voices, requiring us to always use the "I" voice in our papers. None of this "one might think" or "it is believed that" nonsense. "Who's this 'one'?" he would bellow. "Who's doing the 'believing' here? It's *you*! So write '*I* think' and '*I* believe!'" He died of brain cancer in 2013, but as I sit here typing these words that are very much in my own voice, a voice I discovered in his classes, I do not think he is lost.

But ultimately, I agree with a sentiment attributed to Kafka that "the meaning of life is that it ends." And I appreciate the advice from Psalms to "number our days, that we may gain a heart of wisdom."

I used to wonder why, when people were so often trying to kill us, we didn't seek to comfort ourselves by making the afterlife our primary focus. In some ways, that might have been the more humane thing to do. But we never made that choice. Maybe that's one of the reasons why we're still here—because we refused to give up on this world or devalue this life, even if we didn't always get as much of it as we would have liked.

I share these thoughts and opinions with no small amount of humility since, like everyone else, I obviously have no idea what happens next.

Plenty of people I know have confided that they sometimes feel the presence of loved ones they have lost, and I'm deeply moved by these accounts.

I'm also sobered by a fable written by Rabbi Y. M. Tuckachinsky that depicts a set of twins in their mother's womb. For months, they live a quiet, pleasant life, but sensing that things are about to change, they wonder what's in store.

The more spiritually minded twin insists that they will continue on to another life, "a great new world, a whole new realm of being . . . There we will be able to see for great distances, and we will hear through these two things that we have on the sides of our heads! There our feet will be straightened and eventually we will learn how to walk upon them!"

The other, more hard-headed twin thinks this is all ridiculous, retorting that when they leave the womb, "Our world will collapse and sink into oblivion. No more. Nothing. Black void. An end to consciousness. Forgotten. This may not be a comforting thought, but it is the only logical and realistic one."

In this story, I'm definitely more like the second twin, clinging to my current existence, fearful that there is nothing good on the other side.* I hope I'm wrong, but again, none of us really knows.

What we do know, and what Judaism affirms, is that, as it says in the biblical Song of Songs, "Love is strong as death." We never stop loving those we've lost, and in some way they are always with us. But our focus is on this world, this life. That is what Judaism tells us: To choose life so that we may live.

---

* Though I appreciate that worrying about what will happen after I die is sort of like worrying about what was happening before I was born. My prebirth existence/nonexistence doesn't keep me up at night, and maybe I should try to feel the same way about what is beyond the other end of my life.

Again, Why Bother with Judaism?

I f you are Jewish or considering becoming Jewish, this is probably the moment when it would make sense for me to tell you how to *do* Judaism— to prescribe a regimen of Jewish practice for you, listing out which prayers you should learn or instructing you to start celebrating Shabbat.

But as I'm sure is now obvious, I'm still trying to figure out my own Jewish practice, and I have no business telling anyone else how to be Jewish. Instead, I wrote this book in the hope of inspiring you to explore this question for yourself. As my friend Abby Pogrebin notes, "It's a quintessential Jewish act: seeking, grappling. If you're reaching, it's because you believe there's something to grab hold of." By sharing what I've found in my own search, I'm hoping I've shown you that there's something for you to grab hold of in Judaism—that the seeking and grappling will be worth the effort.

But I also wrote this book because I believe that through our individual seeking and grappling, we don't just *discover,* but collectively help *create,* the kind of Judaism that is worth grabbing hold of. From Rabbinic Judaism to Kabbalah, Ḥasidism, and Reform Judaism, at moments of upheaval for the Jewish people—when the religion they were practicing no longer made sense in the context of their times—Jews have created new forms of Judaism to meet the needs of their souls and the circumstances of their lives.

We find ourselves at another time of transition right now. Over the past couple of centuries, and particularly in recent decades, Jews have experienced seismic cultural, political, and demographic shifts. And our engagement with Judaism—the Jewish institutions we join (or don't), the practices and rituals we undertake (or don't), the Jewish learning we do (or don't do)—will inform a larger conversation about the Judaism we're practicing today and the Judaism our great-grandchildren will (or won't) practice generations from now.

Like it or not, Judaism tends to be in the image of the Jews who most actively participate in this conversation; its contours are shaped by responses to their yearnings, questions, and demands. Each of us has the power to vote with our voices and our feet for the kind of Judaism we wish to experience. But that requires us to show up—to classes, services, and gatherings of all kinds—and to do some learning, questioning, and wrestling. To undertake this effort, we must first decide that there is something worth showing up for—something in which we're willing to invest our time, trust, and hope.

That is the paradox at the heart of this book: To create the kind of Judaism that is worth choosing, we need to start by choosing Judaism.

To understand the moment of transformation in which we find ourselves, it's helpful to put it in historical context. Rabbi Benay Lappe, who runs a yeshiva called SVARA in Chicago,* offers a useful framework, which she calls the "crash theory."

---

* SVARA is "a traditionally radical yeshiva" that provides serious Talmud learning for queer and queer-minded people—people who are in some way outsiders and approach Judaism with fresh perspectives.

Lappe argues that each of us has a master story about our life that explains who we are and what we're meant to be doing in the world. But inevitably, that master story crashes: Circumstances change, we change, and the old story no longer makes sense. This happens again and again throughout our lives: Your parents have always wanted you to be a doctor, and you like science and are interested in health and wellness, so you grow up planning to fulfill their dream for you . . . then you take a cooking class, absolutely love it, and decide that you really want to be a chef. Crash! You're happily married, excited to spend the rest of your life with your spouse . . . then one day you find out that your spouse has been cheating on you. For years. Crash!

When your master story crashes, Lappe explains, you have three options:

Option One: Deny the crash and cling to the master story. Grit your teeth through medical school. Pretend not to know about your spouse's infidelity and do your best to carry on. While you get to keep the positive aspects of the master story—your parents' approval, the benefits of married life—you have to suppress a fundamental part of yourself and quash some powerful feelings.

Option Two: Accept the crash, totally reject the old master story, and create an entirely new master story. Drop out of high school, get a job in a restaurant, and focus solely on developing your culinary skills. Divorce your spouse on the spot, decide marriage is a worthless institution, and vow to remain single for the rest of your life. The problem here is that you end up throwing the baby out with the bathwater, losing aspects of the master story that were meaningful for you.

Option Three: Don't deny the crash, but don't wholesale reject the master story either. Take the crash and use it to reexamine the master story—to figure out what works and what doesn't—and then rewrite the master story accordingly: You realize that you miss studying science and are still interested in wellness, so you attend culinary school while also taking classes in biology and nutrition at a nearby community college, and you start your own restaurant devoted to healthy eating. You realize that you like being in a committed relationship, so you try couples counseling, and when that doesn't work, you get a divorce, take some time to heal, and then try to find another partner.

As Lappe explains, religions, including Judaism, also have master stories that crash: Up until the first century, Judaism's master story revolved around worshipping God by making sacrifices at a Temple in Jerusalem. Then the Romans destroyed the Temple. Crash!

In the wake of this crash, notes Lappe, Jews went with one of three options:

Some Jews—including the Temple Priests, who resisted challenges to their power, and Jews known as the "zealots," who insisted on duking it out with the Romans until the bitter end—went with Option One and clung to the master story.

Most Jews went with Option Two and rejected the master story: They abandoned Judaism and assimilated into the Roman Empire.

Various groups of Jews, including the Rabbis, proposed Option Threes. They accepted the crash, realizing that now that the Temple was gone, they would have to rework the master story. The Rabbis' Option Three—which was based on study and rituals performed in homes and synagogues—caught on and eventually became the new master story.

Rabbinic Judaism, Lappe observes, has been remarkably durable, continuing to evolve for about eighteen hundred years through a series of minicrashes (crusades, expulsions, etc.). But then came the Emancipation (the movement in the eighteenth and nineteenth centuries to give Jews in Europe full citizenship). No longer restricted to isolated ghettos, Jews could participate much more fully in secular life, attending universities and pursuing various professions. Lappe argues that these changes precipitated the second major crash for Judaism—one which we're still reeling from today—and once again, Jews chose one of three options.

Some Jews went with Option One and clung to the master story, continuing to live in insular communities, refusing to engage in secular society, and resisting changes to their traditional way of life.

Some Jews went with Option Two, abandoning Judaism and doing their best to assimilate into broader society, even converting to Christianity.

Other Jews got to work creating Option Threes—ways of practicing Judaism that would preserve their traditions but also allow them to participate in modern life. According to Lappe, initial post-Emancipation Option Threes included Reform Judaism, Conservative Judaism, Orthodoxy, and Zionism. And in recent decades, there have been new challenges to those Option Threes, and Jews have been scrambling to come up with new Option Threes in response.

The Holocaust was obviously also a serious crash to Judaism, one which revealed the utter falsity of the post-Emancipation narrative that Jews could assimilate safely into European society and become accepted as full and equal citizens. And it represented a massive crash to Jewish theology, calling into question the very idea of a God who loves and protects the Jewish people.

Another challenge to the Jewish master narrative, I would argue, has to do with Israel.

The biblical Land of Israel has always been central to Judaism. It is at the core of the Jewish founding story. For millennia, it has been the subject of countless Jews' love, devotion, and yearning—even today, we still end our Passover seders by declaring, "Next year in Jerusalem!" And for many Jews, the founding of the State of Israel in 1948 represented the fulfillment of their dream of returning to their ancestral homeland and establishing a state where they would no longer be at the mercy of those who wished to persecute, or even annihilate them.

In the wake of the Holocaust, as the Jewish educator Avraham Infeld notes, the word "Jewish" was frequently followed by the word "refugee"—"there were Jewish refugees everywhere." But with the founding of Israel, which offers birthright citizenship to all Jews, it is essentially no longer possible for a Jew to be stateless. Israel's founding can thus be understood both as a response to the crash of Emancipation and its failed promise (as reflected in the Holocaust)—and as a crash to the master narrative of Jews as a defenseless, stateless people.

Having a state has in many ways been a blessing—modern Israel is a diverse (and raucous) democracy; a hub of technological innovation; and a place where Jewish culture, holidays, and learning are at the center of life. But statehood has also been a challenge, particularly when it comes to the anguishing, decades-long conflicts between Israelis and Palestinians, and Israel and the Arab states that surround it. These issues are mind-bogglingly complicated, involving history, politics, religion, economics, and demographics, among other factors. But too often, the conversation around Israel fails to reflect its complexity, instead devolving into charged exchanges of one-sided talking points and vicious personal attacks.

In recent years, the policies of Israel's government—settlement expansion in the West Bank; the daily treatment of Palestinians; the control that ultra-Orthodox rabbis have over religious affairs, including marriage and conversion to Judaism—have left many Jews, including me, feeling deeply dismayed. As has the disproportionate left-wing focus on singling out and condemning Israel—both here in America, particularly on college campuses, and in Europe and elsewhere—which often disregards the threats of terrorism Israel faces, sometimes amounts to denying Israel's right to exist, and can shade into antisemitism.

Like many Jews, I find myself frustrated with the divisiveness around Israel in the Jewish community. And I'm not a fan of the kind of single-issue Judaism that is focused entirely on supporting Israel, or entirely on criticizing Israel, sometimes at the expense of other Jewish values and concerns. I believe that truly loving and caring about Israel requires grasping the complexities of its existence*—its successes and its shortcomings—and being able to recognize multiple truths and hold strong, conflicting feelings.

I think you can believe that Israel's founding and flourishing is a

---

* This is why I am not focusing more on Israel in this book. To do so properly would require an entire book at the very least, and this is not that book.

modern miracle, one that fills you with pride and awe . . . and also be heartbroken and deeply troubled about the Palestinians who lost their homes and land and became refugees themselves. You can be moved by Jews' connection to the land on which Israel was established . . . while acknowledging that Palestinians have a connection to that land as well. And you can be grateful that Jews have a state, knowing that we've never been safe without one . . . while also being sobered by the pitfalls that come with that responsibility.

Yet another crash to the Jewish master narrative has to do with demographics.

Judaism has traditionally revolved around families and communities. Many of our values, such as our emphasis on ḥesed and tzedakah, presume the existence of a community of which we are part and to which we are obligated. And our holidays, life cycle rituals, and prayer services are generally family and community occasions. In fact, other than the mourning rituals, there are no traditional Jewish life cycle rituals designed to celebrate or support milestones in the life of a single adult who does not have children.

Decades ago, most American Jews married other Jews and raised Jewish children. And synagogues—long the centers of Jewish communities—traditionally focused on meeting the needs of these families.

The problem is that many Jews no longer belong to such families. (Crash!)

Only half of American Jews are currently married (the same as the overall American adult population). And among non-Orthodox American Jews who've gotten married since 2000, the intermarriage rate is 72 percent. Let me repeat that: *72 percent of non-Orthodox American Jews are marrying non-Jews.**

---

* Note: A marriage where the non-Jewish spouse converts is *not* an interfaith marriage since both partners are now Jewish. A couple is considered to be in an interfaith marriage only if the non-Jewish spouse does not convert.

As for children, only 39 percent of American Jews ages twenty-five to fifty-four (excluding ultra-Orthodox Jews) have any children at home.

In response to these trends, many synagogues have adjusted their approach, making concerted efforts to reach out to interfaith couples, and a survey conducted in 2017 found that 85 percent of Reform and Reconstructionist rabbis now perform interfaith weddings (the Orthodox and Conservative movements still do not allow their rabbis to do so). But while the synagogues I've encountered are eager to welcome congregants of all family backgrounds, many still feel like a poor fit for unmarried Jews like me who have aged out of the young singles group and don't have kids to send to Hebrew school or bring to "Tot Shabbat." So it's not surprising that while 39 percent of married Jews belong to a synagogue, just 22 percent of unmarried Jews do.

Furthermore, in part due to intermarriage, conversion, and adoption, there is a significant population of Jews of color in America— 11.2 percent by one estimate, 12 to 15 percent by another[*]—including rabbis, lay leaders, and congregants in communities across the country. And their experiences in synagogues and other Jewish spaces are sometimes not amazing. Being asked "Who are you here with?" gets really old, especially when the answer is "Myself." Ditto for being asked "When did you become Jewish?" or "How are you Jewish?" when the answer is "Born this way" or "None of your business." And being told "Oh, so you're only *half* Jewish" when the word "half" is said in a tone that implies "not really" or "less than" also doesn't help.

Synagogues are certainly not the only forms of Jewish community. But it doesn't appear that the many Jews who have declined to join

---

[*] Note that whether Sephardi and Mizraḥi Jews are counted as Jews of color in surveys depends on how they choose to self-identify. And whether and how Jews of color are counted in general depends on whether and how surveys ask about race and ethnicity in the first place. Unfortunately, Jewish population studies are inconsistent in how they approach these issues, which may well result in undercounting Jews of color.

congregations have all found vibrant Jewish communities elsewhere.* In addition, here in America, declining religiosity and participation in communal organizations are ominous signs for a community-based religion like Judaism. Though while traditional piety may be waning, Jews' hunger for meaning and spiritual connection does not seem to have abated.

So the question is, can we come up with an Option Three Judaism that welcomes Jews of all different backgrounds—and their partners and families of all different backgrounds as well? That doesn't turn off Jews who wish to have a more complex, less polarized conversation about Israel? That offers an approach to theology that, as Rabbi Yitz Greenberg heartbreakingly put it, is "credible in the presence of the burning children"? That provides something more meaningful than secularism and individualism?

In other words, can we create an Option Three Judaism that is responsive to the needs and yearnings of . . . well . . . Jews?

In his book about the Talmud, Jonathan Rosen calls the transition from Temple Judaism to Rabbinic Judaism, which happened over many years, "one of the greatest acts of translation in human history." I can't say how the transition from pre-Emancipation to post-Emancipation, post-Holocaust, post-founding of Israel, etc., Judaism will compare in magnitude. But I imagine that it will also require a great act of translation. And I cannot begin to convey how challenging I think this will be.

For decades, countless Jewish professionals,† educators, rabbis, and others have been coming up with creative ways to translate Judaism.

---

* Thirty-one percent of American Jews belong to a synagogue and 18 percent to a non-synagogue Jewish organization—and there is some overlap between those two categories such that 63 percent of American Jews do *not* belong to either a synagogue or a Jewish organization.

† The term "Jewish professionals" is often used to refer to people who work in Jewish organizations and institutions.

They have been reviving centuries-old practices like hitbodedut and meditation; reimagining holiday celebrations and life cycle rituals; reclaiming traditions like Shabbat; and developing new approaches to studying Jewish texts. They have created Torah wilderness programs, Jewish social justice initiatives, and independent Jewish congregations that have taken innovative approaches to prayer and spirituality.

As I'm sure is now obvious, I am among the most enthusiastic fans—and grateful beneficiaries—of these initiatives. They have made Judaism come alive for me and countless other modern Jews, and I think they are vital to the Jewish future. But I also worry that efforts like these don't always address a more fundamental problem, one that is not particularly sexy and is tremendously difficult to solve: lack of basic Jewish literacy.

Jewish leaders have been raising the alarm about this issue and working to address it for decades, founding and funding Jewish Day schools,* investing in new approaches to Hebrew school, sponsoring adult education programs, and more. Like these leaders, I believe that Jewish literacy is not just one challenge among many, but rather the defining challenge we face, one that looms over every effort we make to translate Judaism for Jews today.

Before I had basic Jewish literacy, I found it difficult to have meaningful experiences with Jewish rituals, texts, and events. I simply didn't have the context or background to understand or appreciate them. Even the most beautiful Shabbat service or dynamic Talmud study session had only a fraction of its potential impact when I didn't understand the point of Shabbat or comprehend the prayers I was reciting and had no idea what the Talmud was or why studying it was important.

Just consider the phrase "the Rabbis said." Say that to a beginner, and you may wind up with a conversation along the following lines:

---

* These are schools that have both a secular curriculum (math, English, science, etc.) and a Jewish curriculum (Hebrew, Torah, Talmud, etc.). The children who attend them tend to come from more traditionally observant families.

Beginner: Wait, who are the Rabbis?

You: Sorry, I should have explained that—they're the scholars who saved Judaism by retranslating it after the Temple was destroyed.

Beginner: The Temple?

You: Oh, right, so two thousand years ago, Judaism revolved around making animal sacrifices at a massive temple in Jerusalem.

Beginner: *What?* Why were Jews sacrificing animals?

You: Well, the Torah laid out a number of mitzvot specifying that animal sacrifices were necessary to worship God.

Beginner: Okay, I know the Torah is the thing on the scrolls in a synagogue, but what exactly is it? And what are mitzvot?

You'll recall that it took me two entire chapters just to explain the meaning of that one phrase: "the Rabbis said."

For me, acquiring a Judaism 101 level of knowledge was like acquiring a net in which I could catch and hold on to Jewish experiences, rather than watching them slip by me, leaving only a shallow impression.

I've also found that having basic Jewish literacy can be a foundation for meaningful interactions with Jews whose practice of Judaism is wildly different from my own. I may not follow Jewish law the way my traditionally observant friends do, but when one of them shares a Hasidic teaching that she loves, or a passage of Talmud that moves her, I have a frame of reference in which to receive what she is telling me, and I may even recognize and already love that story or text myself. I can share with another friend how moved I am by the moment at the burning bush when, after God instructs Moses to rescue the Israelites, Moses protests that he is "slow of speech and slow of tongue," and God responds: "Who gives man speech?" To me, it seems like God is reassuring Moses by telling him, "Who do you think formed that mouth of yours that you're so ashamed of? You were created like this!" My friend will know exactly what I'm talking about, and perhaps also be moved. This is something we share.

There are plenty of divisions—some of them quite fraught—within the Jewish community over how we understand and honor our traditions. But I think the nineteenth-century German-Jewish poet Heinrich Heine made a crucial point when he referred to the Hebrew Bible as "the portable homeland" of the Jewish people.* Even if we've wandered in very different directions, perhaps our sacred texts are a place to which we can all return.

But just learning the basics can be a serious challenge. Each aspect of Judaism is connected to every other aspect of Judaism, and I found that I couldn't really understand the fundamentals of Judaism—holidays, life cycle rituals, prayer, ethics, theology—until I had a basic understanding of Jewish history, the Torah, and the Talmudic process of interpretation. I once complained to a rabbi with whom I was studying that to learn about Judaism, I felt like I needed to read hundreds of books, and read them all at the same time, and even then I would still hardly know anything. "Yes," he replied. "Welcome to the club."

I am a reasonably competent person. I like to think I'm no one's fool. But Judaism often makes me feel foolish, and learning about Judaism as an adult was the second hardest intellectual challenge I have ever undertaken.

The hardest was trying to write about it.

Good writing and storytelling require sacrificing some amount of precision and nuance (though never accuracy) for the sake of clarity, but that is often not the Jewish way. In fact, Judaism traditionally goes in the opposite direction—diving deep into the weeds, striving to be more and more precise and nuanced. And as I wrote, I constantly worried that I was misunderstanding or oversimplifying things or missing some text or counterargument that would undermine whatever point I was making.

In the White House, every speech I wrote was reviewed by fact-checkers, who would scrub every line, and I did my best to replicate that process with this book, asking numerous scholars and rabbis of all denominations to review it. In a moment of particular anxiety, I told

---

* This statement is particularly interesting coming from Heine, who converted to Christianity in an attempt to improve his career prospects.

one of them that I planned to reread the Torah one more time to triple-check my summary of it. "You'd better read the entire Talmud too," he replied, with mock seriousness. "And the later commentaries as well."

Even if that were possible, it would present a new problem. I found that the more I learned, the less clear and coherent I became when writing about Judaism. I found myself beginning to sound like some of the policy experts I worked with in the White House, slipping into jargon, getting lost in the details, and missing the beating heart.

I do not have any solutions to the difficulties of translating Judaism, and I do not think there are any shortcuts to Jewish literacy. This is a four-thousand-year-old tradition that values scholarship and urges us to think for ourselves, and there is a lot of material to sort through. In my experience, the only way to learn is to simply do the work. And that doesn't just mean reading books and studying Jewish texts. There are countless ways to learn about Judaism. We can do so through music, art, theater, poetry, and literature, as well as by celebrating Jewish holidays and life cycle rituals; traveling and living in Israel and Jewish communities around the world; trying out various spiritual practices and ethical practices like Mussar; and simply asking questions—lots and lots of questions. In the appendix to this book, I share some of the books, online resources, and organizations that were most helpful to me when I started exploring or that I wish I had known about back then.

There is no one right way to engage with Judaism—we just have to dive in and get started. We can't leave the future of Judaism solely to rabbis, scholars, and Jewish professionals. While experts can certainly lead the way, the rest of us have to participate too, because if only a small number of highly committed Jews are involved in creating Option Three while the rest of us show up a few times a year or not at all, we may not like what they create.

Also, Judaism needs fresh voices and outsider perspectives. In his book about the future of the Jewish people, *God Is in the Crowd,* Tal Keinan cites a Hebrew proverb that states, "It is the new guest who sees the home's faults." Having grown up with no formal Jewish education, he notes, "my own approach to the home of Judaism was originally that of a guest."

I too approached Judaism as a guest. In my Introduction to Judaism classes, I often related more to the students who were converting than to their Jewish partners who were taking the course to support them. And I can tell you that guests don't just notice a home's flaws, but also its beauty—all the unique and lovely features that its inhabitants take for granted. I think we need more Jews and others to come to Judaism as guests and help make it their—and our—home.

So while I can't tell you how to practice Judaism, I do want to offer some advice on how to start exploring, wrestling, and figuring out what Judaism is, what it means to you, and what it could be for all of us.

APPROACH JUDAISM WITH CURIOSITY, OPENNESS, AND PERSISTENCE

I don't think I'm the only Jew who has viewed Judaism as if it were a dull, distant relative whom I loved in a vague familial way and was required to see a few times a year but had no desire to get to know further. And that's ironic, because many of us approach other people's traditions with great openness and enthusiasm. We delight in celebrating Chinese New Year with the family down the block. We admire our Muslim friends' discipline and spiritual commitment during Ramadan. We love immersing ourselves in other cultures by traveling and studying abroad. And we pride ourselves on being loyal allies to other minority groups.

Here is a thought: What if we approached Judaism with that same eager curiosity, believing that it too is worthy of our respect and trusting that there is something there worth finding?

When I finally opened up to Judaism like this, I found that it began to open up to me. Not every aspect of it, of course. I had to run a number of experiments, trying different synagogues and Jewish meditation retreats; attending various classes, events, and Shabbat dinners; and reading all kinds of books.

Some of these experiments were resounding successes. Others

were depressing failures. Many were awkward for me at first, like I was playacting or doing things that felt too religious—like they were for "real Jews," not seeker/poser/wannabes like me. But I would often remind myself of what the Israelites said when they accepted the Torah: "We will do, and we will understand." The doing came first, then the understanding—not the other way around. That is true of many Jewish things—you have to do them to understand what they have to teach you.

For example, during morning prayers at the first meditation retreat I attended—the one I described in Chapter 3—some of the attendees would put on "tefillin," which are little boxes attached to long leather straps that some Jews wrap around their arms and foreheads during prayer. The boxes contain parchment inscribed with verses from the Torah. This practice derives from language in the Torah that tells us to bind God's words on our hands and between our eyes.

At one point, one of the rabbis leading the retreat offered to run a workshop to demonstrate how to put on tefillin. I hesitated, unsure whether to attend. I thought the people wearing tefillin looked a little silly. In fact, as I watched them during the retreat, I had an image of a man-in-the-sky kind of God looking down, smacking His hand to His forehead, and bellowing, "Guys, what are you doing? It was a *metaphor*!"

But then I figured, why not? And as the rabbi helped me wrap my arm in the straps and talked about the meaning of the verses in the boxes, I have to admit, I was moved. There was something about the feel of the leather encircling my skin and the weight of performing a centuries-old Jewish ritual, especially one rarely undertaken by women before modern times. Who knew?

This experimental approach requires some persistence. While you should never suspend your critical thinking or disregard your gut feelings, you can't just attend one bad service and decide that all Jewish prayer is worthless, or experience one uninspiring holiday celebration and conclude that Jewish holidays are meaningless. That would be like having one bad meal at an Italian restaurant and deciding that all Italian food is awful. Sometimes the problem isn't the cuisine, but the particular restaurant or dish. Another helpful metaphor, courtesy of a friend of mine, has to do with learning to taste wine. When you first drink a fine wine, it might taste bitter. But once you train your taste buds to recognize its more subtle qualities, you may come to appreciate it, maybe even like it.

There are many very fine Jewish things out there—and plenty of not so fine things too—and you have to take the time to sort through them. As a rabbi once told me, "Judaism isn't just taught, it's caught." You have to be willing to be surprised by Judaism. You have to give yourself a chance to catch it.

FIND YOURSELF A TEACHER—IDEALLY, MANY TEACHERS

Jewish learning is not meant to be a solitary endeavor, and it is difficult to find your way through Judaism without some guidance, so as the Rabbis advised, "Establish a teacher for yourself." Personally, I would suggest finding many teachers if possible.

I've found my teachers through classes at synagogues and at the meditation retreats I've attended, as well as informally at Jewish events and through friends. I've learned from my teachers in person, via video chat, and over email. And teachers don't have to be rabbis or scholars, they can simply be other Jews who are learned and willing to share what they know with you.

If you don't have much Jewish education, I would recommend starting with an Introduction to Judaism class. My friends thought it was hilarious that I took not one, but two of these classes. One joked, "When you introduced yourself on the first day, was everyone like, 'Sarah Hurwitz? Okay, who brought the ringer?'" But even though I had attended Hebrew school, had a bat mitzvah, and celebrated major holidays, I was amazed at how much I didn't know.

PUSH THROUGH FEELINGS OF INTIMIDATION
AND EMBARRASSMENT

For years, entering Jewish settings sent me into a state of panicky self-consciousness. I was convinced I was going to inadvertently commit some act of sacrilege that would reveal my ignorance and deepen my shame at being such a crappy Jew. So I would become hypervigilant, trying my best to copy the people around me and hoping no one noticed as I sat down or stood up at the wrong time, or pretended to mouth words to prayers I didn't know, or nodded and smiled uncomprehendingly when people said things like "Should we start benching?"* or "I'm looking forward to the ḥagim"† or "You did a great job on that—yasher koaḥ!"‡

Looking back, I'm reminded of a story in the Talmud about a man who's walking outside on a dark night and comes across a man who is blind, also out walking, holding a torch. The first man asks the blind man why he's carrying a torch when he can't see its light. The blind man replies that as long as he carries the torch, people can see him and aid him.

It took me a long time to summon the courage to pick up a torch. But when I finally did, for the most part, the response I got was not judgment or disdain, but delight. The rabbis I met were thrilled to answer my questions—and even more thrilled that I was asking them at all. The traditionally observant Jews I met were similarly excited that I was interested in learning about Judaism. They relished answering my beginner's questions, and they didn't seem to care that I didn't intend to practice Judaism the way they did.

Picking up a torch can be as simple as saying something like "Sorry, I didn't understand that—I'm new to Judaism/I don't have a lot of Jewish background, and I'm just beginning to learn—can you explain what that means?"

---

* "Benching" is a Yiddish word that refers to reciting blessings after a meal.
† "Ḥagim" is Hebrew for "holidays."
‡ Translated as "may your strength be straight," "yasher koaḥ" is a way of saying "may you continue to have the strength to do wonderful things like this."

Even after five years spent learning about Judaism—even after writing a book about Judaism—I still have moments of self-consciousness, worrying that I'm going to mispronounce a word or botch a ritual. So I continue to wave my torch, and while that's sometimes a little embarrassing, I've found that the light draws many kind and helpful people my way.

THERE IS NO ONE RIGHT WAY TO BE JEWISH

I sent drafts of this book to an entire spreadsheet full of rabbis and scholars, and on multiple occasions, one of these deeply learned, brilliant, committed Jews would insist that a point I was making was dead wrong and terribly offensive; another would tell me that one of my points was absolutely right and incredibly inspiring . . . and they would both be referring to the same point!

I don't think creating a Jewish identity is about picking which of these views I like better and rejecting the other. I prefer an approach that Avraham Infeld compares to making tsimmes, which is a traditional Jewish stew. Just as he adds new ingredients to his tsimmes, each time he's learned about a different way of being Jewish—secular Zionism, Orthodoxy, liberal Judaism—he's woven some aspect of it into his own life. "Each time, rather than replacing what came before with a new, improved version, I added layer upon layer of meaning about what being Jewish means to me," he writes—and his Judaism became deeper and more satisfying as a result.

This is true for me as well. I count among my dearest friends and teachers Jews whose practice revolves around mindfulness meditation and yoga, and Jews who may well think such practices amount to idolatry. I embrace modern feminist approaches to studying Jewish texts and admire the most traditional forms of Shabbat observance and death and mourning rituals. And one of the people I most enjoy talking with about Judaism is a woman who is quite traditionally observant. As divergent as our Jewish paths may be, often, when we're speaking about the Divine or about what most touches us in Judaism, I feel like we are native speakers of the same language.

Judaism has numerous strains and strands. And if we all practiced Judaism the exact same way, and studied the same narrow selection of texts, then very little of it would survive. We need Jews who geek out on Jewish history, Jews who are enthralled by Jewish mysticism, Jews who love nothing more than a passionate debate about Jewish law, Jews who relish creating memorable holiday celebrations and beautiful Shabbat dinners, and countless other kinds of Jews, each of them breathing life into some aspect of our tradition. I believe that this diversity of interests and paths is the key to Jewish survival, and we all have something to learn from each other.

HOWEVER YOU CHOOSE TO DO JUDAISM, DO IT MEANINGFULLY

I recently had a conversation with a friend who was trying to figure out how to incorporate Jewish traditions into his family life—and he was struggling. He and his wife found the services at their local synagogue uninspiring, and neither of them had much Jewish education, so they felt like they didn't have many options. "What counts as doing something Jewish?" he asked. Is volunteering at a homeless shelter Jewish? Eating lunch at a Jewish deli? Having a Friday night dinner with your family where you don't say any Jewish prayers? Does adding the prayers make it a Jewish experience?

I appreciate my friend's commitment to wrestling with all of this, but I don't think the question is whether or not something is Jewish, but rather, how *meaningfully* Jewish it is—whether it's deeply, transformatively Jewish . . . or Jewish in a thinner, more superficial kind of way.

Is it Jewish for me to have a Friday night dinner with loved ones where we all turn off our phones, avoid talking about work, and focus on being fully present with each other? I think it is. But would it be more meaningfully Jewish if we all understood the Jewish thinking about Shabbat and recited the Jewish blessings—or maybe instead of just reciting them, we discussed what they mean and how they might be relevant in our lives today? I think it would be.

Is it Jewish for me to volunteer for a cause I care about? Sure. (It's also Christian, Islamic, etc.) But would it be more meaningfully Jewish if I understood the Jewish thinking about ḥesed and tzedakah and what it means to live out the Jewish ethic of non-indifference? For me, that has certainly been the case.

So while I think helping those in need and having that intentional Friday night dinner with friends are *Jewish experiences,* and are also meaningful *experiences in general,* I do not think they are *meaningful Jewish experiences.* For me, experiences like these *become* meaningful Jewish experiences once I truly understand the Jewish thinking and traditions behind them.

Of course, there's nothing wrong with doing light, fun Jewish things: having a happy hour and serving apple and honey martinis because Rosh Hashanah is coming up, or gathering friends to make chocolate-covered matzah during Passover. Not every contact with Judaism has to be life-altering.

But I've come to realize that if events like these are my only form of engagement with Judaism, then I'm missing out. If all I do is participate in activities that have a veneer of Judaism with little Jewish substance beneath, that's like attending those spin classes that have amazing music and energetic instructors but just sitting on the bike and not pedaling. It might be fun to sit and listen to the music and the motivational talks from the instructors, but I won't walk away in better shape.

I've found that if I want to be transformed by Judaism, I have to put in some effort.

FIGURING OUT HOW TO BE JEWISH IS A LIFELONG PROCESS

Even after all the time I've spent learning and exploring, I'm still trying to find my place in Judaism. And I don't know any Jews whose engagement with Judaism has stayed static over the course of their lives. Someone might be heavily involved with their synagogue youth group and college Hillel, but then drift away after graduation, reengage once they have kids, disengage once the kids leave home, and reengage again once they retire.

I've also found that as I continue to learn, my understanding of Judaism continues to deepen and change. No matter what the topic in Judaism, there is always another book to read, experience to have, or opinion to consider. And after doing some learning about a subject, I might think I'm beginning to understand it. Then after doing some more learning, I realize that my prior understanding was quite shallow, but I feel like now I'm starting to get it. Then I learn some more and realize that I was previously missing out on all kinds of nuances and connections, but now I'm finally getting somewhere. And so on. With Judaism you can always go another level deeper.

My Jewish self is constantly evolving, and it is disconcerting to freeze it in time in these pages. Five years from now, I might write a very different book. Of course, this is a risk no matter what one is writing about. But just know that my Judaism will continue to change, and so will yours.

Creating Option Three will take time, and we probably will not live to see it come to fruition. But that in itself is quite Jewish. A story in the Talmud tells of a man named Ḥoni, who is out walking one day and comes across a man planting a carob tree. Ḥoni asks the man how long it will take for the tree to bear fruit. The man replies that it will take seventy years. Ḥoni is astounded and points out that the man probably won't live long enough to enjoy the fruits of his labor. The man replies, "I found the world provided with carob-trees; as my forefathers planted them for me, I likewise plant them for my descendants."

Jewish tradition focuses a great deal on our obligation to be ancestors and pass Judaism along to future generations. At the end of the Torah, Moses exhorts the Israelites to "love the Lord your God with all your heart and with all your soul and with all your might," and then tells them, "Take to heart these instructions with which I charge you this day. Impress them upon your children." Citing the sixteenth-century Rabbi Moses Alshekh, who argues that these two verses are linked, Rabbi Jonathan Sacks notes, "We can only pass on to our children what we ourselves love."

When I said I wanted to show you why Judaism is worth choosing, I think that's what I really meant: that I hope you will come to love Judaism, or to at least trust that there is something in it to love, if you're willing to search for it. To that end, I've shared with you some of the many things I have come to love about Judaism:

I love the idea that we are created in the Divine image—that, as the Rabbis put it, "there is no person who does not have his hour, and there is nothing which does not have its place." No one is expendable, and we are all here for some purpose, even if we do not know what it is.

I love the way Judaism empowers us, demanding that we be worthy partners for the Divine—that we ask hard questions, think for ourselves, and push back on immorality wherever we find it, even if that means pushing back on God.

I love Judaism's aversion to dogma—how loyal it is to life's complexity, constantly resisting my attempts to shape it into easy or definitive answers.

I love how countercultural Judaism is—its insistence on hard things, on obligations we didn't choose, on our communal ties rather than just our individual needs.

I love that Judaism flies in the face of the strip-mall culture of our time—that depressing array of generic, disposable-quality merchandise—and instead offers something wonderfully durable, enduring, and unique.

I love the primal aspects of Judaism—how we mark our most important holidays by blowing on an animal horn and how holidays start at sundown, prompting us to notice the changing of light and darkness over the course of a year.

I love seeing so many Jewish last names in the ranks of activists and on the rosters of social justice organizations—and I love how, even if they've never read the Torah, so many Jews seem to have absorbed its key message, orienting their hearts toward strangers and embodying the ethic of non-indifference in their lives.

I love our breathtaking story of survival, and I think often of a statistic I came across when working on President Obama's remarks on Holocaust Memorial Day back in 2009. Researchers found that Jews who survived the Holocaust and came to America went on to have more children than Jews who were not survivors. When I shared this fact with a colleague, the human rights activist Samantha Power, who later became Ambassador to the United Nations, she replied: "To think that after all they had endured, they still believed they had a duty to life."

I love how, even when we try to give up on Judaism, it does not give up on us—how, no matter how frustrated or distant we become, something still tugs at us, some thread we did not even realize was there. As a character in a novella by the Yiddish poet Jacob Glatstein put it: "Inside me sits the soul of an ancestor who summons me back."

When describing her relationship to Judaism, Blu Greenberg once wrote, "It has chosen me and I have chosen it back."

It took me a long time to love Judaism enough to choose it back. But I'm glad I did. And if you are Jewish—or seek to become so— I hope that you will come to love and choose Judaism too.

ACKNOWLEDGMENTS

I have thought often, while writing this book, of the ministry of presence/"I will be there with you" aspect of the Divine. Throughout this process, I have been accompanied by people who talked me through moments of fear and self-doubt, took my hand and freed me when I was stuck, and reminded me that even in lonely moments I am never really alone.

I am profoundly grateful to:

Brian Forde and Adam Grant, who believed in this book and my ability to write it long before I did, and who convinced me that I should give it a go. It is not an exaggeration to say that this book exists because of them.

David Axelrod, Melissa Winter, and Jeff Zients, who understood that I needed to write this book and provided advice and support to help me move forward with it.

Former First Lady Michelle Obama, for teaching me so much of what I know about writing and what it means to speak your truth.

My agent, Richard Pine, for his savvy, soulfulness, empathy, wry humor, probing intellect, impeccable judgment, unwavering integrity, and all-around menschiness. No matter what happens, Richard always knows exactly what to do, and he's right there with you in it—not just as an agent, but as a friend. Richard is, quite simply, the best agent in the universe. I treasure his friendship, and I will never stop being grateful that he was willing to work with me.

Richard's fantastic colleagues at Inkwell Management, Eliza Rothstein and Nat Jacks, for all their help, as well as Julie Angell, for her excellent advice and for being a joy to work with.

My first editor, Cindy Spiegel, for understanding this book right from the beginning and giving me the inspiration and encouragement I needed to discover what it was meant to be, and for her brilliance, generosity, and devotion to its success.

My second editor, Whitney Frick, who jumped in without missing a beat and did an utterly phenomenal job carrying this book through to the end. Her formidable smarts, wisdom, insight, and determination were tremendous gifts to me in the homestretch.

Associate editor Rose Fox for her breathtaking competence and abounding kindness and patience with my many questions, to which she always had exactly the right answers.

Melanie DeNardo and Ayelet Gruenspecht, the publicity and marketing dream team, for their boundless energy, creativity, and shared love of spreadsheets.

Donna Cheng, for somehow managing to create a cover that is beautiful and also fits my insanely long title.

Susan Kamil, Tom Perry, Jennifer Rodriguez, Susan M. S. Brown, Greg Mollica, Susan Turner, Maria Braeckel, Erin Richards, and everyone else at Penguin Random House whose passion, dedication, talent, and expertise made this book possible.

Menachem Butler, Max Chapnick, Deena Cowans—and especially Ben Kamine, who went above and beyond to help me in the final stretch—for their superb research.

Kristen Bartoloni and Alex Platkin of Silver Street Strategies for their exceptionally smart and meticulous factchecking—and for their enthusiasm and good humor.

The folks at Sefaria.org, who have worked tirelessly to make Jewish texts accessible online and available in English translation. I have no idea how I would have written this book without that website.

The many fabulous people who took the time to read all or part of this book and offer their feedback. Every page reflects their brilliant edits, corrections, suggestions, pushback, and ideas (though mistakes are 100 percent mine—and note that some of these folks disagree quite strongly with parts of what I've written):

∿ A number of rabbis reviewed my entire manuscript, starting with Shoshana Boyd Gelfand and Burt Visotzky, who both offered to help me within minutes of first meeting me and whom I trusted with my earliest, roughest drafts (and in Shoshana's case, with my final draft as well). Their support, encouragement, and hugely insightful edits and comments were crucial to me in those early days and throughout this process. I am also deeply grateful to Rabbis Yaffa Epstein, Gil Steinlauf, Avi Strausberg, and David Fried (who also drew on his extensive knowledge of Jewish texts to provide thoughtful answers to countless questions) for being willing to review the whole book and offer brilliant feedback. In addition, the following rabbis reviewed at least one chapter, some of them more (and often fielded numerous follow-up questions from me): Jordan Bendat-Appell, Stephanie Bernstein, Ariel Burger, Yoni Ganger, Shai Held, Dan Horwitz, James Jacobson-Maisels, Howard Jaffe, Jen Kaluzny, Patricia Karlin-Neumann, Elie Kaunfer, Jess Minnen, Dani Passow, Scott Perlo, Aaron Potek, Ariel Sholklapper, Suzy Stone, Joseph Telushkin, and Stuart Weinblatt.

∿ Many old friends—and new friends, and incredibly generous friends of friends—brought a range of expertise to reading and commenting on this book. Hilary Cohen, Bill Dauster, Rachel Elkin, Dara Horn, Bonnie Rich, Augusta Ridley, Amanda Sloat, and Chanan Weissman reviewed the entire manuscript, as did Abby Pogrebin, a kindred spirit who has been there from day one, providing lovingly honest feedback and crucial advice and help. Numerous others took the time to offer thoughts on one or more chapters, including Jennifer Berlin, Michelle Boorstein, Erica Brown, Ilona Cohen, Idan Dershowitz, Nick Ehrmann, Marshall Ganz, Cody Keenan, Aliza Kline, Michelle Kuo, Ilana Kurshan, Jen Leib, Anne Neuberger, Shawn Pompian, Tara Schuster, Robert Seltzer, Adam Simon, Terry Szuplat, Colleen Titelbaum, and Laura Yares.

∼ Finally, countless people responded to my questions, some of them complete strangers. I am moved by and appreciative of their kindness.

The friends who sustained me throughout this process, listening sympathetically to my tiresome complaints, delivering much-needed pep talks, and making sure I occasionally left my apartment, particularly Kwaku Akowuah, Jeremiah Baronberg, Jackie Gran, Cameron Krug, Anna Langer, Sara Polon, Shawn Pompian, Amanda Sloat, and Aaron Strauss.

Finally, and most of all, my family, whose boundless love is the foundation upon which I have built my life. I love you beyond all words.

APPENDIX OF RESOURCES FOR GETTING STARTED

When I first started learning about Judaism, I felt overwhelmed. There were so many books! And websites! And organizations! And classes! I often had trouble discerning which resources would be helpful and which would not.

This appendix is an attempt to provide you with a roadmap for getting started. And I want to emphasize the words "getting started." This is *not* a comprehensive list of every excellent Jewish resource out there—such a list would require a book of its own—but simply those that were most accessible and helpful to me at the beginning of my journey, or that I've encountered more recently and wish I'd known about back then.

I'd recommend starting with some of the items in the "Introductory Materials" section to give you a broad web of context. Once you have a handle on the basics, you'll be prepared to dive more deeply into whichever topic(s) most intrigue you.

INTRODUCTORY MATERIALS

Classes: Introduction to Judaism classes are often offered at synagogues and Jewish Community Centers, and taking one is a great way to find your first teacher and connect with others who are exploring

Judaism. I also found the following books and websites to be helpful when I was just starting to learn:

THE "WHAT" OF JUDAISM

~ Rabbi Joseph Telushkin, *Jewish Literacy: The Most Important Things to Know About the Jewish Religion, Its People, and Its History:* This 750-page book is broken up into essays of about two to four pages, and its title is a good description of what it offers.

~ My Jewish Learning (MyJewishLearning.com): You can find basic information on just about any Jewish topic on this site, as well as plenty of resources for deeper learning.

~ Bimbam (Bimbam.com): This website is filled with (often hilarious) videos on Jewish holidays, values, and rituals, as well as videos on the weekly Torah portion, the Talmud, and more. It also has videos for kids.

THE "WHY" OF JUDAISM

~ Rabbi Jonathan Sacks, *A Letter in the Scroll: Understanding Our Jewish Identity and Exploring the Legacy of the World's Oldest Religion;* Rabbi Zalman Schachter-Shalomi with Joel Segel, *Jewish with Feeling: A Guide to Meaningful Jewish Practice;* Harold S. Kushner, *To Life!: A Celebration of Jewish Being and Thinking:* These books offer answers to the "why be Jewish" question, and they've been influential in my own understanding of Judaism.

~ Rabbi Edward Feinstein, *Tough Questions Jews Ask: A Young Adult's Guide to Building a Jewish Life:* While technically for young people, Feinstein's explanations and observations are helpful for adults as well.

THE "HOW-TO" OF JUDAISM

~ Anita Diamant, *Living a Jewish Life: Jewish Traditions, Customs and Values for Today's Families;* Blu Greenberg, *How to Run a*

Traditional Jewish Household: Both of these books offer concrete guidance for Jewish practice (and while I'm not the target audience for Greenberg's book, I found it to be quite insightful).

TORAH

Rabbi Reuven Hammer, *The Torah Revolution: Fourteen Truths that Changed the World:* This book provides an accessible account of some of the Torah's key ideas.

Robert Alter, *The Five Books of Moses:* I appreciate Alter's vivid translations, and find his notes to be quite helpful (often, when I'm wondering, "What on earth does *that* mean?" I just look down, and Alter has provided an answer).

Rabbi Jonathan Sacks' Covenant and Conversation series of commentaries on the weekly Torah portion (online and in book form) and Rabbi Shai Held, *The Heart of Torah: Essays on the Weekly Torah Portion,* vols. 1 and 2: I recommend reading the Torah one weekly portion at a time and reading some of the corresponding essays from Rabbis Sacks and Held, which explore the Torah's spiritual and moral lessons.

TALMUD

Adin Steinsaltz, *The Essential Talmud:* Steinsaltz offers a clear overview of the history and content of the Talmud.

Ilana Kurshan, *If All the Seas Were Ink;* Jonathan Rosen, *The Talmud and the Internet: A Journey Between Worlds:* These books provide fresh takes on the Talmud from two people writing about their own experiences studying it.

Sefaria (sefaria.org): Sefaria is a free website and app that offers a massive library of Jewish texts—biblical, Talmudic, Kabbalistic, and more—many of them in English translation.

HISTORY

Micah Goodman, *A History of Judaism;* Paul Johnson, *A History of the Jews;* Jonathan D. Sarna, *American Judaism: A History:* Each of these books is relatively concise and accessible given the scope of what they cover, and together, they provide a basic grounding in Jewish history.

GOD

JEWISH THEOLOGY OVERVIEW

~ Rabbi Jamie S. Korngold, *The God Upgrade: Finding Your 21st-Century Spirituality in Judaism's 5,000-Year-Old Tradition:* This is a relatable journey through various Jewish God conceptions.

~ Rabbi Elliot J. Cosgrove, ed., *Jewish Theology in Our Time: A New Generation Explores the Foundations and Future of Jewish Belief:* This is a collection of provocative essays about the Divine.

SPECIFIC THEOLOGIES/THINKERS

~ Harold S. Kushner, *When Bad Things Happen to Good People*

~ Kenneth Seeskin, *Maimonides: A Guide for Today's Perplexed*

~ Jay Michaelson, *Everything Is God: The Radical Path of Nondual Judaism*

~ Shai Held, *Abraham Joshua Heschel: The Call of Transcendence*

~ Rabbi Bradley Shavit Artson, *God of Becoming and Relationship: The Dynamic Nature of Process Theology*

ETHICS

Rabbi Joseph Telushkin, *A Code of Jewish Ethics,* vols. 1 and 2, and *Words That Hurt, Words That Heal: How to Choose Words Wisely and Well:* Rabbi Telushkin distills a tremendous amount of Jewish law into clear prose peppered with anecdotes that make the material come alive.

Rabbi Donniel Hartman, *Putting God Second: How to Save Religion from Itself:* This book is an argument for how to resolve tensions between ritual and ethics (spoiler alert: ritual should serve ethics, not be in opposition to it).

Alan Morinis, *Everyday Holiness: The Jewish Spiritual Path of Mussar:* A user-friendly introduction to Mussar with instructions on how to try it for yourself.

SPIRITUAL PRACTICE

Lawrence A. Hoffman, *The Way into Jewish Prayer:* This is a solid introduction to, and overview of, traditional Jewish prayer.

Rabbi Mike Comins, *Making Prayer Real: Leading Jewish Spiritual Voices on Why Prayer Is Difficult and What to Do About It:* This book includes excerpts from dozens of thoughtful rabbis about their struggles and successes with prayer.

Rabbi Marcia Prager, *The Path of Blessing: Experiencing the Energy and Abundance of the Divine:* This book about the role and practice of blessings in Judaism also offers broader insights about Jewish spirituality.

Yael Shy, *What Now?: Meditation for Your Twenties and Beyond:* Personal yet substantive, this engaging introduction to meditation includes concrete instructions to help you get started. While the examples are geared toward people in their twenties, this book is useful for people of all ages.

Alan Lew, *Be Still and Get Going: A Jewish Meditation Practice for Real Life:* This is a remarkable book about Jewish meditation that offers spiritual wisdom grounded in the Torah and other sacred texts.

Or Halev; Institute for Jewish Spirituality: I have done meditation retreats with both of these organizations, as well as webinars and online classes not just on meditation, but on many other forms of Jewish spiritual practice.

SHABBAT

Rabbi Abraham Joshua Heschel, *The Sabbath:* If you read just one book on Shabbat, this should be it.

OneTable (onetable.org): This website provides ritual resources, hosting tips, and access to Shabbat experts to help twenty- and thirty-somethings create meaningful Shabbat dinners.

HOLIDAYS

Rabbi Jonathan Sacks, *Ceremony and Celebration: Introduction to the Holidays,* and Rabbi Irving Greenberg, *The Jewish Way: Living the Holidays:* Each of these books provides an overview of the holidays, as well as an exploration of their moral and spiritual meanings.

Abigail Pogrebin, *My Jewish Year: 18 Holidays, One Wondering Jew:* A personal account by a thoughtful, funny Jew who spent a year observing all of the Jewish holidays.

Alan Lew, *This Is Real and You Are Completely Unprepared: The Days of Awe as a Journey of Transformation:* This book is filled with profound insights about the High Holy Day season. I know people who read it every year.

Rabbi Jonathan Sacks, *The Jonathan Sacks Haggada: Collected Essays on Pesaḥ:* This book includes both a Haggadah and a series of essays exploring the meaning of Passover.

Haggadot.com: This website helps you make your own Haggadah.

DEATH AND MOURNING

Anita Diamant, *Saying Kaddish: How to Comfort the Dying, Bury the Dead, and Mourn as a Jew,* and Maurice Lamm, *The Jewish Way in Death and Mourning:* These books both explain the death and mourning rituals and are invaluable for mourners and anyone wishing to understand the Jewish approach to death. Lamm's is from a more traditional perspective and provides more detail.

Jack Riemer, ed., *Jewish Reflections on Death* and *Jewish Insights on Death and Mourning:* These books offer essays about death and mourning from Jews of all different backgrounds.

Neil Gillman, *The Death of Death: Resurrection and Immortality in Jewish Thought:* An account of how Jewish thinking about the afterlife has evolved over the centuries.

NOTES

INTRODUCTION: WHY BOTHER WITH JUDAISM?

xii **As Rabbi Joseph Telushkin** Dennis Prager and Joseph Telushkin, *The Nine Questions People Ask About Judaism* (New York: Touchstone, 1986), 135–136.

xiii **"pediatric Judaism"** Rabbi Lawrence A. Hoffman, *Rethinking Synagogues: A New Vocabulary for Congregational Life* (Woodstock, V.T.: Jewish Lights, 2006), 96.

xiii **94 percent of American Jews** Pew Research Center, *A Portrait of Jewish Americans: Findings from a Pew Research Center Survey of U.S. Jews,* October 1, 2013, 52, http://www.pewresearch.org/wp-content/uploads/sites/7/2013/10/jewish-american-full-report-for-web.pdf.

xiii **22 percent of them, including** Ibid., 7.

xiii **A full two-thirds** Ibid., 67.

xiii **There is also a trend** Pew Research Center, *A Portrait of Jewish Americans,* 10.

xiv **Though the Orthodox population** Pew Research Center, *A Portrait of American Orthodox Jews: A Further Analysis of the 2013 Survey of U.S. Jews,* August 26, 2015, 2–3, http://www.pewresearch.org/wp-content/uploads/sites/7/2015/08/Orthodox-Jews-08-24-PDF-for-web.pdf.

xiv **The reverse seems to be rare** Ibid., 10.

xvii **"Life has a gap in it"** Sarah Polley, *Take This Waltz,* 2011, https://www.imdb.com/title/tt1592281/quotes?ref_=tt_ql_trv_4.

xxi "**Listen to the truth**" Moses Maimonides, *Eight Chapters: Introduction to Pirkei Avot,* Introduction. My translation with assistance from others.

xxii **As Rabbi Danya Ruttenberg points out** Danya Ruttenberg, *Surprised by God: How I Learned to Stop Worrying and Love Religion* (Boston: Beacon Press, 2008), 98.

xxii "**constructing a safe, tidy, unsurprising God**" Frederica Mathewes-Green in Mark Matousek, "Should You Design Your Own Religion?" *Utne Reader,* July–August 1998, https://www.utne.com/community/shouldyoudesignyourownreligion.

xxiii **Each, Ruttenberg notes** Ruttenberg, *Surprised by God,* 98.

xxiv **One of the best answers** Rabbi Jonathan Sacks, *A Letter in the Scroll: Understanding Our Jewish Identity and Exploring the Legacy of the World's Oldest Religion* (New York: Free Press, 2000), 42–43.

xxv "**Intrigued, you open it**" Ibid., 43–44.

xxv **By contrast, being Jewish** Ze'ev Maghen, *John Lennon and the Jews: A Philosophical Rampage* (New Milford, C.T.: Toby Press, 2014), 161–162.

xxv **Understanding our family's story** Sacks, *A Letter in the Scroll,* 45.

xxvii **Generations ago, being of** Herbert Gans, "The Coming Darkness of Late-Generation European American Ethnicity," *Ethnic and Racial Studies* 37, no. 5 (2014): 757–65.

xxvii **And a recent study of people** Mark Hugo Lopez, Ana Gonzalez-Barrera, and Gustavo López, *Hispanic Identity Fades Across Generations as Immigrant Connections Fall Away,* Pew Research Center, December 20, 2017, 4–5, http://www.pewhispanic.org/wp-content/uploads/sites/5/2017/12/Pew-Research-Center_Hispanic-Identity-Report_12.20.2017.pdf.

xxvii "**The purpose of Jewish existence**" Joseph Telushkin, preface to Prager and Telushkin, *The Nine Questions People Ask About Judaism,* 16.

xxix **a "civilization"** See Mordecai M. Kaplan, *Judaism as a Civilization: Toward a Reconstruction of American-Jewish Life* (London: Forgotten Books, 2015; New York: Thomas Yoseloff, 1957).

1 | IN THE BEGINNING AND IN THE IMAGE

5 "**a great nation**" Genesis 12:2. All biblical translations are from the following unless otherwise noted: Jewish Publication Society, *JPS Hebrew-English Tanakh,* 2nd ed. (Philadelphia: Jewish Publication Society, 1999).

5 "**For you have wrestled with God**" Genesis 32:29, common translation.

6 "**slow of speech**" Exodus 4:10.

10 "**never a lacuna, never a gap**" Erich Auerbach, *Mimesis: The Representation of Reality in Western Literature,* trans. Willard R. Trask (Princeton: Princeton University Press, 2003), 6–7.

10   **"thoughts and feeling remain unexpressed"** Ibid., 11.

11   **"Abraham took the wood"** Genesis 22:6–8.

11   **"merely to read"** Dara Horn, "Jacob: Some Notes on Character Develop-
      ment and Repentance," in Beth Kissileff, ed., *Reading Genesis: Beginnings*
      (London: Bloomsbury T & T Clark, 2016), 169.

12   **"You shall surely open your hand"** Deuteronomy 15:8, translation
      from Rabbi Jill Jacobs, *There Shall Be No Needy: Pursuing Social Jus-
      tice Through Jewish Law and Tradition* (Woodstock, V.T.: Jewish Lights,
      2010), 11.

12   **"seventy faces to the Torah"** *Numbers Rabbah* 13:16, translation from
      Sefaria Community Translation, Sefaria.org.

12   **"Turn it [the Torah] over"** *Pirkei Avot* 5:22. Unless otherwise noted, all
      translations of Pirkei Avot come from *Sage Advice: Pirkei Avot with Trans-
      lation and Commentary by Irving (Yitz) Greenberg* (New Milford, C.T.:
      Maggid Books, 2016).

12   **"hesitant and uncertain"** Paul Johnson, *A History of the Jews* (New York:
      Harper Perennial, 1988), 28.

13   **"Now that I am withered"** Genesis 18:12.

13   **"Was it for want of graves"** Exodus 14:11.

13   **"The thing you are doing"** Exodus 18:17–18.

13   she **"had stopped having the periods"** Genesis 18:11.

13   **Some Jews, who I assume** Pew Research Center, *U.S. Public Becoming
      Less Religious,* November 3, 2015, 58, http://www.pewforum.org/wp
      -content/uploads/sites/7/2015/11/2015.11.03_RLS_II_full_report.pdf.

15   **"God created man in His image"** Genesis 1:27.

15   **"The pronoun for God is God"** Rabbi Danya Ruttenberg (@TheRaDR),
      "The pronoun for God is God," Twitter, November 9, 2018, 10:11 A.M.,
      https://twitter.com/TheRaDR/status/1060958030030872576.

15   **This belief that every single one** See Jerusalem Talmud, *Nedarim* 9:4;
      Rabbi Yitz Greenberg, quoted in Shalom Freedman, comp., *Living in the
      Image of God: Jewish Teachings to Perfect the World, Conversations with
      Rabbi Irving Greenberg as Conducted by Shalom Freedman* (Northvale,
      N.J.: Jason Aronson, 1998), 31.

15   **"three inalienable dignities"** Rabbi Yitz Greenberg, interview with Daniel
      Libenson and Lex Rofeberg, "The Third Era—Irving 'Yitz' Greenberg,"
      100th episode in the podcast *Judaism Unbound,* podcast audio, January 12,
      2018, http://www.judaismunbound.com/podcast/2018/1/4/judaism
      -unbound-episode-100-the-third-era-yitz-greenberg-2. Drawing on Mish-
      nah *Sanhedrin* 4:5.

16   **"Anyone who destroys a life"** Mishnah, *Sanhedrin* 4:5, translation from
      Open Mishna, Sefaria.org.

17   **"Our glorious diversity"** First Lady Michelle Obama, "Remarks by
      the First Lady at the National School Counselor of the Year Event,"
      Speech, The White House, Washington, D.C., January 6, 2017, https://
      obamawhitehouse.archives.gov/the-press-office/2017/01/06/remarks-first
      -lady-national-school-counselor-year-event.

18   **"Be fruitful and multiply"** Genesis 1:28. Note that I substituted the more
      commonly known King James translation, "Be fruitful and multiply," for
      the JPS translation, "Be fertile and increase."

18   **"The task they are given"** Rabbi Reuven Hammer, *The Torah Revolution:
      Fourteen Truths That Changed the World* (Woodstock, V.T.: Jewish Lights,
      2011), 63.

18   **"Humans," she notes** Christine Hayes, "Lecture 4: Doublets and Con-
      tradictions, Seams and Sources: Genesis 5–11 and the Historical-Critical
      Method," *RLST 145: Introduction to the Old Testament (Hebrew Bible),*
      transcript of online lecture, Open Yale Courses, Yale University.

19   **"The king grants a covenant"** Yoram Hazony, *The Philosophy of Hebrew
      Scripture* (Cambridge: Cambridge University Press, 2012), 94.

19   **"senior partner"** Irving Greenberg, "The Third Great Cycle of Jewish
      History," *Perspectives: A CLAL Thesis* (New York: CLAL: National Jewish
      Center for Learning and Leadership, 1987), 4, https://rabbiirvinggreenberg.
      com/wp-content/uploads/2013/02/1Perspectives-3rd-Great-Cycle-1987
      -CLAL-1-of-3.pdf.

19   **"men, women, children, and the strangers"** Deuteronomy 31:12.

19   **"you shall be to Me"** Exodus 19:6.

19   **"Surely, this Instruction"** Deuteronomy 30:11–14. In the final verse, JPS
      renders the Hebrew word "hadavar" as "the thing." But others have trans-
      lated it as "the word," and I have made this substitution.

20   **"You shall not ill-treat"** Exodus 22:21–23.

21   **"for he is needy"** Deuteronomy 24:15.

21   **God puts forth measures** Deuteronomy 15:1–3.

21   **requiring landowners to leave a portion** Leviticus 19:9–10, 23:22; Deu-
      teronomy 24:19–21.

21   **"If you take your neighbor's garment"** Exodus 22:25–26.

21   **"is not part of"** Rabbi Shai Held, "Love Your Neighbor," lec-
      ture, 2017 Limmud NY Conference, https://www.youtube.com/
      watch?v=h2tibgsGPCg.

21   **Some scholars have suggested** See Frank Anthony Spina, "Israelites as
      Gerim, 'Sojourners,' in Social and Historical Context," in Carol L. Mey-
      ers and M. O'Connor, eds., *The Word of the Lord Shall Go Forth: Essays
      in Honor of David Noel Freedman in Celebration of His Sixtieth Birthday*
      (Winona Lake, I.N.: Eisenbrauns, 1983), 322, 323–325.

22   **And as Held points out** Held, "Love Your Neighbor."

22   **"You shall not oppress a stranger"** Exodus 23:9.

22   **"the stranger who resides with you"** Leviticus 19:34. Note that the JPS translation renders the Hebrew word "ezraḥ" as "citizen," but Rabbi Held argues that a more accurate translation is "native born," and I have made that substitution. See Held, "Love Your Neighbor."

22   **"love your neighbor as yourself"** Leviticus, 19:18. JPS renders the Hebrew word "reakha" as "fellow," but I substituted the more commonly known translation "neighbor."

22   **Whatever "love" entails** Held, "Love Your Neighbor."

22   **"befriends the stranger"** Deuteronomy 10:18–19.

22   **"El-roi," meaning "God of seeing"** Genesis 16:13.

22   **"God who sees me"** Rabbi Shai Held, *The Heart of Torah: Essays on the Weekly Torah Portion: Genesis and Exodus,* vol. 1 (Philadelphia: Jewish Publication Society, 2017), xxv.

22   **"You can't love a God"** Held, "Love Your Neighbor."

22   **As Held points out, the Torah** Ibid.

23   **"It was not Abraham"** Avraham Weiss, *Holistic Prayer: A Guide to Jewish Spirituality* (New Milford, C.T.: Maggid Books, 2014), 5.

24   **a number of commentators** Dr. Moshe Lavee and Dr. Shana Strauch-Schick, "The 'Egyptian' Midwives: Recovering a Lost Midrashic Text and Exploring Why It May Have Been Forgotten," https://thetorah.com/the -egyptian-midwives/.

24   **"God dealt well with the midwives"** Exodus 1:20.

24   **"It is not because you are"** Deuteronomy 7:7–8.

26   **Jewish tradition holds that the souls** Babylonian Talmud, *Shevuot* 39a. Unless otherwise noted, for quotations from the Talmud, I use the English translation from the William Davidson digital edition of the Koren Noé Talmud, with commentary by Rabbi Adin Even-Israel Steinsaltz, posted on Sefaria.com.

2 | THE PROCESS OF JUDAISM

29   **"I am the great-great-granddaughter"** First Lady Michelle Obama, "Remarks by the First Lady at the Santa Fe Indian School Commencement," Commencement Address, Santa Fe Indian School, Santa Fe, N.M., May 26, 2016, https://obamawhitehouse.archives.gov/ the-press-office/2016/05/26/remarks-first-lady-santa-fe-indian-school -commencement.

32   **"the sole institution in which"** Shaye J. D. Cohen, *From the Maccabees to the Mishnah,* 3rd ed. (Louisville, K.Y.: Westminster John Knox, 2014), 11.

32 **and began referring to themselves** Joseph Blenkinsopp, "Temple and Society in Achaemenid Judah," in *Second Temple Studies, Persian Period*, vol. 1, Philip R. Davies, ed., *Journal for the Study of the Old Testament, Supplement Series* 117 (Sheffield, England: Sheffield Academic Press, 1991), 47.

33 **Prayer services were timed around** H. H. Ben-Sasson, ed., *A History of the Jewish People* (Cambridge, M.A.: Harvard University Press, 1985), 317.

33 **and were in no way considered** Martin Goodman, *A History of Judaism* (Princeton: Princeton University Press, 2018), 70.

33 **the congregations faced toward the Temple** Ben-Sasson, ed., *A History of the Jewish People,* 317–318.

34 **How loudly must one recite it?** Mishnah, *Berakhot* 2:3.

34 **How carefully must one articulate** Ibid.

34 **When, exactly, should it be said?** Mishnah, *Berakhot* 1:1–2.

34 **In what position** Mishnah, *Berakhot* 1:3.

34 **Is it permissible to interrupt** Mishnah, *Berakhot* 2:1.

34 **They also considered what one** Mishnah, *Berakhot* 4:5.

34 **Later Rabbis asked** Babylonian Talmud, *Berakhot* 16a.

34 **At one point, the Rabbis recounted** Babylonian Talmud, *Eruvin* 13b.

35 **pushing him to sharpen** Babylonian Talmud, *Taanit* 7a.

35 **they insisted that this Oral Torah** *Pirkei Avot* 1:1

36 **"what might have happened"** Lawrence Kushner, *God Was in This Place & I, i Did Not Know: Finding Self, Spirituality and Ultimate Meaning* (Woodstock, V.T.: Jewish Lights, 2016), 17.

36 **The first imagines that they reached** Babylonian Talmud, *Sota* 37a.

36 **The other midrash is about** Babylonian Talmud, *Sanhedrin* 39b. My translation with assistance from others.

37 **"Judaism is based upon"** Abraham Joshua Heschel, *God in Search of Man: A Philosophy of Judaism* (New York: Farrar, Straus and Giroux, 1976), 274.

38 **The Torah itself prohibits amendments** Deuteronomy 4:2, 13:1.

38 **For instance, the Torah offers** Deuteronomy 21:18–21. I substituted "rebellious," which I prefer, over "defiant" in the JPS translation.

38 **Yet, through pages of sometimes torturous** Babylonian Talmud, *Sanhedrin* 68b–72a.

38 **Two of the Rabbis even declared** Babylonian Talmud, *Sanhedrin* 71a.

38 **"God makes unenforceable laws"** Adam Kirsch, "Put to Death for Crimes Yet to Be Committed," *Tablet Magazine,* October 3, 2017, https://www.tabletmag.com/jewish-life-and-religion/246300/daf-yomi-213-put-to-death-for-crimes-yet-to-be-committed.

38   **"if anyone maims his fellow"** Leviticus 24:19–20.

39   **"should not enter your mind"** Babylonian Talmud, *Bava Kamma* 83b.

39   **Rather, through a series** Babylonian Talmud, *Bava Kamma* 83b–84a.

39   **demanding testimony from at least** Deuteronomy 17:6.

39   **as well as proof that someone** Mishnah, *Makkot* 1:9.

39   **"Jews, contrary to general understanding"** Jonathan Rosen, *The Talmud and the Internet: A Journey Between Worlds* (New York: Picador, 2000), 30.

40   **"Jews became the people of"** Ibid., 14.

41   **"There are no weekly meetings"** Rabbi Bradley Shavit Artson, "God: An Introduction," in Rabbi Bradley Shavit Artson and Deborah Silver, eds., *Walking with God* (Bel Air, C.A.: Ziegler School of Rabbinic Studies, 2007), 12, https://www.aju.edu/ziegler-school-rabbinic-studies/our-torah/walking-series.

42   **There are about 14 million** Pew Research Center, *The Changing Global Religious Landscape,* April 5, 2017, 10, http://www.pewforum.org/wp-content/uploads/sites/7/2017/04/FULL-REPORT-WITH-APPENDIXES-A-AND-B-APRIL-3.pdf.

42   **were oddly contradictory** See Paul Johnson, *A History of the Jews* (New York: Harper Perennial, 1988), 309; Dennis Prager and Joseph Telushkin, *Why the Jews?: The Reason for Antisemitism, the Most Accurate Predictor of Human Evil* (New York: Touchstone, 2016), 3; Rabbi Jonathan Sacks, *A Letter in the Scroll: Understanding Our Jewish Identity and Exploring the Legacy of the World's Oldest Religion* (New York: Free Press, 2000), 195.

43   **with the first Jewish settlers** Jonathan D. Sarna, *American Judaism* (New Haven: Yale Univ. Press, 2004), 1–2.

43   **a handful of Jews** Ibid., 1.

43   **in 2017, antisemitic incidents rose** Anti-Defamation League, *2017 Audit of Anti-Semitic Incidents: 2017 Year in Review,* 4, https://www.adl.org/media/11174/download.

43   **Between late January 2017** Anti-Defamation League, *Quantifying Hate: A Year of Anti-Semitism on Twitter,* May 7, 2018, https://www.adl.org/resources/reports/quantifying-hate-a-year-of-anti-semitism-on-twitter.

43   **the "lachrymose theory" of Jewish history** Salo Baron, "Ghetto and Emancipation: Shall We Revise the Traditional View?" *The Menorah Journal* 14, no. 6 (June 1928): 526.

47   **"the anthropocentric nature of revelation"** Rabbi Donniel Hartman, *Putting God Second: How to Save Religion from Itself* (Boston: Beacon Press, 2016), 123.

48   **Revelation thus cannot be viewed** Ibid.

48   **"Scripture is thus inherently constituted"** Ibid.

48   **"The Torah has a very strong"** Rabbi Alan Lew, *This Is Real and You Are*

Completely Unprepared: The Days of Awe as a Journey of Transformation (Boston: Little, Brown, 2003), 199.

48   **The Code of Hammurabi, for example** See Code of Hammurabi 196–205.

49   **According to this midrash** Babylonian Talmud, *Menaḥot* 29b.

49   **"Which narrative will ultimately prevail?"** Hartman, *Putting God Second,* 42.

50   **"opium of the people"** Karl Marx, *Critique of Hegel's "Philosophy of Right,"* Joseph O'Malley, ed. and trans., Annette Jolin, trans. (Cambridge: Cambridge Univ. Press, 1977), 131.

50   **"Theirs was a system"** Rosen, *The Talmud and the Internet,* 61.

3 | FREEING GOD FROM "HIS" HUMAN-SHAPED CAGE IN THE SKY

52   **One recent study found** Pew Research Center, *A Portrait of Jewish Americans: Findings from a Pew Research Center Survey of U.S. Jews* October 1, 2013, 74, http://www.pewresearch.org/wp-content/uploads/sites/7/2013/10/jewish-american-full-report-for-web.pdf.

60   **Rabbi Edward Feinstein shares a story** Rabbi Edward Feinstein, *Tough Questions Jews Ask: A Young Adult's Guide to Building a Jewish Life,* 2nd ed. (Woodstock, V.T.: Jewish Lights, 2014), 6–7.

61   **"In the midst of life"** Arthur Green, *Radical Judaism: Rethinking God and Tradition* (New Haven: Yale University Press, 2010), 4–5.

61   **"overview effect"** See Frank White, *The Overview Effect: Space Exploration and Human Evolution* (Boston: Houghton Mifflin, 1987).

61   **"I would suggest that science is"** Carl Sagan, *The Varieties of Scientific Experience: A Personal View of the Search for God,* ed. Ann Druyan (New York: Penguin, 2006), 31.

63   **An often-cited medieval midrash** *Exodus Rabbah* 5:9.

63   **"If various people can and do"** Rabbi Elliot Dorff, "God in Modern Jewish Thought," in Rabbi Bradley Shavit Artson and Deborah Silver, eds., *Walking with God* (Bel Air, C.A.: Ziegler School of Rabbinic Studies, 2007), 95–96, https://www.aju.edu/ziegler-school-rabbinic-studies/our-torah/walking-series.

65   **Righteous people who suffer** Babylonian Talmud, *Berakhot* 7a.

65   **It's a mystery** *Pirkei Avot* 4:15.

65   **There are certain natural laws** Babylonian Talmud, *Avodah Zarah* 54b.

65   **regarding the giving of the Torah** *Pirkei Avot* 3:14.

65   **"It is like a man who"** Mekilta, Beshallah 4, translation from George Foot Moore, *Judaism in the First Centuries of the Christian Era: The Age of Tannaim,* vol. 2 (Peabody, M.A.: Hendrickson, 1997), 203–204.

66   **"The difference between God's intelligence"** Kenneth Seeskin, *Mai-*

monides: *A Guide for Today's Perplexed* (Millburn, N.J.: Behrman House, 1991), 29.

66 **"We do not say this heat"** Moses Maimonides, *The Guide for the Perplexed,* trans. M. Friedländer, 2nd ed. (London: Routledge & Kegan Paul, 1904), part 1, chs. 56, 79, http://www.sacred-texts.com/jud/gfp/gfp066.htm.

66 **"It is as if God is"** Seeskin, *Maimonides,* 36.

66 **Seeskin invites us to imagine** Ibid., 36–37.

67 **"The point is not to comprehend"** Ibid., 79.

67 **"There is none beside Him"** Deuteronomy 4:35.

67 **"The whole world is filled"** Numbers 14:21, translation from Jay Michaelson, *Everything Is God: The Radical Path of Nondual Judaism* (Boston: Trumpeter, 2009), 52.

67 **"There is therefore absolutely nothing"** *Likutim Yekarim* 14d, quoted in *Sefer Baal Shem Tov,* VeEthChanan13, translation from Rabbi Aryeh Kaplan, *The Light Beyond: Adventures in Hasidic Thought* (New York: Menzaim, 1981), 37.

68 **"I will be what I will be"** Exodus 3:14.

68 **"I am becoming that which"** Email from Rabbi Jonathan Kligler, November 15, 2017.

68 **"The closer I feel to life"** Rabbi Alexander M. Schindler, "Here and Hereafter," in Rifat Sonsino and Daniel B. Syme, *What Happens After I Die: Jewish Views of Life After Death* (New York: Union of American Hebrew Congregations Press, 1990), 71.

68 **"the great force of life"** Eitan Fishbane, "God as the Breath of Life," in Rabbi Elliot J. Cosgrove, ed., *Jewish Theology in Our Time: A New Generation Explores the Foundations and Future of Jewish Belief* (Woodstock, V.T.: Jewish Lights, 2013), 12.

68 **"the inner force of existence itself"** Green, *Radical Judaism,* 19.

68 **A more accessible explanation** As recounted in Michaelson, *Everything Is God,* 87–88.

68 **"in some mysterious way Being"** Green, *Radical Judaism,* 20.

69 **"to return to the experience"** Michaelson, *Everything Is God,* 8.

69 **"How might we approach strangers"** Ibid., 184.

69 **"If every moment, every object"** Rabbi James Jacobson-Maisels, "Non-Dual Judaism," in Cosgrove, ed., *Jewish Theology in Our Time,* 34.

69 **"a sort of invisible superman"** Mordecai M. Kaplan, *The Meaning of God in Modern Jewish Religion* (New York: Behrman's Jewish Book House, 1937), 88.

69 **"man normally veers in the direction"** Mordecai M. Kaplan, *Questions*

Jews Ask: Reconstructionist Answers (New York: Reconstructionist Press, 1956), 84.

69 **"the power that makes for salvation"** Kaplan, *The Meaning of God in Modern Jewish Religion,* 40.

70 **"God is the force"** Rabbi Elliot Dorff, "God in Modern Jewish Thought," in Artson and Silver, *Walking with God,* 97.

70 **"He or She, limited by"** Martin Buber, *I and Thou,* trans. Walter Kaufmann (New York: Touchstone, 1996), 59.

70 **"You" who "fills the firmament"** Ibid.

70 **"deep calls unto deep"** Psalms 42:7. Quoted in Martin Buber, *Between Man and Man,* trans. Ronald Gregor Smith (New York: Macmillan, 1966), 204.

70 **"Every particular Thou is a glimpse"** Martin Buber, *I and Thou,* trans. Ronald Gregor Smith (New York: Scribner Classics, 2000), 77.

71 **"The man who steps"** Buber, *I and Thou,* trans. Kaufmann, 158.

71 **"unknown and indifferent to man"** Abraham Joshua Heschel, *The Prophets* (New York: Harper Pernnial, 2001), 298.

71 **As a result of this move** Shai Held, *Abraham Joshua Heschel: The Call of Transcendence* (Bloomington, I.N.: University of Indiana Press, 2013), 21.

71 **"righteous indignation"** Heschel, *The Prophets,* 363.

71 **Understanding God in this way** Abraham Joshua Heschel, *Man Is Not Alone: A Philosophy of Religion* (New York: Farrar, Straus and Giroux, 1976), 48.

72 **"transcendent loan"** Ibid.

72 **"radical amazement"** Abraham Joshua Heschel, *God in Search of Man: A Philosophy of Judaism* (New York: Farrar, Straus and Giroux, 1976), 45.

72 **And we have a feeling of "indebtedness"** Ibid., 112.

72 **"It did not really matter"** Viktor E. Frankl, *Man's Search for Meaning* (Boston: Beacon Press, 2006), 77.

72 **"the human project now becomes"** Held, *Abraham Joshua Heschel,* 19.

72 **"relentless self-assertion"** Ibid., 43.

72 **"move from ego-centeredness"** Ibid., 4.

72 **"are caused by bad luck"** Harold S. Kushner, *When Bad Things Happen to Good People* (New York: Anchor Books, 2004), 147–148.

72 **"neither causes nor prevents tragedies"** Ibid., 154.

72 **God *does* inspire human beings** Ibid., 142, 155.

73 **"I believe that God gives us"** Ibid., 141.

73 **Kushner acknowledges that his detractors** Rabbi Harold Kushner, "Encountering the Living God," in Rabbi Edward Feinstein, ed., *Jews and Judaism in the 21st Century: Human Responsibility, the Presence of God,*

and the Future of the Covenant (Woodstock, V.T.: Jewish Lights, 2007), 81–82.

73 **"God-as-person"** Feinstein, *Jews and Judaism in the 21st Century,* 104.

73 **So instead of saying that** Rabbi Harold M. Schulweis, "From God to Godliness: Proposal for a Predicate Theology," *Reconstructionist,* February 1975, 1, http://hmsi.info/wp-content/uploads/2017/01/from-god-to -godliness-proposal-for-predicate-theology.pdf.

73 **"express Godliness"** Feinstein, *Jews and Judaism in the 21st Century,* 104.

73 **"Does God console me"** Ibid.

74 **"We aren't human *beings*"** Rabbi Bradley Shavit Artson, *God of Becoming and Relationship: The Dynamic Nature of Process Theology* (Nashville, T.N.: Jewish Lights, 2016), 82.

74 **"God works through persuasion and invitation"** Ibid., 17.

74 **At every moment, God offers** Ibid., 41.

74 **We have the freedom** Ibid., 11–12, 17.

74 **"God is persistently, tirelessly luring creation"** Ibid., 125.

74 **"Who am I that I should"** Exodus 3:11–12.

76 **"You can safely assume you've created"** Anne Lamott, *Bird by Bird: Some Instructions on Writing and Life* (New York: Anchor Books, 1995), 22.

76 **"what appears to the mind"** Michaelson, *Everything Is God,* 181.

77 **"the mystery that is rendered banal"** Jay Michaelson, "Surrendering to the Preposterousness of Prayer," in Rabbi Mike Comins, *Making Prayer Real: Leading Jewish Spiritual Voices on Why Prayer Is Difficult and What to Do About It* (Woodstock, V.T.: Jewish Lights, 2010), 36.

77 **"If to believe in God means"** Martin S. Buber, *Meetings: Autobiographical Fragments,* 3rd ed., ed. and trans. Maurice S. Friedman (London: Routledge, 2002), 53.

77 **"I am sometimes asked"** Rabbi Jeremy Gordon, "More Theos, Less Ology," in Cosgrove, *Jewish Theology in Our Time,* 54.

78 **"Their way of thinking typically prefers"** Rabbi Lawrence A. Hoffman, ed., *My People's Prayer Book: Traditional Prayers, Modern Commentaries,* vol. 1, *The Sh'ma and Its Blessings* (Woodstock, V.T.: Jewish Lights, 1997), 70–71.

78 **"theology and atheism go out"** Michaelson, *Everything Is God,* 179.

78 **"one God or fewer"** Ibid., 129.

79 **Yet I often find** Rabbi Rachel Timoner, *Breath of Life: God as Spirit in Judaism* (Brewster, M.A.: Paraclete Press, 2011), ix–x.

79 **"for you have wrestled with God"** Genesis 32:29. Note, this is not the JPS translation, but rather a commonly used translation.

79 **"Far be it from You"** Genesis 18:25.

80   **"turn from Your blazing anger"** Exodus 32:12.

80   **"And consider one of my favorite"** Babylonian Talmud, *Bava Met-zia* 59a–b, translation of final line from Rabbi Joseph Telushkin, *Jewish Literacy: The Most Important Things to Know About the Jewish Religion, Its People, and Its History,* rev. ed. (New York: William Morrow, 2008), 156.

81   **"atheists replace God"** Dennis Prager and Joseph Telushkin, *The Nine Questions People Ask About Judaism* (New York: Touchstone, 1986), 38.

81   **Pre-Holocaust Germany** Paul Johnson, *A History of the Jews* (New York: Harper Perennial, 1988), 470.

81   **"No you're not, that job"** Avraham Infeld, Informal talk given to participants on Schusterman REALITY Global trip to Israel, Jerusalem, August 29, 2015.

82   **"They think that God is"** Malala Yousafzai, "Sixteenth Birthday Speech at the United Nations," Speech on "Malala Day" at the United Nations, New York, N.Y., July 12, 2013, https://www.malala.org/newsroom/malala -UN-speech.

83   **"A Jew dare not"** In Milton Himmelfarb, ed., *The Condition of Jewish Belief: A Symposium Compiled by the Editors of Commentary Magazine* (New York: Macmillan, 1966), 179.

4 | MITZVOT AND THE SPIRITUALITY OF DOING

85   **"Better that they"** Jerusalem Talmud, *Ḥagigah* 1:7, translation from Dennis Prager and Joseph Telushkin, *The Nine Questions People Ask About Judaism* (New York: Touchstone, 1986), 18.

86   **"A Jew is asked to take"** Abraham Joshua Heschel, "The Meaning of Observance," in Jacob Neusner, ed. *Understanding Jewish Theology: Classical Issues and Modern Perspectives* (Binghamton, N.Y.: Global Publications, 2001), 100. Previously published in *The Jewish Frontier* (April 1954), 22–28.

87   **"Similarly, there is a wonderful"** *Midrash Shmuel,* ch. 4, translation from Rabbi Jill Jacobs, *There Shall Be No Needy: Pursuing Social Justice Through Jewish Law and Tradition* (Woodstock, V.T.: Jewish Lights, 2010), 163–164.

89   **"the systematic effort of the rabbis"** Rabbi Bradley Shavit Artson, "Mitzvot: Imperatives of a Loving Heart," in Rabbi Bradley Shavit Artson and Rabbi Patricia Fenton, eds., *Walking with Mitzvot* (Bel Air, C.A.: Ziegler School of Rabbinic Studies, 2011), 8, https://www.aju.edu/ziegler-school -rabbinic-studies/our-torah/walking-series.

89   **it is related to a word** Rabbi Moshe Smolkin, "Mitzvot and the Spirit," in Ibid., 52.

91 **"a series of practices to bring"** Rabbi James Jacobson-Maisels, "Non-dual Judaism," in Rabbi Elliot J. Cosgrove, ed., *Jewish Theology in Our Time: A New Generation Explores the Foundations and Future of Jewish Belief* (Woodstock, V.T.: Jewish Lights, 2013), 38.

91 **"make a fence for the Torah"** *Pirkei Avot* 1:1.

91 **For example, the Talmud includes** Babylonian Talmud, *Bava Metzia* 83a.

92 **"a scoundrel within the limits"** Ramban on Leviticus, 19:2, translation from Elliot N. Dorff, *To Do the Right and the Good: A Jewish Approach to Modern Social Ethics* (Philadelphia: Jewish Publication Society, 2002), 117.

92 **Orthodox Jews—who are 10 percent** Pew Research Center, *A Portrait of Jewish Americans: Findings from a Pew Research Center Survey of U.S. Jews,* October 1, 2013, 48, http://www.pewresearch.org/wp-content/uploads/sites/7/2013/10/jewish-american-full-report-for-web.pdf.

92 **The Conservative movement—to which** Ibid.

92 **Reform Judaism, the largest movement** Ibid.

92 **Like Reform Jews, Reconstructionists** Ibid.

92 **"The ancient authorities are entitled to"** Mordecai M. Kaplan, *Not So Random Thoughts: Witty and Profound Observations on Society, Religion, and Jewish Life by America's Leading Jewish Thinker* (New York: Reconstructionist Press, 1966), 263.

93 **That said, an increasing number** Ibid.

94 **"It is not your responsibility"** *Pirkei Avot* 2:16, translation from Open Mishna, Sefaria.org.

5 | BECOMING A GREAT PERSON

98 **"Let there be light"** Genesis 1:3.

98 **"Death and life"** Proverbs 18:21.

98 **"The Holocaust did not begin"** Susannah Heschel, Introduction, Abraham Joshua Heschel, *Moral Grandeur and Spiritual Audacity: Essays Edited by Susannah Heschel* (New York: Farrar, Straus and Giroux, 1997), viii.

98 **"Unless you, or someone dear"** Rabbi Joseph Telushkin, *Words That Hurt, Words That Heal: How the Words You Choose Shape Your Destiny,* rev. ed. (New York: William Morrow, 2019), 3–4.

98 **"Anyone who humiliates another"** Babylonian Talmud, *Bava Metzia* 58b.

99 **The Rabbis approvingly cite the example** Babylonian Talmud, *Sanhedrin* 11a.

99 **"Do not go about as a"** Leviticus 19:16. Note that "go about as a talebearer among" is an alternative translation JPS provides in a footnote.

99 **"In a small town"** Rabbi Joseph Telushkin, *A Code of Jewish Ethics,* vol. 1, *You Shall Be Holy* (New York: Bell Tower, 2006), 337–338.

100 **"If a man takes a sword"** *Midrash Psalms,* 120:4, translation from Telushkin, *A Code of Jewish Ethics,* vol. 1, 338–339.

100 **"A gossip always seeks out"** *Orchot Tzaddikim,* trans. Seymour J. Cohen (Jerusalem: Feldheim, 1974), 437.

102 **Another example, courtesy of** Nachum Amsel, *The Jewish Encyclopedia of Moral and Ethical Issues* (Northvale, N.J.: Jason Aronson, 1994), 5.

103 **Each person has what Mussar expert** Alan Morinis, *Everyday Holiness: The Jewish Spiritual Path of Mussar* (Boulder, C.O.: Trumpeter, 2007), 19.

104 **These days, our culture is focused** David Brooks, "The Moral Bucket List," *The New York Times,* April 11, 2015.

104 **"Years pass and the deepest parts"** Ibid.

105 **The Hebrew word for sin** Rabbi Reuven Hammer, "The Jewish View of Sin," *My Jewish Learning,* https://www.myjewishlearning.com/article/the -jewish-view-of-sin/.

105 **"Sin crouches at the door"** Genesis 4:7.

106 **And they even state that in** Jerusalem Talmud, *Kiddushin* 4:12.

106 **"for the ingratitude and haughtiness"** Elliot N. Dorff, *Love Your Neighbor and Yourself: A Jewish Approach to Modern Personal Ethics* (Philadelphia: Jewish Publication Society, 2003), 25.

106 **One of the best-known Talmudic** Babylonian Talmud, *Shabbat* 33b.

107 **were it not for the evil** *Genesis Rabbah* 9:7.

107 **There's even a charming story** Babylonian Talmud, *Yoma* 69b.

107 **So as Rabbi Harold Kushner notes** Harold S. Kushner, *To Life!: A Celebration of Jewish Being and Thinking* (New York: Grand Central, 1994), 53–54.

107 **Kushner offers the following examples** Ibid., 55–65.

109 **"That which is hateful to you"** Babylonian Talmud, *Shabbat* 31a. This translation is not from Sefaria.org, but is a commonly used one.

109 **Another sage, the renowned Rabbi Akiva** Jerusalem Talmud, *Nedarim* 30b.

109 **Rabbi Donniel Hartman refers to** Rabbi Donniel Hartman, *Putting God Second: How to Save Religion from Itself* (Boston: Beacon Press, 2016), 20.

109 **"from his perch of royal power"** Ibid., 23.

109 **This same ethic of non-indifference** Ibid., 27–40.

109 **If we see someone we know** Leviticus 19:17.

109 **If we find someone's lost property** Deuteronomy 22:1–3.

109 **"stand idly by"** Leviticus 19:16, translation from Hartman, *Putting God Second,* 31.

109 **"drowning in a river"** Babylonian Talmud, *Sanhedrin* 73a.

110 **"turn justice into wormwood"** Amos 5:7.

110 **"defraud men of their homes"** Micah 2:2.

110 **"trample the heads of the poor"** Amos 2:7.
110 **It's as if, notes Rabbi Telushkin** Rabbi Joseph Telushkin, *Biblical Literacy: The Most Important People, Events, and Ideas of the Hebrew Bible* (New York: William Morrow, 1997), 12.
111 **"is Mine"** Leviticus 25:23.
111 **insisting in the Torah that** Leviticus 19:9–10; Deuteronomy 24:19, 21.
111 **every seven years, they should let** Exodus 23:10–11.
111 **Further, every seven years, all debts** Deuteronomy 15:1–3.
111 **and every fifty years** Leviticus 25:10–13.
112 **Hillel actually developed a loophole** Mishnah, *Shevi'it* 10:3, translation from Sefaria Community Translation, Sefaria.org.
112 **"When a poor person comes"** Babylonian Talmud, *Shabbat* 151b.
112 **"is consistent with the reality"** Rabbi Jill Jacobs, *There Shall Be No Needy: Pursuing Social Justice Through Jewish Law and Tradition* (Woodstock, V.T.: Jewish Lights, 2010), 51.
113 **"If there is among you"** Deuteronomy 15:7–8, translation from Jacobs, *There Shall Be No Needy,* 11.
113 **"The overarching Jewish attitude toward"** Jacobs, *There Shall Be No Needy,* 12.
113 **And in Maimonides' frequently cited list** Moses Maimonides, *Mishneh Torah,* "Gifts to the Poor," 10:7–14.
113 **To that end, the Talmud instructs** Babylonian Talmud, *Bava Metzia* 75b.
114 **The Rabbis even urged rich people** Babylonian Talmud, *Moed Katan* 27a.
114 **The poor are even expected** Babylonian Talmud, *Gittin* 7b.
114 **working at an unpleasant job** Babylonian Talmud, *Pesaḥim* 113a.
114 **living as frugally as possible** Babylonian Talmud, *Pesaḥim* 112a.
114 **But rather than worrying** *Leviticus Rabbah* 34:7, translation from Rabbi Joseph Telushkin, *A Code of Jewish Ethics,* vol. 2, *Love Your Neighbor as Yourself* (New York: Bell Tower, 2009), 238.
114 **the rate of fraud** Emelyn Rude, "A Very Short History of Food Stamp Fraud in America," *Time,* March 30, 2017, http://time.com/4711668/history-food-stamp-fraud/.
115 **For example, when we visit** Maimonides, *Mishneh Torah,* "Mourning," 14:6.
115 **though if the person is in** Josef Karo, *Shulhan Arukh,* "Yoreh Deah," 335:3.
115 **And we shouldn't just visit once** Maimonides, *Mishneh Torah,* "Mourning," 14:4.
115 **The Rabbis viewed acts of ḥesed** Babylonian Talmud, *Sotah* 14a.
116 **These experiences have often reminded me** Babylonian Talmud, *Berakhot* 5b.

116 **One example occurred on September 11** Katharine Lackey, "An Oasis of Kindness on 9/11: This Town Welcomed 6,700 Strangers amid Terror Attacks," *USA Today,* September 8, 2017, https://www.usatoday.com/story/news/nation/2017/09/08/gander-newfoundland-september-11-terror-attacks-kindness-come-from-away/631329001/; Michael Schulman, "Stuck in Gander, Newfoundland," *The New Yorker,* March 27, 2017, https://www.newyorker.com/magazine/2017/03/27/stuck-in-gander-newfoundland.

118 **"be fruitful and multiply"** Genesis 1:28. Note that I substituted the more commonly known King James translation "Be fruitful and multiply" for the JPS translation, "Be fertile and increase."

118 **"See, I give you every"** Genesis 1:29.

118 **"every tree that was pleasing"** Genesis 2:9.

118 **"Of every tree of the garden"** Genesis 2:16.

118 **"Every creature that lives"** Genesis 9:3.

118 **"eat flesh with its life-blood"** Genesis 9:4.

118 **God later tells the Israelites** Leviticus 11.

118 **God then further prohibits** Exodus 23:19, 34:26; Deuteronomy 14:21.

118 **and killing a baby animal** Leviticus 22:28.

118 **And God insists that** Deuteronomy 22:6–7.

119 **We're also told not to yoke** Deuteronomy 22:10.

119 **not to muzzle an ox** Deuteronomy 25:4.

119 **We must also let all our** Exodus 20:10, 23:12; Deuteronomy 5:14.

119 **if we see our enemy's donkey** Exodus 23:5.

119 **"How can a man of Israel"** Rabbi Yehezkel Landau, *Responsa of Noda BiYehuda II,* Yoreh Deah, Teshuva 10, translation from Sefaria Responsa Anthology, Sefaria.org.

120 **"For there is no difference"** Moses Maimonides, *The Guide for the Perplexed,* 3:48, translation from Telushkin, *A Code of Jewish Ethics,* vol. 2, 303.

120 **"teach us the trait of mercy"** Ramban on Deuteronomy 22:6, translation from Sefaria Community Translation, Sefaria.org.

120 **"If the Law provides"** Maimonides, *The Guide for the Perplexed,* ch. 48, 372.

121 **"Now go study"** Babylonian Talmud, *Shabbat* 31a.

121 **"Study is greater"** Babylonian Talmud, *Kiddushin* 40b.

121 **And as Rabbi Jonathan Sacks** Rabbi Jonathan Sacks, *Ceremony and Celebration: Introduction to the Holidays* (New Milford, C.T.: Maggid Books, 2017), 191.

121 **"in danger of verbalizing my moral"** Quoted in Adrienne Rich, "The Burning of Paper Instead of Children," *The Will to Change: Poems 1968–1970* (New York: W.W. Norton, 1971), 15.

122 **"In a place where there are"** *Pirkei Avot* 2:5. I substituted "strive," used in other translations, for "try" in Greenberg's translation.

6 | PRAYER AND MORE

123 **"The problem is that our ancient"** Rabbi Zalman Schachter-Shalomi with Joel Segel, *Jewish with Feeling: A Guide to Meaningful Jewish Practice* (Woodstock, V.T.: Jewish Lights, 2013), 5.

123 **"If you say *'Modeh ani'"*** Rabbi Jeff Roth, quoted in Rabbi Mike Comins, *Making Prayer Real: Leading Jewish Spiritual Voices on Why Prayer Is Difficult and What to Do About It* (Woodstock, V.T.: Jewish Lights, 2010), 174.

124 **"in our synagogues, people who are"** "The Spirit of Jewish Prayer," in Abraham Joshua Heschel, *Moral Grandeur and Spiritual Audacity: Essays Edited by Susannah Heschel* (New York: Farrar, Straus and Giroux, 1997), 103.

124 **"wrapping your tongue around a fossil"** Judith Shulevitz, *The Sabbath World: Glimpses of a Different Order of Time* (New York: Random House, 2011), 60.

124 **"Praised are You"** "Maariv Aravim," in Elyse D. Frishman, ed., *Mishkan T'filah: A Reform Siddur* (New York: Central Conference of American Rabbis, 2007), 6.

125 **"I read to them"** Comins, *Making Prayer Real,* xviii.

126 **"Does God answer prayer?"** Lawrence A. Hoffman, *The Way into Jewish Prayer* (Woodstock, V.T.: Jewish Lights, 2010), 17.

126 **"If praying was reliable"** Eugene B. Borowitz, *Liberal Judaism* (New York: Union of American Hebrew Congregations, 1984), 431.

126 **"asleep to some extent"** Rabbi Shefa Gold, "Longing: Fuel for Spiritual Practice," in Comins, *Making Prayer Real,* 52.

127 **"Listen, are you breathing"** "Have You Ever Tried to Enter the Long Black Branches," in Mary Oliver, *New and Selected Poems,* vol. 2 (Boston: Beacon Press, 2005), 142.

127 **"the axe for the frozen sea"** Franz Kafka to Oskar Pollak, January 27, 1904, in Franz Kafka, *Letters to Friends, Family, and Editors,* Richard and Clara Winston, trans. (New York: Schocken Books, 1977), 16. Note that Kafka was referring to books.

128 **"Jewish diary of the centuries"** Rabbi Lawrence A. Hoffman, ed., *My People's Prayer Book: Traditional Prayers, Modern Commentaries,* vol. 1, *The Sh'ma and Its Blessings* (Woodstock, V.T.: Jewish Lights, 1997), 1.

129 **"I call out to God"** Rabbi Aryeh Ben David, "Does Prayer Work?" in Comins, *Making Prayer Real,* 22.

129 **"is not to feel good"** Jay Michaelson, *Everything Is God: The Radical Path of Nondual Judaism* (Boston: Trumpeter, 2009), 123.

129 **Rather, as Rabbi Shai Held observes** Rabbi Shai Held, "Living and Dreaming with God," in Rabbi Elliot J. Cosgrove, ed., *Jewish Theology in Our Time: A New Generation Explores the Foundations and Future of Jewish Belief* (Woodstock, V.T.: Jewish Lights Publishing, 2013), 18.

130 **"Even if our mouths"** "Nishmat Kol Chai," in Frishman, *Mishkan T'filah,* 220.

130 **"Poetry is the official palace language"** Anne Lamott, *Help, Thanks, Wow: The Three Essential Prayers* (New York: Riverhead Books, 2012), 79.

131 **"Is such the fast I desire"** Isaiah 58:5, 6–8.

131 **"A famous Ḥasidic master"** As recounted in Rabbi Donniel Hartman, *Putting God Second: How to Save Religion from Itself* (Boston: Beacon Press, 2016), 19–20.

132 **"Prayer is meaningless unless"** "On Prayer," in Heschel, *Moral Grandeur and Spiritual Audacity,* 262.

132 **"Even without words"** Susannah Heschel, "Op-Ed: What Selma Means to the Jews," *Jewish Telegraph Agency,* January 28, 2015, https://www.jta .org/2015/01/18/opinion/op-ed-what-selma-meant-to-the-jews.

133 **"is the indigenous Jewish practice"** Ariel Burger, "Hitbodedut, A Brief Introduction," unpublished article, 4.

133 **"When you're telling the truth"** Lamott, *Help, Thanks, Wow,* 6.

133 **"The seal of God is truth"** Babylonian Talmud, *Shabbat* 55a, *Sanhedrin* 64a, translation from Rabbi Joseph Telushkin, *A Code of Jewish Ethics,* vol. 1, *You Shall Be Holy* (New York: Bell Tower, 2006), 398.

134 **Hebrew, as Rabbi Marcia Prager** Rabbi Marcia Prager, *The Path of Blessing: Experiencing the Energy and Abundance of the Divine* (Woodstock, V.T.: Jewish Lights, 2003), 26.

134 **For example, explains Prager** Ibid., 40, 43.

134 **Given its connections** Ibid., 40–41.

134 **"Has there ever been an experience"** Ibid., 44.

134 **You can see what the poet** Hayim Nahman Bialik, "On 'Language and Nation,'" Speech, Hovevei Sfar Ever, Moscow, April 2017, https:// benyehuda.org/bialik/dvarim02.html.

134 **"in the interaction between"** Reuven Kimelman, "The Shema Liturgy: From Covenant Ceremony to Coronation," in Joseph Tabory, ed., *Kenishta: Studies of the Synagogue World,* vol. 1 (Ramat-Gan: Bar-Ilan University Press, 2001), 28.

134 **Let's take a look at** Rabbi Elie Kaunfer, "The Other in Jewish Prayer," Lecture, Adas Israel Synagogue, May 8, 2018. See also audio of Kaunfer's lectures on prayer posted on Hadar.org and his forthcoming book, *Come Closer: Literary Interpretations of the Amidah.*

135 **"O Lord, open my lips"** "The Amidah," translation in Rabbi Jonathan

Sacks, ed. and trans., *The Koren Siddur,* 2nd ed. (Jerusalem: Koren, 2016), 108.

135 **"the God of your father"** Exodus 3:6.

136 **"the great, the mighty"** Deuteronomy 10:17–19.

136 **"I am a shield to you"** Genesis 15:1.

136 **"How shall I know"** Genesis 15:8.

136 **As Rabbi Bradley Shavit Artson explains** Comins, *Making Prayer Real,* 155.

137 **As Rabbi Zalman Schachter-Shalomi noted** Schachter-Shalomi, *Jewish with Feeling,* 82.

137 **"O my luve's"** Robert Burns, "A Red, Red Rose," in *The Complete Works of Robert Burns: Containing His Poems, Songs, and Correspondence,* Allan Cunningham, ed. (Boston: Phillips, Sampson, and Company, 1855), 264, http://www.gutenberg.org/files/18500/18500-h/18500-h.htm#songsCXLIX.

137 **"And they [the angels] call"** "The Amidah," translation in Sacks, *The Koren Siddur,* 112.

138 **Or let's take the Torah excerpt** "The Shema," translation from Ibid., 98.

138 **But if they worship other gods** Ibid., 98, 100.

138 **"the first step to prayer"** Hoffman, *The Way into Jewish Prayer,* 18.

139 **"counts the number of the stars"** Psalm 147, translation in Sacks, *The Koren Siddur,* 74.

139 **"Night brings out predators"** Rabbi Lawrence A. Hoffman, "Anxiety and Opportunity: The Mood of Nighttime Prayer," in Rabbi Lawrence A. Hoffman, ed., *My People's Prayer Book: Traditional Prayers, Modern Commentaries,* vol. 9, *Welcoming the Night: Minchah and Ma'ariv (Afternoon and Evening Prayer)* (Woodstock, V.T.: Jewish Lights, 2010), 2.

140 **"spread over us Your canopy"** "Hashkiveinu," translation in Sacks, *The Koren Siddur,* 250.

140 **But as Rabbi Sheila Peltz Weinberg** Rabbi Sheila Peltz Weinberg, informal talk at meditation retreat, n.d.

140 **As the old story goes** Recounted by Rabbi David J. Wolpe in Comins, *Making Prayer Real,* 177.

140 **"At first, the mundane surrender"** Jay Michaelson, "Surrendering to the Preposterousness of Prayer," in Comins, *Making Prayer Real,* 37.

140 **"Let's not get bogged down"** Lamott, *Help, Thanks, Wow,* 2–3.

141 **In fact, one midrash lists** *Deuteronomy Rabbah* 2:1, translation from Anne Brener, "Choosing Life: Prayer and Healing," in Comins, *Making Prayer Real,* 26.

142 **I love the story** Rabbi Elie Kaunfer, "Making Prayer Meaningful: Two Approaches," ELI Talk, https://elitalks.org/making-prayer-meaningful-2 -approaches; Rabbi Elie Kaunfer, *Empowered Judaism: What Independent*

Minyanim Can Teach Us About Building Vibrant Jewish Communities (Woodstock, V.T.: Jewish Lights, 2012), 49.

143 **"who has imparted Godly wisdom"** Translation from Prager, *The Path of Blessing,* 172.

143 **"who makes varied creatures"** Translation from Ibid.

143 **"who has given us life"** Translation from Ibid., 173.

143 **"in which we thank God"** "Asher Yatzar," translation from Jules Harlow, ed., *Siddur Sim Shalom for Weekdays* (New York: Rabbinical Assembly, 2005), 4.

143 **Reuven stepped into it** *Exodus Rabbah,* 24:1, translation from Lawrence Kushner, *God Was in This Place & I, i Did Not Know: Finding Self, Spirituality and Ultimate Meaning* (Woodstock, V.T.: Jewish Lights Publishing, 2016), 28–29.

144 **Rabbi Max Kadushin deemed this approach** Max Kadushin, *Worship and Ethics: A Study in Rabbinic Judaism* (Binghamton, N.Y.: Global Publications, 2001), 13–17.

144 **It appears to date back** Aryeh Kaplan, *Jewish Meditation: A Practical Guide* (New York: Schocken Books, 1985), 41–42.

144 **"wait one hour and then pray"** Mishnah, *Berakhot* 5:1, translation from Open Mishnah, Sefaria.org.

145 **There are also Jewish texts** Kaplan, *Jewish Meditation,* 45–49.

146 **And that moment when you realize** Herbert Benson with Miriam Z. Klipper, *The Relaxation Response,* rev. ed. (New York: Quill, 2001), xxviii.

146 **"We inhabit the most basic elements"** Alan Lew, *Be Still and Get Going: A Jewish Meditation Practice for Real Life* (New York: Little, Brown, 2005), 26.

147 **one school of thought even views** Babylonian Talmud, *Shabbat* 10a.

147 **"When I pray I talk to God"** In Burton L. Visotzky, *Reading the Book: Making the Bible a Timeless Text* (Philadelphia: Jewish Publication Society, 2005), 228.

149 **"the pitiful prison"** Abraham Joshua Heschel, *Man's Quest for God* (Santa Fe, N.M.: Aurora Press, 1998), 33.

149 **The first is from Rabbi Menachem** Martin Buber, *Tales of the Hasidim, Book Two* (New York: Schocken Books, 1991), 278.

149 **"A young, uneducated shepherd"** Rabbi Jamie S. Korngold, *The God Upgrade: Finding Your 21st-Century Spirituality in Judaism's 5,000-Year-Old Tradition* (Woodstock, V.T.: Jewish Lights, 2011), 183.

150 **"Those who honestly search"** "The Spirit of Jewish Prayer," in Heschel, *Moral Grandeur and Spiritual Audacity,* 126.

7 | GIVING SHABBAT A CHANCE

152 **"God finished the work"** Genesis 2:2.

152 **But the renowned medieval rabbi** Rashi on Genesis 2:2.

152 **"Remember the sabbath day"** Exodus 20:8–11.

153 **The Rabbis even went so far** Babylonian Talmud, *Berakhot* 57b.

153 **Much as Pharaoh insisted** Walter Brueggemann, *Sabbath as Resistance: Saying No to the Culture of Now* (Louisville, K.Y.: Westminster John Knox, 2017), 3–4, 13.

153 **To convince us to purchase** Ibid., 13–14.

153 **To keep up, we need** Ibid., 14.

154 **"without pause, without space or rest"** Rabbi Sheila Peltz Weinberg, "Shabbat and Right Concentration," in *Jewish Mindfulness Meditation Teacher Training Program Curriculum Binder* (New York: Institute for Jewish Spirituality, 2016), 6.

155 **don't work or make others work** Exodus 20:10.

155 **don't kindle fire** Exodus 35:3.

155 **don't "leave [your] place"** Exodus 16:29.

155 **If you poke holes** Mishnah, *Shabbat* 2:4.

155 **If a deer happens to enter** Mishnah, *Shabbat* 13:6.

155 **What about a lion?** Babylonian Talmud, *Shabbat* 106b.

155 **What should you do if** Babylonian Talmud, *Shabbat* 107a.

156 **"May God bless you and keep you"** Numbers 6:25.

156 **"Be who you are"** Marcia Falk, *The Book of Blessings: New Jewish Prayers for Daily Life, the Sabbath, and the New Moon Festival* (San Francisco: HarperSanFrancisco, 1996), 124.

157 **To answer this question** Babylonian Talmud, *Shabbat* 49b.

157 **the type of wood** Exodus 27:1.

157 **the kind of cloth** Exodus 26:1.

157 **The Rabbis counted thirty-nine different** Mishnah, *Shabbat* 7:2.

157 **They decided that getting a haircut** Babylonian Talmud, *Shabbat* 94b.

157 **Watering and fertilizing plants are forbidden** Babylonian Talmud, *Moed Katan* 2b.

157 **They even put restrictions on *handling*** Babylonian Talmud, *Shabbat* 122b.

158 **They also forbade activities even *associated*** Babylonian Talmud, *Shabbat* 143b.

158 **"mountains hanging by a hair"** Mishnah, *Ḥagigah* 1:8, translation from Rabbi Shraga Silverstein, Sefaria.org.

160 **"God blessed the seventh day"** Genesis 2:3.

161 **"sanctuary in time"** Abraham Joshua Heschel, *The Sabbath* (New York: Farrar, Straus and Giroux, 1975), 29.

161 **"the goal is not to have"** Ibid., 3.

162 **"God rested on the seventh day"** Brueggemann, *Sabbath as Resistance,* 29.

162 **"not as creators but creations"** Rabbi Jonathan Sacks, *A Letter in the Scroll: Understanding Our Jewish Identity and Exploring the Legacy of the World's Oldest Religion* (New York: Free Press, 2000), 138.

162 **We live in what** Rabbi Zalman Schachter-Shalomi with Joel Segel, *Jewish with Feeling: A Guide to Meaningful Jewish Practice* (Woodstock, V.T.: Jewish Lights, 2013), 37–38.

163 **"Remember that you were a slave"** Deuteronomy 5:15.

163 **"Six days you shall labor"** Exodus 20:9.

164 **"Those occasional Shabbat dinners"** Blu Greenberg, *How to Run a Traditional Jewish Household* (New York: Fireside, 1985), 28.

165 **"let everyone remain where he is"** Exodus 16:29.

165 **"We can't see the picture"** Alan Lew, *Be Still and Get Going: A Jewish Meditation Practice for Real Life* (New York: Little, Brown, 2005), 39.

165 **"Why *did* God stop, anyway?"** Judith Shulevitz, *The Sabbath World: Glimpses of a Different Order of Time* (New York: Random House, 2011), 217.

166 **"The Shabbat is more than"** Rabbi Irving Greenberg, *The Jewish Way: Living the Holidays* (New York: Touchstone, 1993), 139–140.

166 **The Torah tells us that God** Exodus 31:17.

166 **"He got His soul back"** Harold S. Kushner, *To Life! A Celebration of Jewish Being and Thinking* (New York: Grand Central, 1994), 97.

166 **Rabbi Zalman Schachter-Shalomi explains** Schachter-Shalomi, *Jewish with Feeling,* 48.

166 **In her book on Shabbat** Shulevitz, *The Sabbath World,* 24–26.

166 **Students at the Princeton Theological Seminary** John M. Darley and C. Daniel Batson, "'From Jerusalem to Jericho': A Study of Situational and Dispositional Variables in Helping Behavior," *Journal of Personality and Social Psychology* 27, no. 1 (1973): 100–108, http://citeseerx.ist.psu.edu/viewdoc/summary?doi=10.1.1.315.252.

167 **And as Shulevitz points out** Judith Shulevitz, "How the Sabbath Keeps the Jewish People," *The Forward,* April 2, 2010, https://www.haaretz.com/1.5099822.

168 **Some commentators have interpreted the prohibition** Isaiah Horowitz, *Shenei Luchot HaBerit,* vol. 3, Eliyahu Munk, trans. (New York: KTAV Publishing, 2000), Torah Shebikhtav, Vayakhel, Pekudei, Derekh Chayim. On Sefaria.org.

169 **"Six days you shall labor"** Exodus 20:9.

169 **The midrash asks** Mekhilta de'Rabbi Yishmael, 20:9, translation from Dov Peretz Elkins, ed., *A Shabbat Reader: Universe of Cosmic Joy* (New York: Union of American Hebrew Congregations Press, 1997), 5.

169 **There is a story in** Babylonian Talmud, *Shabbat* 119b.

170 **"Look how clever the Rabbis were"** Greenberg, *How to Run a Traditional Jewish Household,* 40.

8 | JEWISH HOLIDAYS AND THE POWER OF A WELL-PLACED BANANA

173 **"The world was awakened and shattered"** Rabbi Dan Moskovitz, "The Banana on the Seder Plate: A Ritual to Reflect on the Refugee Crisis During the Passover Seder," Religious Action Center of Reform Judaism, March 2016, http://www.rac.org/sites/default/files/Banana%20On%20 Seder%20Plate%20Mar%202016.pdf.

175 **"One could, in fact, teach"** Blu Greenberg, *How to Run a Traditional Jewish Household* (New York: Fireside, 1985), 301.

176 **As Rabbi Jonathan Sacks points out** Jonathan Sacks, *Ceremony and Celebration: Introduction to the Holidays* (New Milford, C.T.: Maggid Books, 2017), 287.

176 **"the festival of Jewish identity"** Rabbi Jonathan Sacks, *The Jonathan Sacks Haggada: Collected Essays on Pesaḥ,* 2nd ed., trans. Jessica Sacks (New Milford, C.T.: Maggid Books, 2016), 20.

177 **One commentator, comparing the Haggadah** David Arnow, "The Haggadah Is a Cubist Composition," in *My People's Passover Haggadah: Traditional Texts, Modern Commentaries,* vol. 1, ed. Rabbi Lawrence A. Hoffman and David Arnow (Woodstock, V.T.: Jewish Lights, 2008), 4.

178 **"Even were we all wise"** Sacks, *The Jonathan Sacks Haggada,* 30.

178 **"The children of Israel groaned"** Ibid., 56.

178 **"Now we are here"** Ibid., 24.

178 **"The Lord acted for me"** Ibid., 40.

178 **"It was not only our ancestors"** Ibid., 90.

179 **"Everyone who elaborates on discussing"** This translation/interpretation is attributed to the fourteenth-century Spanish rabbi David ben Joseph Abudarham. See Hoffman and Arnow, *My People's Passover Haggadah,* 176.

181 **"Wherever you go, I will go"** Ruth 1:16.

181 **And once you convert, the Rabbis** Babylonian Talmud, *Shevuot* 39a.

181 **the Rabbis claimed that all Jews** Ibid.

182 **"You shall not subvert the rights"** Deuteronomy 24:17–18.

182 **"When you gather the grapes"** Deuteronomy 24:21–22.

182 **Remembering "that you were once slaves"** Deuteronomy 5:15.

182 **"Remembering 'that you were once slaves'"** Sacks, *Ceremony and Celebration,* 168.

182 **"You shall not oppress a stranger"** Exodus 23:9.

182 **As Rabbi Shai Held points out** Rabbi Shai Held, "Love Your Neighbor," lecture, 2017 Limmud NY Conference, https://www.youtube.com/watch?v=h2tibgsGPCg.

183 **"Wherever you live, it is probably"** Michael Walzer, *Exodus and Revolution* (New York: Basic Books, 1984), 149.

183 **two-thirds of the white people** Arthur Liebman, *Jews and the Left* (New York: Wiley, 1979), 68.

183 **And in a recent survey** Pew Research Center, *A Portrait of Jewish Americans: Findings from a Pew Research Center Survey of U.S. Jews,* October 1, 2013, 55, http://www.pewresearch.org/wp-content/uploads/sites/7/2013/10/jewish-american-full-report-for-web.pdf.

183 **"When a classmate of mine"** Joshua Israel, "Governor Richards Fought the Good Fight," *Brandeis University Magazine,* Fall 2006, 96.

184 **"We assist refugees today"** Mark Hetfield, "Why a Jewish Organization Is Suing to Stop the Muslim Ban," February 15, 2017, https://www.aclu.org/blog/immigrants-rights/why-jewish-organization-suing-stop-muslim-ban?redirect=blog/speak-freely/why-jewish-organization-suing-stop-muslim-ban.

185 **Maimonides viewed it as** Moses Maimonides, *Mishneh Torah,* "Repentance," 3:4, translation from *Book of Mishnah Torah Yod Ha-Hazakah,* trans. Simon Glazer, vol. 1 (New York: Maimonides Publishing, 1927), on Sefaria.org.

185 **"A great shofar sounds"** "Unetaneh Tokef," translation from *The Koren Rosh Hashana Maḥzor,* 3rd ed., trans. Chief Rabbi Lord Jonathan Sacks (Jerusalem: Koren, 2016), 566.

186 **"There was a great and mighty"** 1 Kings 19:11–12. Note that I substituted "a still, small voice" from the King James translation for "a soft murmuring sound" from the JPS translation.

186 **Blu Greenberg, drawing from the writings** Greenberg, *How to Run a Traditional Jewish Household,* 330–331.

187 **"to zero in on pockets"** Abigail Pogrebin, *My Jewish Year: 18 Holidays, One Wondering Jew* (Bedford, N.Y.: Fig Tree Books, 2017), 26.

187 **"the beginning of Teshuvah"** Alan Lew, *This Is Real and You Are Completely Unprepared: The Days of Awe as a Journey of Transformation* (Boston: Little, Brown, 2003), 52.

188 **"when the walls come tumbling down"** Ibid., 109.

189 **"the worst thing you can do"** Harold S. Kushner, *To Life!: A Celebration of Jewish Being and Thinking* (New York: Grand Central, 1994), 111.

189 **"And so let holiness rise up"** "Unetaneh Tokef," translation by Joel M. Hoffman in Rabbi Lawrence A. Hoffman, *Who by Fire, Who by Water: Un'taneh Tokef* (Woodstock, V.T.: Jewish Lights, 2013), 29.

189 **"who will live"** Ibid., 30.

189 **"who by water"** "Unetaneh Tokef," translation by Sacks in *The Koren Rosh Hashanah Maḥzor,* 568.

190 **"resign as general manager"** Larry Eisenberg, *"It's Me, O Lord": Standin' in the Need of Prayer!* (Tulsa, O.K.: Fun Books, 1992), 111.

190 **"You [God] will remember everything"** "Unetaneh Tokef," translation by Joel M. Hoffman in Hoffman, *Who by Fire, Who by Water,* 29.

190 **"As the tape begins"** Lew, *This Is Real and You Are Completely Unprepared,* 139.

191 **"slow to anger; quick to forgive"** "Unetaneh Tokef," translation by Hoffman in Hoffman, *Who by Fire, Who by Water,* 31.

191 **"For You [God] do not desire"** "Unetaneh Tokef," translation by Sacks in *The Koren Rosh Hashana Maḥzor,* 570.

191 **"This is how God is different"** Lew, *This Is Real and You Are Completely Unprepared,* 148.

191 **"Truly, it was You"** "Unetaneh Tokef," translation by Sacks in *The Koren Rosh Hashana Maḥzor,* 572.

193 **Believe it or not, it's** Joel M. Hoffman, "How Was Your Flight?" in Hoffman, *Who by Fire, Who by Water,* 97.

193 **"help the hardship of the decree"** "Unetaneh Tokef," translation by Hoffman in Hoffman, *Who by Fire, Who by Water,* 31.

193 **if we do such activities** Babylonian Talmud, *Rosh Hashanah* 16b.

193 **On this "Day of Atonement"** Leviticus 23:27–28, 32.

194 **"For perhaps as much as five"** Rabbi Kenneth R. Berger, "Five Minutes to Live," Sermon, Congregation Rodeph Sholom, Tampa, F.L., September 16, 1986, https://www.sdiworld.org/sites/default/files/educational-event/five-minutes-to-live-rabbi-kenneth-berger-z22l-yom-kippur-sermon-sept-1986%20%282%29.pdf.

194 **This sermon is especially poignant because** Samuel G. Freedman, "A Rabbi's Enduring Sermon on Living Your Last Five Minutes," *The New York Times,* October 1, 2016, https://www.nytimes.com/2016/10/02/us/a-rabbis-enduring-sermon-on-living-your-last-five-minutes.html.

195 **"to bring us to the point"** Lew, *This Is Real and You Are Completely Unprepared,* 228.

195 **"Man is founded in dust"** "Unetaneh Tokef," translation by Sacks in *The Koren Rosh Hashana Maḥzor,* 572.

195 **One of the Rabbis** Babylonian Talmud, *Shabbat* 153a.

196 **"Why, when we fasted"** Isaiah 58:3.

196 **"Because on your fast day"** Isaiah 58:3–7.

198 **Also, the Talmud points out** Babylonian Talmud, *Taanit* 16a.

198 **"It is necessary to find"** As recounted by Yaakov Yosef of Polnoye, *Sefer Ben Porat Yosef,* 43b, translation from Rabbi Lawrence Kushner, "On Hitting Yourself," in Rabbi Lawrence A. Hoffman, ed., *We Have Sinned: Sin and Confession in Judaism* (Woodstock, V.T.: Jewish Lights, 2012), 193.

199 **"Even that behavior we took"** Lew, *This Is Real and You Are Completely Unprepared,* 127.

199 **"The thought of starting"** Greenberg, *How to Run a Traditional Jewish Household,* 333.

199 **And the Talmud claims that** Babylonian Talmud, *Bava Batra* 14a–b.

200 **"In the place where penitents stand"** Babylonian Talmud, *Sanhedrin* 99a.

200 **"You shall live in booths"** Leviticus 23:42–43.

201 **"gives us no shelter"** Lew, *This Is Real and You Are Completely Unprepared,* 265.

201 **"it exposes the idea"** Ibid., 266.

201 **"You shall rejoice"** Leviticus 23:40.

202 **It looks like the Rabbis** Rabbi Burton Visotzky, "On Hanukkah," in Pogrebin, *My Jewish Year,* 115.

9 | LIFE CYCLE RITUALS

206 **In fact, as Rabbi Harold Kushner** Harold S. Kushner, *To Life! A Celebration of Jewish Being and Thinking* (New York: Grand Central, 1994), 215.

208 **"I have put before you"** Deuteronomy 30:19.

208 **"Remember us for life"** "The Amidah," translation in *Maḥzor Lev Shalem: Rosh Hashanah and Yom Kippur* (New York: Rabbinical Assembly, 2016), 82.

210 **"For dust you are"** Genesis 3:19.

210 **As historian Deborah Lipstadt** Deborah Lipstadt, "The Lord Was His," in Jack Riemer, ed., *Jewish Reflections on Death* (New York: Schocken Books, 1976), 48.

211 **The Rabbis had a debate** Babylonian Talmud, *Shabbat* 152b.

211 **"an act that seemed impossibly intimate"** Rabbi Rachel Barenblat, "Facing Impermanence," in Richard A. Light, *Jewish Rites of Death: Stories of Beauty and Transformation* (Santa Fe, N.M.: Terra Nova Books, 2016), 58.

211 **"When a person enters the world"** *Ecclesiastes Rabbah* 5:14, translation from Rifat Sonsino and Daniel B. Syme, *What Happens After I Die?: Jewish Views of Life After Death* (New York: Union of American Hebrew Congregations Press, 1990), 3–4.

212 **"Since I didn't know whose remains"** Rochel U. Berman, *Dignity Beyond Death: The Jewish Preparation for Burial* (Jerusalem: Urim Publications, 2005), 151.

213 **"to utter over him [the dead]"** Josef Karo, *Shulḥan Arukh,* "Yoreh Deah," 344:1, translation from Josef ben Efrayim Karo, *Code of Hebrew Law: Shulḥan 'Aruk—Yoreh Deah,* trans. Chaim N. Denburg (Montreal: Jurisprudence Press, 1954), on Sefaria.org.

214 **Judaism provides what author Anita Diamant** Anita Diamant, *Saying Kaddish: How to Comfort the Dying, Bury the Dead, and Mourn as a Jew* (New York: Schocken Books, 1998), 97.

214 **"To eat means to live"** Jack Riemer, "Introduction: Jewish Insights on Death," *Jewish Insights on Death and Mourning,* ed. Jack Riemer (Syracuse, N.Y.: Syracuse University Press, 2002), 11–12.

215 **"*Shiva* is for one thing only"** Diamant, *Saying Kaddish,* 112–113.

215 **"an adjustment of one's body"** Maurice Lamm, *The Jewish Way in Death and Mourning,* rev. ed. (Middle Village, N.Y.: Jonathan David Publishers, 2000), 108.

215 **"The purpose of the condolence call"** Ibid., 133.

215 **Jewish law even advises visitors** Karo, *Shulḥan Arukh,* "Yoreh Deah," 385:2.

218 **"Magnified and sanctified"** Rabbi Jonathan Sacks, ed. and trans., *The Koren Siddur,* 2nd ed. (Jerusalem: Koren, 2016), 60.

219 **As Rabbi Elie Kaunfer points out** Rabbi Elie Kaunfer, "The Mourner's Kaddish Is Misunderstood," in *My Jewish Learning,* https://www.myjewishlearning.com/article/the-mourners-kaddish-is-misunderstood/.

219 **This seems to be the point** *Deuteronomy Rabbah* 11:10, translation from Hillel Halkin, *After One-Hundred-and-Twenty: Reflecting on Death, Mourning, and the Afterlife in the Jewish Tradition* (Princeton, N.J.: Princeton University Press, 2016), 213.

220 **"The one thing that had seemed"** Shoshana Wolok, "Stronger Than Death," in Rabbi Herbert A. Yoskowitz, ed., *The Kaddish Minyan: From Pain to Healing,* 2nd ed. (Fort Worth, T.X.: Eakin Press, 2003), 56.

220 **"Grief is the price we pay"** Queen Elizabeth II, "Text of the Queen's Message to New York," *The Guardian,* September 21, 2001.

220 **Jewish law lays out specific instructions** Babylonian Talmud, *Moed Katan* 26a–b.

220 **"In time even the rough stitch"** Rabbi David Stern, "To Tear and to Sew," in Rabbi Lawrence A. Hoffman, ed., *May God Remember: Memory and Memorializing in Judaism* (Woodstock, V.T.: Jewish Lights, 2013), 211.

221 **but as Rabbi Immanuel Jakobovits noted** As recounted by Rabbi Jonathan Sacks in Rabbi Jonathan Sacks, "Do Remember the Past, but Do Not

Be Held Captive by It," July 17, 2004, http://rabbisacks.org/do-remember -the-past-but-do-not-be-held-captive-by-it/.

221 **The Hebrew word translated as "bond"** David J. Wolpe, "Why Stones Instead of Flowers?" in Riemer, ed., *Jewish Insights on Death and Mourning,* 129.

222 **"While flowers may be a good"** Ibid.

222 **"There is no craving for death"** Abraham J. Heschel, "Death as Homecoming," in Riemer, ed., *Jewish Reflections on Death,* 68.

223 **Rather, as Rabbi Neil Gillman explained** Neil Gillman, *The Death of Death: Resurrection and Immortality in Jewish Thought* (Woodstock, V.T.: Jewish Lights, 2015), 75–77.

224 **"Now, however, pious Jews"** Ibid., 87.

224 **Rabbi Gillman explains that the Rabbis** Ibid., 119–120, 140.

225 **One Rabbi claimed that in the** Babylonian Talmud, *Berakhot* 17a.

225 **utopia where each grape would produce** Babylonian Talmud, *Ketubot* 111b.

225 **and trees would produce new fruit** Babylonian Talmud, *Shabbat* 30b.

227 **This idea is beautifully captured** As recounted by Rookie Billet, "We Will Get Better, We Must Get Better," in Riemer, ed., *Jewish Insights on Death and Mourning,* 288.

227 **Rabbi Lamm includes in his book** Lamm, *The Jewish Way in Death and Mourning,* 276.

227 **"I look at rituals"** Berman, *Dignity Beyond Death,* 116.

229 **For example, the Talmud claims** Babylonian Talmud, *Yevamot* 97a.

229 **I also appreciate, as many commentators** Gillman, *The Death of Death,* 238; Lamm, *The Jewish Way in Death and Mourning,* 241–242.

230 **"number our days"** Psalms 90:12, translation from New King James Version.

231 **I'm also sobered by a fable** Y. M. Tuckachinsky, "The Birth," in Riemer, ed., *Jewish Insights on Death and Mourning,* 311–312.

231 **"Love is strong as death"** Song of Songs 8:6, translation from New King James Version.

CONCLUSION

232 **"It's a quintessential Jewish act"** Abigail Pogrebin, *My Jewish Year: 18 Holidays, One Wondering Jew* (Bedford, N.Y.: Fig Tree Books, 2017), 29.

233 **Rabbi Benay Lappe, who runs** Rabbi Benay Lappe, "An Unrecognizable Jewish Future: A Queer Talmudic Take," ELI Talk; https://elitalks.org/ unrecognizable-jewish-future-queer-talmudic-take; Rabbi Benay Lappe, Lecture, Sukkot Retreat, Isabella Freedman Jewish Retreat Center, Octo-

ber 3, 2015. See also http://www.svara.org/the-crash-talk/ for other talks, articles, and resources on Lappe's crash theory.

236 **In the wake of the Holocaust** Avraham Infeld with Clare Goldwater, *A Passion for a People: Lessons from the Life of a Jewish Educator* (Jerusalem: Melitz, 2017), 58.

238 **Only half of American Jews** Pew Research Center, *A Portrait of Jewish Americans: Findings from a Pew Research Center Survey of U.S. Jews,* October 1, 2013, 35, http://www.pewresearch.org/wp-content/uploads/sites/7/2013/10/jewish-american-full-report-for-web.pdf.

238 **the same as the overall American** Abigail Geiger and Gretchen Livingston, "8 Facts About Love and Marriage in America," *Pew Research Center,* https://www.pewresearch.org/fact-tank/2019/02/13/8-facts-about-love-and-marriage/.

238 **And among non-Orthodox American Jews** Gregory A. Smith and Alan Cooperman, "What Happens When Jews Intermarry," Pew Research Center, November 12, 2013, https://www.pewresearch.org/fact-tank/2013/11/12/what-happens-when-jews-intermarry/.

239 **As for children, only 39 percent** Sylvia Barack Fishman and Steven M. Cohen, "Family, Engagement, and Jewish Continuity among American Jews," The Jewish People Policy Institute, June 5, 2007, 18, http://jppi.org.il/new/wp-content/uploads/2017/06/Raising-Jewish-Children-Research-and-Indicators-for-Intervention.pdf.

239 **a survey conducted in 2017** InterfaithFamily, *Report on InterfaithFamily's 2017 Survey on Rabbinic Officiation for Interfaith Couples,* 1, https://www.interfaithfamily.com/wp-content/uploads/2018/08/Rabbi-Officiation-Report-Final.pdf.

239 **So it's not surprising that** Pew Research Center, *A Portrait of Jewish Americans: Findings from a Pew Research Center Survey of U.S. Jews,* October 1, 2013, 60, http://www.pewresearch.org/wp-content/uploads/sites/7/2013/10/jewish-american-full-report-for-web.pdf.

239 **11.2 percent by one estimate** Steinhart Social Research Institute, *American Jewish Population Estimates 2015: Summary and Highlights,* September 22, 2016, 2.

239 **12 to 15 percent by another** Ari Y. Kelman, Aaron Hahn Tapper, Izabel Fonseca, Aliya Saperstein, *Counting Inconsistencies: An Analysis of American Jewish Population Studies, with a Focus on Jews of Color,* 5, https://jewsofcolorfieldbuilding.org/wp-content/uploads/2019/Counting-Inconsistencies-052119.pdf

239 **Unfortunately, Jewish population studies are inconsistent** Ibid., 9–15.

240 **Thirty-one percent of American Jews belong** Pew Research Center, *A Portrait of Jewish Americans,* 60. The 63 percent figure is not in the

report but was calculated from its data by the Pew Research Center per my request.

240 **"credible in the presence of"** Irving (Yitzchak) Greenberg, "Cloud of Smoke, Pillar of Fire: Judaism, Christianity, and Modernity After the Holocaust," Steven T. Katz, Shlomo Biderman, Gershon Greenberg, eds., *Wrestling with God: Jewish Theological Responses During and After the Holocaust* (New York: Oxford University Press, 2007), 506.

240 **"one of the greatest acts"** Jonathan Rosen, *The Talmud and the Internet: A Journey Between Worlds* (New York: Picador, 2000), 15.

242 **"slow of speech"** Exodus 4:10.

242 **"Who gives man speech?"** Exodus 4:11.

243 **"the portable homeland"** Heinrich Heine, "Geständnisse," *in Düsseldorfer Heine Ausgabe,* vol. 15 (Hamburg: Hoffman and Campe, 1982), 44. Translation from Hindy Najman, *Losing the Temple and Recovering the Future: An Analysis of 4 Ezra* (Cambridge, U.K.: Cambridge University Press, 2014), 67.

244 **In his book about the future** Tal Keinan, *God Is in the Crowd: Twenty-First-Century Judaism* (New York: Spiegel & Grau, 2018), x–xi.

246 **"We will do"** Exodus 24:7, commonly used translation.

247 **"Establish a teacher for yourself"** *Pirkei Avot,* 1:16.

248 **Looking back, I'm reminded of** Babylonian Talmud, *Megillah* 24b.

249 **I prefer an approach that** Infeld, *A Passion for a People,* 5, 13–14.

252 **A story in the Talmud tells** Babylonian Talmud, *Taanit* 23a, translation from Abraham Cohen, *Everyman's Talmud: The Major Teachings of the Rabbinic Sages* (New York: Schocken Books, 1975), 187.

252 **"love the Lord your God"** Deuteronomy 6:5.

252 **"Take to heart these instructions"** Deuteronomy 6:6.

253 **"We can only pass on"** Rabbi Jonathan Sacks, *A Letter in the Scroll: Understanding Our Jewish Identity and Exploring the Legacy of the World's Oldest Religion* (New York: Free Press, 2000), 7.

253 **"there is no person"** *Pirkei Avot* 4:3.

254 **Researchers found that Jews who survived** William Helmreich, "Don't Look Back: Holocaust Survivors in the U.S.," Jerusalem Center for Public Affairs, October 1, 1991, http://jcpa.org/article/dont-look-back-holocaust-survivors-in-the-u-s/.

254 **"Inside me sits the soul"** Jacob Glatstein, *The Glatstein Chronicles, Book Two: Homecoming at Twilight,* ed. Ruth R. Wisse, trans. Maier Deshell and Norbert Guterman (New Haven: Yale University Press, 2010), 283–284.

254 **"It has chosen me"** Blu Greenberg, *How to Run a Traditional Jewish Household* (New York: Fireside, 1985), 27.

INDEX

ABOUT THE AUTHOR

From 2009 to 2017, SARAH HURWITZ worked in the White House, serving as head speechwriter for First Lady Michelle Obama and as a senior speechwriter for President Barack Obama. Prior to working in the Obama administration, Hurwitz was the chief speechwriter for Hillary Clinton on her 2008 campaign for president, and a speechwriter for Senator John Kerry and General Wesley Clark during the 2004 presidential election. Hurwitz is a graduate of Harvard College and Harvard Law School.

ABOUT THE TYPE

This book was set in Times Roman, designed by Stanley Morison (1889–1967) specifically for *The Times* of London. The typeface was introduced in the newspaper in 1932. Times Roman had its greatest success in the United States as a book and commercial typeface, rather than one used in newspapers.